Additional Thoughts on *The Stones Applaud*

"Terri left us an extraordinary book about growing up with CF in Allentown, Pa., and about her years at Children's Hospital, the Phillips Exeter Academy, and at Harvard. As she entered each new stage of her life, some authority figure—a doctor or a school administrator—assured her she would fail, telling her, in effect, why didn't she just go home and die? . . . In a narrative that is alternately revealing, emotionally wrenching, fun, and at times darkly cynical, Terrri discusses her refusal to surrender to the disease and to society's low expectations of CF patients."

Alex Beam
as published in the *Boston Globe*, January 15, 1992

"We witnessed Teresa's tenaciousness and the love and support from her family to do all they could to let her live out her dreams. We are inspired and blessed by the honesty and candidness her book reveals. Although reading *The Stones Applaud* brought many tears, they were tears that heal. We know there are many who will be deeply touched by Teresa's life."

Harris and Debbie Weinstein,
whose son Brett died of cystic fibrosis in 1999

"The voice of the author of *The Stones Applaud* is that of a gifted, deeply likeable woman who is a keen observer of human behavior, maintains an incisive sense of humor, holds strong opinions, and is driven to participate fully in life. As she chronicles her own progressive insights related to CF, we find remarkably few people outside her immediate family who take advantage to know Teresa Mullin after hearing she has cystic fibrosis. She finds the impact of social isolation to be one of the most painful aspects of CF. The time is long overdue for all of us to understand that one of the most important things we can do for children diagnosed with chronic medical conditions is to treat them like everyone else and normalize their life to the degree possible. Teresa Mullin is a powerful advocate who opens the window very widely to that future."

John D. Van Brakle, MD
Chairman and Forrest G. Moyer Distinguished Chair of Pediatrics
Lehigh Valley Hospital, Allentown, Pennsylvania

"Although Teresa and I were about ten years apart in age, our experiences of the public acceptance, understanding of, and growing up with CF did not differ. Reading *The Stones Applaud*, I found many similarities—the same doctor, hospital experiences, struggles to suppress a cough, unexplained alienation of a good friend, determination of not letting CF hold you back, tragedy of losing friends to CF—and one major commonality: the trials and tribulations of living with a life-threatening disease all the while trying to live a 'normal' life among a not-so-understanding or civil world. Yes, life with CF is difficult and a challenge. Yet, I cannot live with CF any other way than to really live life as much and when I can. I believe Teresa had the same determination; we would have much enjoyed each other and the fight against cystic fibrosis. Perhaps with this book, people will begin to understand."

Lynn M. Pancoast,
who lives with cystic fibrosis

"*The Stones Applaud* is a great and compelling book. Teresa's writing makes people understand what the person with a terminal illness is going through and what their family is going through."

Bobby Gunther Walsh
WAEB Radio

THE
STONES
APPLAUD

HOW CYSTIC FIBROSIS SHAPED MY CHILDHOOD

TERESA ANNE MULLIN

Providence House Publishers
PROVIDENCE PUBLISHING CORPORATION
FRANKLIN, TENNESSEE

Printed in the United States of America

11   10   09   08   07   1   2   3   4   5

Library of Congress Control Number: 2006939000

ISBN: 978-1-57736-363-7

Cover and page design by LeAnna Massingille

"Bloody Foreland" was originally published in *Sheltering Places* by Gerald Dawe
(Belfast: Blackstaff Press, 1978) and reissued in a limited edition, with illustrations
by Noel Connor, in *Sheltering Places & Company* (Staffs: Rudyard Press, 1994).
Used by gracious permission of the author. All rights reserved.

In the years since Teresa penned *The Stones Applaud*, medical treatments and
knowledge of cystic fibrosis have changed, so some of the things she experienced
are no longer part of the lives of those with the disease today. This is her story as
she lived it and her personal perspectives of life with cystic fibrosis; while it is
factual, some of the names of individuals have been changed.

PROVIDENCE HOUSE PUBLISHERS
an imprint of
Providence Publishing Corporation
238 Seaboard Lane • Franklin, Tennessee 37067
www.providence-publishing.com
800-321-5692

In loving memory of

Teresa Anne Mullin and Susan Patricia Mullin Boyle.

We will hold you tenderly in our hearts forever.

Edward Michael Mullin Jr., MD
Patricia Mary (Dugan) Mullin
Major Edward "Ted" Parks Mullin, USMC
Elizabeth Mary Mullin
Timothy Michael Mullin
Lieutenant Commander Sean Patrick Boyle, USN
Mary Terese (Scherberger) Dugan

Teresa Mullin and a friend perch atop cliffs jutting out into the North Atlantic during a trip to Ireland. The cliffs' lonely struggle to withstand the waves inspired Teresa to title her biography, The Stones Applaud, *a line from Gerald Dawe's poem, "Bloody Foreland."*

BLOODY FORELAND
For Christabel Bielenberg

No man could stand here long
where the Atlantic rises up
and the Foreland hangs across . . .

the huge stones rumble:
there is only one life here
watching and knowing
like the gull
hovering and screaming,
to plunge
and glide
and cry again
that shrill pitch
like widows' keening . . .

once, in the city,
sauntered into
the wrong kitchen-house,
them all in black
in a dark parlour
baying to the moon
an archaic death. . . .

the stones applaud.
You cannot turn
and walk and speak
of our past
as something
natural.

Gerald Dawe
(Used with permission)

Foreword: A Note From Teresa's Parents

We were married at St. Joseph's Catholic Church in Garden City, New York, on June 15, 1968. We moved to Phillips Street on Boston's Beacon Hill. Ed was a surgical intern and Pat was a registered nurse at Massachusetts General Hospital. Our first baby was due to be born on Easter Sunday, 1969.

Apparently anxious to arrive, Teresa Anne Mullin came into the world at ten minutes past noon on Ash Wednesday, February 19, 1969—a full six weeks premature. Four pounds at birth, she was down to three pounds, eleven ounces within two days. Teresa was a miracle—a true joy—from the day she was born. Named after her two grandmothers, Mary Terese (Scherberger) Dugan and Annemarie Kathryn (Gallagher) Mullin, Teresa was welcomed into a large and loving family. Her first four years were filled with all the fun activities of early childhood.

Shortly after Teresa's fourth birthday, she developed a cough that would not go away. Following visits to several doctors, a fellow surgical resident at Duke University Hospital, where Ed was a urology resident, suggested that Teresa undergo a sweat test—a diagnostic test for cystic fibrosis. Teresa will tell you the rest of the story.

Edward Michael Mullin Jr., MD
Patricia Mary (Dugan) Mullin

CHAPTER
ONE

The hospital garden loomed out in front of us. It was a carefully landscaped courtyard between buildings at Children's Hospital in Boston, and many of us went there to escape the tension of the hospital wards. So many times I had gone there to forget.

Round and round we went, past the clumps of flowers, the stone benches, the handful of trees. The cheery garden-statue animals peeked at us from all corners.

I was afraid to speak to my friend, unsure of what either of us had to say.

I heard the wheels of her chair grating against the pavement and thought our motion protected me from words. I absently took us in circles.

Then came her command.

"Stop the damn wheelchair!" she shouted, loudly enough that if there had been anyone else in the garden, she would have created a scene.

"Oh, right. Sorry," I fumbled, desperately trying to effect nonchalance.

The chair's uncooperative brakes allowed it to speed down a small incline on the path, almost throwing Nellie onto the grass. She did not laugh or smile, just shook her head.

Nellie said she wanted flowers. As we illegally plucked bunches from different parts of the garden, we dodged the security guards who kept passing through. The deception brought the hint of a smile to my accomplice's face.

I welcomed the diversion. Did we have enough white ones? Did she like purple? Would pink and red clash or complement each other?

We finished arranging flowers, and then the moment gripped us both.

Nellie's chair stood parked near an empty fountain with seals that would spout water later in spring. We stared across at the hospital building from which we had emerged. The rows of windows bore witness to little activity within, and an overwhelming stillness crowded around us. We met our fears alone.

"How do you do it?" Nellie's question came slowly, and without inflection. With these words she declared her own waning strength.

"Well, I . . ." I groped for an appropriate answer that would somehow encourage Nellie but found none.

I had always considered Nellie more worldly and sophisticated than I would ever be. Since her family spoke Italian, and little English, she constantly acted as translator, bridging the gap between two cultures several times each day. She had lived in Europe, traveled extensively, and spoke several languages.

Hospital staff often told me she looked up to me and felt slightly jealous, as well as proud, of my academic career. If we knew mutual admiration, we also knew empathy. Nellie knew I found my first year at Harvard difficult.

"I think it would be so uncool to have CF and be at Harvard," she had said months earlier on the telephone. It was "so uncool to have CF" no matter what, but Nellie referred specifically to the awkwardness and the hard times: missing classes, coughing in lecture halls, and explaining to the countless people who asked about cystic fibrosis. She saw Harvard as a prohibitive world that shunned people like us; she was not entirely wrong but her scope remained blessedly narrow. Had she had more time for such observations, she might have found Harvard to be the least of our problems.

When Nellie had called me at school, she caught me scrambling to prepare for winter finals and blaring a classical radio station that provided good study music. The station abruptly adopted talk show format, and I found myself listening to someone who called himself a cough specialist and insisted he knew remedies for all coughs. "Health-conscious men and women could usually prevent the development of a serious cough," he said. I repeated these words to Nellie and continued to update her as the show progressed.

After first agreeing this specialist made claims a bit too lofty for a late-night talk show, we both began crying on the phone. Although the program had nothing to do with our problem— except that the specialist had not seen fit to include chronic coughs in his discourse—it served as a reminder. Scientists had barely confronted the lung disorder we had been born with; our arcane struggle seemed strangely exempt from the possibility of modern intervention.

In the garden Nellie waited for me to finish my sentence. After I stood silent for several long seconds, her words flooded the space around us.

She was lost, afraid, unable to keep fighting. Worse, she had lost faith in her doctors. They had given up on her, and every-thing was a pretense, she said. She felt alone; feared that when her trial came, there would be no one to save her.

I could do nothing, say nothing; I looked blankly at the hospital wall. The colors of spring became gray to us, and the garden courtyard an airless shaft.

Words had to be found, and I tried.

"What made this different?" I asked. She had been through many challenging times.

"No, this was different," she insisted. Her face remained expressionless, but her voice held terror.

"Come on, come on, you can't give up," I said breezily, as though I were making her guess the contents of a Christmas present. "Hey, think about all your unfinished business. You must have some goals, some role model," I said, almost impatiently.

"You," she said simply. I swallowed hard and tried to laugh.

"Yeah, right. No, I mean like a real role model."

"You're it," came the answer.

"No, no, no. Thanks, but you know I'm not together enough to be anybody's role model. I mean there's gotta be somebody out there, in the wild blue yonder, that you really admire."

"Geraldine Ferraro."

"Really? That's so cool," I gushed. "Yeah, she's an impressive lady. So, politics, huh? You going to enter politics?"

She laughed the same way she had when I erroneously tried to tell her there might be clinical applications for treating CF within five to ten years of finding the defective gene. Not applicable, the laugh meant. Now I knew this was not a false alarm. Nellie—the invincible Antonella—was on the verge of giving up. I hated CF for bringing one of the bravest people I knew to her knees. For both our sakes, I would have to act this well.

"Don't laugh, I'm serious about this. If CF weren't a factor and you weren't in the hospital now, would you be getting ready to go into politics?"

She nodded and cried a little. It was something anyway; she briefly bore the hardened look of a fighter.

"Wouldn't it be wild not to have CF?" she asked.

I nodded stupidly, surprised by the question.

Wild indeed.

Cystic fibrosis first received its name in 1938. At that time, doctors believed it mainly affected the pancreas and fittingly called it cystic fibrosis of the pancreas. Since many patients died in infancy, it took several years to detect the respiratory problem that now accounts for most patient casualties.

The cystic fibrosis gene causes the cellular chloride channel to draw chloride into the cell but block its exit. In the natural process of osmosis, the chloride then draws moisture from mucus into the cell, leaving behind thick, sticky mucus. The intractable mucus gradually accumulates in the lungs of a cystic fibrosis patient, despite efforts to clear it. The mucus becomes infected, usually with two or three different strains of bacteria, and damages the lungs. Over time the infections, barely challenged by the best of our antibiotics, destroy the lungs. The heart develops extra muscles to accommodate the ailing lungs but finally can work with them no more.

Cystic fibrosis has no stealth about it. It can be easily diagnosed through a test that measures the chloride content in a patient's perspiration. The infections, which begin in patients of varying ages, seem usually to take more than ten years to work their destruction once they have laid claim to the lungs. Researchers have grown quite familiar with the most common strains of bacteria, have named them, and have included them in countless studies.

One in about twenty-five hundred Americans is born with the CF gene, giving us a current population of thirty thousand patients in this country. This group includes seven thousand adults who struggle daily to push past the perception of CF as a pediatric illness. More than six hundred people in the United States die from CF each year, possibly as many as eleven hundred. No one has successfully tracked the progress of all thirty thousand, so we have no precise data about the death rate or life expectancy. We know, however, that the median life span has reached twenty-one years and may have reached the twenty-six years reported by the Cystic Fibrosis Foundation.

In addition to harboring lung infections, CF patients do not produce the pancreatic enzymes necessary for adequate digestion. Around 1977, a drug company introduced an artificial enzyme that most patients now swallow before eating. The new enzyme, better than anything that had gone before it, helped patients gain weight and strength. Still, a CF patient needs exceptionally high amounts of protein and calories each day. Despite their best efforts, many patients remain grossly underweight and have little of the strength they need to fight respiratory infections. The problem can be severe, and in a small percentage of patients, it is the cause of death.

Besides the pancreatic enzymes and the high-protein, high-calorie diet, we have an array of other treatments now in use. To combat the lung infections, most patients regularly take two or three different oral antibiotics. These drugs are mainly broad spectrum antibiotics, which do not specifically target lung infections. Because the oral antibiotics do not penetrate the secretions and do not completely kill any of the infections, they can only be useful in the short-term. Intravenous antibiotics work more effectively than oral ones, and CF patients often enter hospitals to spend two weeks or more receiving IV antibiotics. Some patients inhale IV antibiotics in aerosol form; this technique has not had many years to prove itself but appears to be helpful. In addition, almost all patients benefit from the use of aerosolized bronchodilators, which expand the airways to make breathing easier and facilitate efforts to clear the lungs.

The most common method of treatment in this country, and the most manifest symbol of the primitive American approach to the disorder, is chest percussion. The treatment originated with ancient civilizations who pounded the chests of their sick in the hope of making them well. Today, physical therapists or trained family members use cupped hands to systematically bang a patient's designated lung areas for an hour or more each day. The percussion stimulates coughing, which clears any easily mobile secretions from the airways. This works well in young patients who have relatively clear airways. Older patients fare less well, however, because the pressure of the percussion on worn airways becomes ineffective, and in some cases, harmful. Therapists and patients throughout Western Europe and Australia have long forsaken chest percussion except in cases of emergency. Instead of the percussion, European doctors teach patients to adhere to exercise regimens and to use breathing techniques to dislodge secretions. They believe the breathing techniques, the most popular of which is called "autogenic drainage," enable patients to reach farther down into the airways than is possible by coughing. Except for a few progressive hospitals, most American CF centers have resisted the move to breathing techniques.

Of course, all our treatments put together still do not save lives. The simplest control would be an effective means of either thinning the secretions or killing the infections. The last half-century has born witness to the fact that this control will not be easily gotten. While we have become well-acquainted with the physiology of the disorder, patients often wonder about the political and economic conditions that may be keeping our answer from us. Patients hold little faith in promises of genetic miracles; we believe the age of high technology has robbed clinical researchers of the prestige and support they deserve.

The part of CF the world notices most is the terrible cough patients carry everywhere we go. The cough cannot be controlled, and though some patients cough more than others, all of us have suffered embarrassment at the hands of an unpredictable and noisy cough. The infections in a CF patient's lungs cannot be transmitted to someone without CF. Many European doctors believe, however, that CF patients can catch infections from each other. Although many European hospitals make an effort to prevent what they call "cross-infection" in CF patients, American hospitals have yet to subscribe to the theory, which would cost them greatly if proven true.

CF seems to have its highest population among people of Anglo or Irish descent, although the disorder is spread throughout the world. The explanation for its genetic source descends into the folkloric and will probably always remain uncertain. I have my own favorite version, pieced together from the musings of doctors throughout the field: Several centuries back, a colony of European fishermen kept falling prey to a mystery illness much like cholera. The CF gene, which causes the immune system to go haywire in its efforts to repair the lungs, somehow developed then as the means of fighting off the illness. While cholera causes the cellular chloride channel to generate an excess of secretions, the CF gene will only let the channel work in an inward direction. The fishermen would have lived in a cold and misty climate, which is the kind of weather in which CF patients seem to have the greatest longevity. Sometimes I try to picture the men, their ships and nets, and the locale that may have shaped our genetic misfortune. Of course, we will never know for sure what happened.

And, while we live and deal daily with our genetic misfortune, we are also confronted by a society mostly uneducated about CF, especially in America, which often attempts to dismiss us and our futures. My hope is that my story will both encourage others with CF to remain strong in their fight for life and motivate those who are healthy to validate and support, not pity and look down on, those who are fighting. And, perhaps, those who are healthy will even be motivated to fight for us in the search for a cure.

CHAPTER
❧ TWO

On January 11, 1974, while Richard Nixon struggled to save his presidency, Skylab IV circled overhead in its orbit, and the Osmonds and David Cassidy filled the airwaves, Patricia Mullin herded her two small children into the car. That Friday morning fell smack in the middle of North Carolina's feeble attempt at winter.

After ten minutes in the blue '64 Buick LeSabre, my mother stopped at the house of a neighbor who had offered to look after ten-month-old Ted for the morning. Then Mom and four-year-old me continued on to Duke University Hospital, where my father, Edward, a urology resident, distractedly attended rounds.

Both my parents dreaded the test scheduled to determine whether I had cystic fibrosis. As doctor and nurse, they knew from textbooks that CF killed most patients before they grew old enough to understand it.

My parents had first become alarmed when I developed what my father called "a cough that wouldn't quit." For several weeks, local pediatricians tried to make sense of my cough and my unusually slight build. They had alternately diagnosed celiac disease, pneumonia, post-nasal drip, severe allergies, and asthma. Finally, a fellow resident of my father's suggested I be taken to have a sweat test.

That morning, a brusque technician boosted me atop an examination table, where I sat impatiently crinkling the paper sheet underneath me. She took hold of one of my arms and attached two pieces of gauze to it, topping both with small electrodes. A current ran between the two electrodes and stimulated sweat, which the gauze collected. The procedure made my arm itch so much I could barely stand it; I repeatedly made this known to the technician.

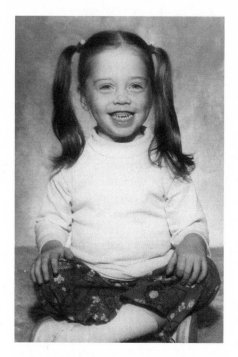

Teresa, age three

The sweat samples showed a high salt content, one of the trademarks of cystic fibrosis. Pediatrician Lois Pounds sent me away with a nurse, then led my mother into a small office. While I tried to play nicely with the chattering nurse, Pounds leaned across her desk and told my mother the test proved positive.

My father answered his page and rushed to the clinic. He stepped into the office and stood against the wall behind my mother. He heard the same diagnosis his wife had moments earlier, and then the couple fought for their composure. Dad did not feel sure he could leave the clinic without fainting; he feared he might cause a scene before other doctors. When Pounds left my parents alone, they filled the tiny room with sobs.

When she could speak through her tears, my mother proposed that they buy a tape recorder that afternoon. Pounds had not conveyed much optimism: few cystic fibrosis patients then lived to be teenagers and the diagnosis found me already about to turn five. So my parents wanted to record my voice and take plenty of pictures. Failing to sense the tension around us, I sat cheerfully during the ride home.

My mother's parents, Mary Terese and Parks Dugan, kept in close touch with us from their home in Garden City, New York. Grandmother, who like Mom had worked as a nurse before having children, knew enough to be concerned. After the test, she and my mother spoke long-distance for more than an hour in a conversation I would not have understood had I been listening. Later that day, Grandmother called the American Lung Association whose staffers politely told her they had never heard of cystic fibrosis.

That same day the doctor gave me what seemed to be a new toy: a portable air compressor to turn medications into a mist I could inhale. That night my mother placed it on the dining room table and handed me the mouthpiece. I puffed away, enjoying myself, while my parents watched solemnly; I thus began the daily treatment they knew would become a regular part of my life.

The nebulizer (1974)

After five minutes, I jumped up from my seat at the end of the table, usually reserved for Daddy at dinner time.

"Okay, that's enough," I announced, pushing the

mouthpiece into my mother's hands. She quietly but firmly handed it back to me, explaining that the doctor told her I needed to use this machine to stay well.

Bored and unhappy, I sat back down, stopping every three or four minutes to appeal my sentence. I could not understand why Mommy and Daddy looked so serious and thought maybe I had not behaved myself at the doctor's office. A shrewd strategist, I tried apologizing for the unknown offense. I grew confused, however, when my parents insisted I had been a good girl all day long.

Then the long-term routine began. Each morning and evening, I would spend about half an hour inhaling a solution intended to dilate my airways and help me mobilize the secretions. My parents put the solution into an odd-looking, small plastic gadget they called a nebulizer. They then used a long pliable plastic tube to connect the handheld nebulizer to an air compressor. When the compressor forced air through the nebulizer, the solution became a fine aerosol which I inhaled. The strange-looking procedure led visitors to say tiring

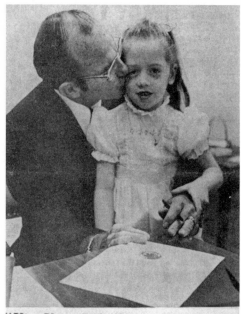

"Kiss Your Baby"

Durham Mayor James Hawkins plants a kiss on the cheek of Teresa Mullin, 5, chosen as the poster child for a Durham County Cystic Fibrosis Foundation awareness drive. Teresa, daughter of Dr. and Mrs. Edward Mullin of Durham, has CF and wants to point out to parents that children with the lung disease have ex- cessively salty sweat. The drive May 12-18 is to encourage parents to kiss their youngsters, the easiest way to discover the saltiness of the skin. Letters have been sent by foundation members to all day care centers and nursery schools in the city and county to ask their participation in the campaign.
—Photo by Cooper

Teresa in her first appearance as a CF poster child

things, like "Smoking the peace pipe again?" I took to rolling my eyes at anyone who tried to comment.

For the second part of the treatment, my parents took turns pounding my chest for half an hour. They would cup their hands in order to trap air as they clapped down on my different lung areas. The chest percussion, by far the worst part of the treatment in a five-year-old's mind, caused enough pressure to loosen some secretions. I rarely failed to scream and cry and beg my parents to stop. The percussion hurt and took up play time, and I did not understand the point of it all.

"You're hurting me!" I would shout, never noticing their own pain. "How 'bout, let's read a storybook?"

"I'm sorry, honey, but we have to do this to keep you well."

"Oh, Daaaddy," I would plead when my father clapped me, always supposing that one day I might sound desperate enough to make him stop. The idea of "keeping me well" held little meaning for me.

Often my parents tried to make the treatments into a game, pretending to be drummers. Sometimes we sang songs, and they would do the percussion to the rhythm of the song. We also spent treatment time listening to records and playing guessing games.

I did not learn of the alternatives to chest percussion until trips to Europe during my college years. Tens of thousands of lives likely would have been improved by knowledge of breathing techniques. European therapists advertised their methods in journals and at meetings, but U.S. doctors had no interest. If the American medical community more readily accepted foreign wisdom, my parents and I might have spent our time very differently in the days after my diagnosis.

Along with chest percussion, I adopted a strict, high-protein, high-calorie, low-fat diet. Suddenly most of my favorite foods became forbidden: no more ice cream, hot dogs, peanut butter, fried chicken, french fries, or chocolate. I could not even use butter anymore. I wistfully remembered the good old days when I could pick out almost anything at the grocery store.

"What's left?" I asked my mother one of the first times we discussed my new diet. At first she could not answer.

Teresa and Ted

"Gumdrops!" she said finally, trying to sound triumphant. "You can eat all the gumdrops you want." The moment she said it I knew I never wanted to see another gumdrop. Doctors would recommend a reduced-fat intake, one of the most difficult new requirements facing me, until they realized several years later that patients who could tolerate it fared much better with a high-fat diet.

For a while I could not pronounce the thing that had started infringing on my diet and play time, but I tested my new word on strangers anyway.

"Gee, Mommy, I wish I didn't have stick stick fy-roshus," I would say loudly in waiting rooms or grocery stores. At five I only meant to show off my impressive vocabulary.

After my diagnosis, I generally avoided hospitals except for my routine weekly allergy shots, for which I developed a unique distraction. Once I yelled, "Take that thing out of me!" during the injection. I began repeating it and kept so busy awaiting my cue that I never felt the full effect of the needle. I had trained my regular nurse to expect the exclamation but once startled an unwary replacement. My ritual ended shortly afterward, partly because I decided five-year-olds should act mature enough to impress the medical personnel who so often talked down to them. I had begun to resent doctors and nurses for using a different voice to address me than they did to speak to Mom.

CHAPTER
❧ THREE

After my father finished his Duke urology fellowship in 1976, we moved to Allentown, Pennsylvania, so he could enter private medical practice there with a friend. My sister Susan, born in 1975, tested positively for CF while just a few weeks old. Doctors at Duke referred Susan and me to Dr. Nancy Huang at St. Christopher's Hospital in Philadelphia.

Soon after moving we traveled ninety minutes to see Dr. Huang, who quickly conveyed to me a sense of crisis about my condition. She immediately increased my treatments from twice to three times daily and urged strict adherence to the low-fat diet. She also decided to admit me to St. Christopher's for my first course of intravenous antibiotics.

That hospital stay became the threshold to a different way of life. Two-week periods in the hospital would become so frequent that I would have difficulty keeping count of their total number, which had neared fifty by the time I reached college. I would spend two years of cumulative time in hospitals before I reached age twenty.

Among cystic fibrosis specialists, Huang kept a high profile as a disciplinarian prepared to innovate boldly should she think it necessary. I could see the passion she brought to her work and yet I did not understand then how cystic fibrosis could consume her professional life. Too young to raise important questions with her, I debated her instead about her preference for syringes rather

Susan, Teresa, and Ted (1976)

than butterfly needles when she drew my blood. She also insisted on samples from my veins, when I had repeatedly told her I would have preferred a finger stick.

As Huang prepared me for that first admission, she knew I feared the needles most. I had endured allergy shots and blood tests from veins, but did not want to sample the different and much more intimidating IV needles and arterial blood tests. Because of the IV, which would mean spending two weeks with a needle stuck in my arm, I resisted entering the hospital as long as my parents would let me. To allay my needle fear before that first hospital stay, Huang led my parents and me around a forty-bed floor, crowded with many of her patients. She wandered around like a news anchor with a camera crew following behind her, interviewing patients every few feet.

"Tell us, please, what your IV feels like."

"Can you show your IV to this little girl?"

"That needle doesn't hurt, does it?"

I did not feel akin to any of the patients I met that day. They were sick, and I was not. My parents had protected me from statistics and dismal medical forecasts, so I imagined myself living with a quirky asthma-like disorder. I did not understand the strange connection between my salty sweat, chest percussion, and my low-fat diet, and I did not care. Because I knew so little, I spent much of my early childhood exasperated with adults who made me do apparently pointless things, such as entering the hospital. Through our entire tour of the ward, I feverishly tried to think of a way to reach my unreasonable parents. I had to make them realize I did not belong here. Finally, however, I decided to make my parents happy and undergo the seemingly futile exercise of hospitalization.

I resolved during that first stay to calculate the number of needles I had already endured and to keep a tally from that point onward. I intended to arrive at some enormous number with which to impress people. I soon stopped the count after five hundred because it had grown tedious.

During my first admission at St. Chris', I felt relieved to acquire a twenty-three-year-old roommate. I did not want to room with "some silly little kid." I wonder now how my roommate felt about sharing her space with a seven-year-old.

Every night my mother and I faced the same argument. My roommate would watch television until eleven, and my mother, staying at the hospital with me, would make sure I had closed my eyes several hours earlier. She even pulled the bedside curtains closed so I could not see the television. I had tried to downplay the age difference between my roommate and me and considered the enforced bedtime a serious blow to my credibility.

"I'll be in bed anyway, Mom. I just won't be asleep."

"Yes, you will be asleep."

"But I'm not going to be tired."

"I'm sorry, honey, but children your age should be asleep earlier than eleven."

Neither of us realized my childhood had begun ebbing away during those first hospital days. I grew impatient with bureaucracy and understaffing; I learned how to fill my IV chamber because if I didn't and Mom was at dinner, the line would clot off, requiring a new needle. I realized some people could handle needles better than others and set about politicking whenever possible to get the more skilled to start IVs and take blood tests. I knew if I could become a favorite of the IV team, who placed most IV needles, they would probably save me from the poor aim of interns and doctors.

I met a few people I didn't like because they seemed pompous and insincere. I worked to keep them as allies, however, smiling at all the right points in our conversations. I knew the doctors and nurses who came to talk to Mom wanted me to appear childishly happy.

I developed my first crush on a tall, blonde CF patient down the hall. He must have been sixteen years old and sat reading newspapers all day. I worried that we might not have anything in common, but on the occasions I felt brave enough, I dragged Mom with me to his room to say hello.

While I did not entirely like this first glimpse of the adult world, when I left St. Christopher's after two weeks, I had aged.

Of all the things I left behind in Durham, I missed "The Quiet Place" most. My parents and I would walk to The Quiet Place, a muddy, wooded area away from everything, to sit on big rocks, drink soup from a thermos, and carry on the deepest conversations my young mind could manage. I never knew the precise location of The Quiet Place because the winding paths that got us there confused me, but I despaired once when we walked all the way through it and found ourselves in a housing development. My parents had been teaching me how to use binoculars and asked me to tell them what I could see in the distance. I grew despondent when I focused on a stop sign I thought to be new; a developer had corrupted our paradise.

I didn't think we'd find anywhere to hike in Allentown, and I suspected we probably would not be allowed to keep chicks in our backyard. The trees in our new neighborhood stood less than half the size of the ones to which I'd grown accustomed. In Durham we

Brother Ted in The Quiet Place

Teresa in the Duke Gardens

had a wonderful, hilly backyard that bordered on a small forest. When they had started tearing down our "forest" in Durham, I at least found a new playmate in the little girl whose family moved into a newly built house behind us. She and I spent hours perched atop my swing set, arguing over which songs to sing. My friend always wanted to sing what she'd learned in kindergarten—ditties about witches and fire trucks. I kept trying to teach her all the words Karen Carpenter, whom I'd seen in concert, sang on the first album of singles she and her brother released. I also preferred Elton John and Simon and Garfunkel to kindergarten songs, mainly because my parents listened to them so often.

Besides forests, I worried about finding picnic places in Allentown. No spot could improve on the Duke Gardens, a place where Mom and Dad could admire the flowers and I could scamper about freely until I sat down to eat. While sitting on the huge, grassy inclines there, I'd finally learned to balance the plate at an angle at which nothing would spill. Then I would leap up again to run down the huge hill at great speed before turning to trudge back triumphantly to the picnic blanket.

I also expected ponies to be scarce in Allentown. My family had taken to feeding carrots to a neighbor's pony down the street from us in Durham. We had called him Pogo, after my beloved pogo stick. I knew we would often wish to visit him from the distance of our new home.

I even missed the small mountains of Asheville, North Carolina, where we had lived for two three-month periods during a training rotation of my father's. There, a walk around the block took us up and down slopes and gave us a view of a miniature valley. The southern ways of Asheville beguiled me; I learned how to clog dance and came home from first grade with a twang in my speech. I told my mother I needed to bring a "pin" to school to "raght with." She almost sent me back with a clothes pin rather than the required writing utensil.

As I struggled to adapt to my new home, all these things made Allentown seem dull by comparison. At least now that we all had our own bedrooms, Teddy would stop trying to knock down my Barbie townhouse the way he had when the three of us roomed together in the old house. I could get the canopy bed I'd wanted. And across the street from our house, we found a park with a good slide.

The event that made Allentown seem like a home to me came during third grade. That year my mother, drawing on the goodwill of townspeople, organized the first annual Cystic Fibrosis Bike-A-Thon in the Lehigh Valley. She began by convincing the local CF parents group it needed to sponsor a large fund-raiser for the Cystic Fibrosis Foundation. Then for several months she spent a few hours on the telephone each day, tirelessly coordinating groups of volunteers, finding businesses to distribute sponsor sheets, and arranging the route.

While my mother worked hard, I kept busy as well. I encouraged all my friends to participate. I recorded an ad, featuring the wistful line "please help us," to be broadcast by a local radio station. Ted and I knocked on hundreds of doors and asked everyone we spoke to if they would sponsor us. Most people agreed to sponsor me for between fifty cents and five dollars per mile.

Our family received a response that made me take a second look at the town. Local college students, friends' mothers, and elderly friends from church all offered to help in any way they could. Disc jockeys and frat brothers alike all made me feel that they wanted to join my fight. I felt baffled by their eagerness to help; privately I wondered if they didn't have something better to do than work so hard to raise money to help those

Teresa and Susan getting ready for the CF Bike-A-Thon

of us with this asthma-like thing I thought I had. Nonetheless, the community impressed me with its show of support for our cause.

One night before the bike-a-thon, my family and I sat watching local news footage of small children straddling their bikes near the route. My mother had somehow landed a bike-a-thon preview story in the local press. I had been one of those children, along with Ted on a big wheel and Susan on a tricycle. We had eagerly sought all possible publicity for the event.

Suddenly the news anchor filled a throwaway line with a phrase that blotted out everything else for me.

". . . the killer disease, cystic fibrosis."

I turned to my mother.

"Hey, Mom, the lady just made a mistake."

I was irate and prepared to call the station. The anchor had screwed up and now all my friends who had watched would behave strangely toward me at school. It might take me months to straighten things out; and this had happened just when I felt my classmates had accepted "the new girl."

"Didn't she? Didn't she, Mom?"

My mother took too long to respond, and then suddenly at age nine, I left childhood behind me forever. I felt disbelief and shock and cursed my fleeting naivete. Through all that time spent talking to doctors, I had suspected nothing. I vowed I would never be so stupid again. I would be tough.

I accused my parents of lying to me. No, they responded, they had been waiting for the right time to tell me. I fired question after question at them. I wanted to know everything they could tell me. I asked how long I had to live.

"It doesn't work like that," my mother said. "Researchers are working very hard every day—you have to believe they're going to find a cure sometime soon. In the meantime, we're going to do everything we can to keep you healthy."

I felt confident then that the more money I raised for the bike-a-thon, the more money I would direct toward the kind of research that would save Susan and me. In my innocence, I knew nothing about organizational overhead costs or institutional priorities that might dilute the effect of my efforts. I assumed every penny would go toward the cure. So I rode hard for all of us with CF, driven wildly by desperation. My parents had known the same motivating force—it had made them stop cars at street corners in Durham, where they had been dispatched by local fund-raisers to seek donations for the Cystic Fibrosis Foundation.

I rode fifteen miles, with no preparation before the event. The exertion caused one of my lungs to collapse. The lung fortunately reinflated itself, giving me a rare uncomplicated recovery. (Most patients with a collapsed lung, or pneumothorax, need special attention in a hospital.) Except for the overpowering chest pain I suffered the day after the event, we had no way of knowing what had happened until my X-rays looked odd to the doctors at St. Chris's a few weeks later. Despite the pneumothorax, I thought my bike ride had been worth it—I raised eight hundred dollars. As a whole, that first bike-a-thon raised about eight thousand dollars for the Cystic Fibrosis Foundation.

My mother sparked what has reportedly become the biggest bike-a-thon on the East Coast. The people of Allentown showed us we could depend on them. Strangers had made our cause theirs.

I would remain restless in my new home and would begin, after that newscast, to project myself into a faraway and purposeful future; I had no delusions that I suffered alone or was special. I just knew we all should propel ourselves into tomorrow as best we could. I vaguely wanted to go live in a big city where I would somehow work hard to be useful to society and to people like Susan and me. Of course, I hoped that by the time I could call myself a grown-up, I would be relieved of CF and free to fight other battles. I did not know what these other battles might be but felt sure that if I no longer had a fight on my hands, someone else would need my help.

Teresa, Ted, and Susan with their CF Bike-A-Thon trophies they won

Growing up, I would not always have the courage or maturity to keep this vision in front of me, but my first instinctive analysis of the situation made me want to help change things. Despite my conservative Catholic upbringing, I had forged inside me a primitive liberalism, based on my observation that we did not live in a fair world. I could imagine myself a well-dressed woman rushing places to do something worthwhile; I did not have the experience to supply more details than that.

After our bike-a-thon, Allentown became for me, as much as any place could, a calm harbor in which to spend the next few years.

CHAPTER
❦ FOUR

Back at St. Christopher's in 1978, I experienced the first of many Halloweens I would spend in the hospital. Huang admitted me because I had grown sick enough to warrant a routine course of IV antibiotics. The unplanned time in the hospital would not interfere too much with my fourth-grade school work, but I felt disappointed about missing trick-or-treat.

For Halloween someone donated several dozen plastic Wizard of Oz masks and capes to St. Chris's so that children dressed as the story's four travelers filled the halls that day. I refused to don a lion suit, but hospital staff costumed me anyway and dragged me to the festivities in the underground cafeteria.

After walking all through the hospital to cheer older patients and the bed-bound, about 150 miniature Oz characters assembled in the basement to march in a huge circular parade. I had no desire to march around, but they ordered me to join the parade. I kept looking for someone in charge who would listen to me; I felt much too old for this childish display. In a pediatric hospital, however, no one treated nine-year-olds very differently from eight, seven, or even six-year-olds. Later I realized I could probably have played sick to be exempt from the ridiculous march to the basement and subsequent parade. As the Scarecrow said, "If I only had a brain!"

After the parade and games, hospital staff started distributing candy. I watched everyone else receive chocolate, and for a moment I forgot the humiliation of the lion suit. When my turn arrived, however, I got a bag of peppermints and an apologetic explanation: no chocolate for people on low-fat diets. I shook my mane and roared.

Upstairs, most nurses dressed in togas made from hospital sheets. The menu called our soup "witches' brew," but it looked the same to us. Most younger patients happily became Dorothy or the Tin Man, but my eleven-year-old roommate and I looked forward to the dance the teenagers would attend that night in the hospital cafeteria. Though an activity director had declared us both underage, we planned to wander in anyway, figuring no one would object to a few extra guests.

We had been told to stay away from the dance, so that night we hesitated before leaving our floor. My friend's mother finally convinced us we would have more fun downstairs than in our room, and she accompanied us to the cafeteria door.

Later the three of us cursed our poor timing. The activity director, dressed as a clown and wearing a bulky red nose, stood at the entry as we approached. He reprimanded us and forced us to step back onto the elevator. My friend, her mother, and I held our ground as long as we could, and her mother tried to distract the clown so the two of us would be able to slip past him. We could see costumed figures dancing inside, and we pleaded with him to let us join them.

"Sorry, you know this is just for the teens. Please go back upstairs now."

My friend's mother tried to convince him that we would not run around or make noise, that we just wanted to stand in a corner and watch the dancing. This would hardly be our night on the town.

The nose shook firmly from side to side.

"I used to like clowns," my roommate said, as we angrily boarded the elevator.

"Me too."

Upstairs we comforted ourselves with candy that Girl Scout troops had brought in during the week. We had gotten the candy by sacrificing our dignity when we let visiting Scouts show us pity in their every gesture. In the back of my mind, I resented them without knowing why. "Here you go, little girl," the Scouts who were our age would say, turning their noses up in apparent self-satisfaction when the troop leader could not see. I had spent the previous two years in a Brownie troop and knew I would not have patronized anyone if I had brought them candy.

In addition to the Scout candy, my fourth-grade teacher Donna Trumbo had taken a classwide collection of candy and sent me a huge box of goodies. The box sadly contained no chocolate because my teacher told everyone I could not eat it. Fortunately, however, it did not contain any gumdrops. After we'd failed to crash the dance, my roommate and I rummaged through the candy, fighting amicably over the best pieces.

Every evening, the clown or another activity director would escort all the mobile and willing patients to the cafeteria for dinner. Such trips often brought me my only contact with older patients. The clown and others worked hard to keep the teenagers and the group of us they called preteens on opposite ends of a caste system. I didn't understand what made teenagers so special. They could go into the Teen Room and shut the door behind them. We small fry needed special permission to enter the room and could be made to leave if, for example, the teenagers decided to watch a television program they considered us too young to view.

Meanwhile, we had free run of the Play Room, a small space full of easels, giant paintbrushes, and baby food jars full of paint. We could paint, build things out of Popsicle sticks, or play with four-year-olds. My friends and I had more fun catching up with school work.

At dinner I could sit at the same table with my professed betters—anyone over the age of twelve. I tended not to say much unless asked a direct question. The teenagers gossiped and complained to each other about various aspects of hospital life. They all seemed to have a "stick" quota, or number of needles they would tolerate. One boy said that during a hospital stay, he would allow two needles per each hand and two per arm, blood tests included. That meant the IV team would face a challenge if the patient's quota had been met. Patients had been known to kick and scream, and a man in his twenties customarily locked himself in a bathroom (gravely inconveniencing about forty other patients) rather than let anyone put another needle to his skin.

Some of these patients would pull the IVs out of their arms in a misplaced protest against the disorder. Others refused to take pills or follow the diet. They ate greasy (and for them indigestible) pizza instead of hospital fare. Some would smoke or smuggle alcohol into the hospital. They would ignore any suggestion from a person in white. I can only guess that either they believed denial would cure their problems or they had grown too numb to care.

I did not understand or fully observe this irresponsible behavior. I took an older patient named Denise as a role model: She seemed to be so much a part of the healthy world and I wanted that for myself. I would not learn until several years later that when Denise died, it was largely because she had rarely obeyed her doctors.

These patients in their teens and early twenties resisted treatment with so much conviction that I misunderstood their calm and their certainty: I thought they cooperated fully with doctors and had settled into the best lives with CF they could make for themselves. They seemed grounded in the fight at hand and they seemed wise. My mother spent much of the hospital stay with me, and I would tell her how much I looked up to them. She knew the truth but kept from me what I could not have accepted.

Once, for a whole dinner, I wrestled with a question I wanted to ask.

"If the doctor said it would help you, wouldn't you get another stick, even if you didn't want any more needles?"

I never asked. Worse than getting an IV restarted for the eighth time, worse even than eating cafeteria food, was the prospect of looking silly in front of the teenagers.

After I left St. Chris's in November, Huang said I should stay home from school on a long-term basis to avoid catching infections from my classmates. CF patients have a reduced resistance to infection, and Huang believed that by staying away from other children, I would reduce my risk of getting sick. I had already proven to her I had a serious case of a disorder that varies among patients, and she deemed the measure necessary if I hoped to remain in stable condition. My parents and I did not feel qualified to challenge Huang; we balked privately at this advice but did not question it.

Officials from the Catholic school I attended told my mother they would make no exceptions to their policy of not providing tutors for absent students. For several weeks my parents suggested that I transfer to a public school so I could receive tutoring. I chose to stay at St. Thomas More, however, because I did not like the prospect of becoming even more alienated from the school to which I'd eventually return.

Christmas passed, and then Huang said I should continue to remain at home. I vaguely felt I had been cheated and wondered if she had planned all along to keep me out of school the entire year. Soon after we realized my absence from school would likely last through June, we made some arrangements with our telephone company. On a cold morning early in winter, two technicians arrived with the ugly, gray intercom device that would keep my academic career on schedule: I could complete fourth grade by listening to my classes.

Plugged into a regular telephone jack, the "box" allowed me to hear the sounds of my classroom. I heard teachers teach and students answer questions; I could also hear unplanned fourth-grade giggles or the commotion made while students entered formation for the lunch line. I pressed a rectangular button on the box to make a noise alerting the teacher when I had something to say. Then I held down the button to speak. In the beginning, I never volunteered answers, because while other students raised their hands silently, every time I pressed the button, the click noise boomed out into the classroom.

The movie about the boy who grew up living in a sterile, plastic bubble had recently aired on television, and my mother and I noted at the time that the young man had used a television monitor to communicate with his schoolmates.

"Don't I even get a screen to look at, like he did?" I asked my mother.

"I guess that only happens on television," she answered.

I could not help but think that my sitting at home talking to a metal box also belonged only on television. The box suddenly changed fourth grade into a surreal experience.

In the midst of the intercom nonsense, my fourth-grade teacher Donna Trumbo launched the best campaign she could to keep me involved with her class. She often called upon me when I "clicked" and treated my answers as though I had given them in the classroom. She casually described visual images whenever I needed them to understand a round of laughter or an illustrative launching point for a day's lesson. Trumbo simultaneously helped me maintain a presence among my classmates and provided me with enough information to leave me almost unhindered by the intercom arrangement.

Once my teacher invited me to help clean her classroom after school, just so I could get back into the building. The threat of infection went home with the students, we thought, so my visit would be permissible. Still, the few remaining fourth-graders in the room looked out for me: we vacuumed, clapped erasers, straightened desks, and cleaned the blackboard, all without coming within six feet of each other.

Trumbo, a worldly woman in her thirties with a wonderfully sarcastic sense of humor, helped me keep a bemused detachment that saw me through the year. Talking to her made me realize the arrangement would not last forever. Trumbo seemed slightly out of place among the conservative St. Thomas faculty, many of whom were nuns or older women with grown-up families. When she regularly arrived at school with wet hair because her permanent could not withstand a hair dryer, another teacher would issue matronly warnings that Trumbo might catch cold. While some teachers condescended to their small charges, Trumbo did not change her manner when she addressed us.

Though my parents and I never complained about the tutoring policy to Trumbo, she visited our

Teresa and Ms. Trumbo

house regularly to help me on her own time. She refused payment and stopped her car in front of our mailbox once to return a check my mother had managed to lodge under a windshield wiper. My teacher and I spent hours absorbed in a game of Chinese checkers she had brought me near the beginning of my exile. When American history or long division grew too weighty for us, we focused on the colorful game board and marbles.

Without Trumbo, my isolation would have been complete. Although I once attended a slumber party and occasionally visited school, I followed Huang's instruction to avoid most contact with my peers. At first I tried to keep in touch with some of my friends and called them at home. Our conversations grew increasingly awkward because fourth-graders tend to discuss only the business of day-to-day life, and I had no news to tell. I could sound interested in what my friends did, or hear the latest in birthday party gossip, but had little to say except that I felt fine and missed everyone. In the interest of my staying popular—I had been in the social mainstream in second and third grade—my mother suggested I keep the intercom activated after classes to offer a "dial-a-joke" service to my classmates. Her humor escaped me.

Without academic or extracurricular activities to draw me out of the house—I had even sacrificed my beloved ballet lessons—I often found that my only outing all week would be attending Sunday Mass in a church only one mile from our house. Sometimes after Mass, I glimpsed classmates leaving church with their families; I would think about how quickly our worlds had diverged.

My days soon became indistinguishable. I would sit up straight at my mother's white wicker desk, watching my two fish spin around in their bowl. Ms. Trumbo had given me sweet

Goldilocks and mafioso Bugsy as Christmas presents. I listened to classroom conversations and tried to click my button at least twice during each class.

When my classmates traveled to rooms without phone jacks—as they did for music, art, gym classes, and the library—someone would turn off the box. Occasionally I used the time for homework, but more often I would experiment in the kitchen or watch daytime television, favoring *All My Children*. My mother had grown up in New York going to school with Susan Lucci, one of the show's leading actresses, and that seemed reason enough to watch it.

Apart from the time I devoted to academics, I idled and daydreamed my way through fourth grade. I read as many books as possible so I could lose myself in them. I repeatedly imagined my return to school. I lived in the future because my present had stranded me in a fortress I could not escape.

CHAPTER
❂ FIVE

In the fall, I, thank goodness, began fifth grade with my classmates and finally felt some semblance of normality returning to
my life. I reduced the previous year to nothing more than a bad
dream. I would forget quickly and start anew.

In mid-October I needed another course of IV antibiotics and
entered Allentown Hospital because of its close proximity to
home. Huang would unofficially call the shots from Philadelphia
while I remained near school and my family. I did not want to fall
behind in school work or lose touch with the fifth grade in this
year of new beginnings. Cards poured into my hospital room, one
from a classmate who wrote, "I'm so glad that you won't have to
use the box anymore."

During my stay in Allentown Hospital, I came to know well
a group of student nurses who worked there. Some of them I
knew already because my parents had occasionally hired them to
babysit for Ted, Susan, and me. The rest grew familiar when they
began gathering regularly in my room to watch *General Hospital*.
One of the students had convinced me to tune in to the soap, and
thereafter they all flocked to the one place on the pediatric ward
where they could see the show. During commercial breaks, the
students took turns explaining the plot's history to me.

For Halloween the students costumed themselves while I
chose not to join the festivities. I found the peace a great relief

A blissful Halloween

*The newspaper captioned this as Teresa receiving a tray full of holiday cheer—
although Teresa didn't necessarily agree!*

after marching as the Cowardly Lion. Some classmates sent in candy, but apart from the massive visitor influx into my room, the stay remained quiet and without commotion.

I found my way into a local paper on Halloween as the centerpiece in a picture of dressed-up student nurses. The caption said the students had brought me "holiday cheer." Newspaper in hand, I quizzed the students as they came into my room the next day: Could they define holiday cheer, and had they brought it to me? I thought I had as much as I wanted on my own.

During that admission and another, and during all the times they babysat the three of us, I grew to know that class of student nurses very well. When they graduated, a bunch of them chipped in to buy me a copy of their yearbook, which included a picture of me taken during Halloween.

My hospital stay lasted three weeks, during which I developed pneumonia that went undetected by pediatricians. The Allentown doctors had always appeared unfazed during rounds, attributing all symptoms to CF. I had struggled with an increasingly frequent cough, but they told us not to be concerned. Had I been older, I might have suspected they had written off my case as hopeless. I would learn later that too many doctors treat CF as passively as these unknowing pediatricians.

When my parents and I returned to the St. Chris's clinic, doctors there hurriedly roused us to action. After viewing my X-ray films, one of Huang's colleagues drew us into a conference room. She pointed to the films and said that with lungs as congested as mine, I had no choice but to immediately undergo a bronchial lavage. During a lavage, pulmonary doctors would extend an instrument down my trachea to suction as much fluid as they could from my lungs. Once a fully orthodox method of treatment, the lavage has since been blacklisted as a procedure that causes more harm than good when it stirs the bacteria and stimulates a new wave of infection.

When the doctor gestured to my X-rays, she stunned me with her nonchalance. No one before had treated my condition as routine business. She sought my parents' approval, and not mine, for surgery that would violate my chest while I lay fully anesthetized. She seemed reconciled to the fact that CF had compromised me and my life would be harder now. I could not fault her for her attitude or advice; she did what the situation required. But even as a new initiate, I knew I never wanted to accept the grim world before me or be part of it.

In an effort to bring good from a troubling situation, I agreed to help a clinic nurse prepare a book about the surgery for future patient use. Initially we planned to film the operation but could not get permission. The lavage became such a traumatic experience, however, that I later apologetically refused to help with the book. I did not want to recall any of my experience and hardly felt I could say anything to reassure others.

For me the experience began the night before when I had to stop eating after midnight. Mom, who stayed at the hospital most of the time, had recommended I stay awake late into the night so that I would sleep much of the next day away. One of my roommates in a four-bed room did the same in preparation for surgery of her own the next day. Our room became a social center that night as teenagers filled chairs and a vacant bed, joining us while they ate their midnight snacks.

I would have enjoyed this chance to mingle with the teenagers, some of whom I had forgiven for kicking me out of the Teen Room, except that they ate their food in such a very palpable manner. They had Cokes, pizza, crackers, and sandwiches, none of which would have been exceptional on an ordinary night but I so wanted to eat. The teens became an intermittent chorus of "yum" and "good stuff" and "here, want some?" I had sent Mom on an eleventh hour mission to the vending machine for canned pasta, but the machine had been broken. One teen recited to my mother his entire recipe for sticky buns, which I fortunately did not like.

In the morning I could not get used to the way I had become an inanimate object to so many wearers of white. They carted me away, and I parted with my mother at the elevator. No one addressed me or explained anything. I looked at their faces and tried to form a question, just so I could hear them talk. When the anesthesiologist put a mask on my face, she barely spoke to me and then walked away. Despite the obvious need for me to surrender to the anesthesia, I did not feel comfortable without direction. After all, perhaps the doctor hadn't expected me to go under right away and she had given me too much anesthetic. I could not see her anywhere and did not want to close my eyes until I knew she had control of the situation.

So I quietly spoke through the mask, trying to get someone's attention.

"Um, excuse me . . . um . . . over here . . . I have a question . . . hello . . . excuse me . . ."

Finally the doctor came to my side.

"I just want to make sure it's all right if I close my eyes now," I said.

She gave an affirmation and chuckled before turning away from me.

Then I remember waking up with a metal rod in my throat. They pulled it out quickly as I opened my eyes and gagged. No one had mentioned that I would be awakened with the equipment still down my throat, and I felt sure someone had made a mistake.

I remained groggy while they wheeled me to the recovery room. In the understaffed recovery area, a handful of nurses made their way among several partially dormant children. Their main function seemed to be to force us to drink fluids, which we spit up all over the place. I soon covered my hospital gown with red punch. The nurses laughed. I asked, pleaded, demanded to be taken back upstairs. I wanted to see my mother. The nurses laughed. I decided hospitals must assign mean nurses to recovery rooms so that we would not have to encounter them while fully awake.

When finally I returned upstairs, I told my dad, who had driven to town, about the horrible rod in my throat. He said they had not made a mistake but had done what they needed to do to trigger the important gagging reflex. Anyone coming out of anesthesia needs to sputter a bit to make the transition to consciousness safely.

The sensation had frightened me because I believed the doctors were unintentionally choking me. Dad said most patients do not recall those first moments of gagging, but I told him I did not care; someone should have told me.

This handful of frustrating episodes, along with the chest pain I felt after the operation, soured the lavage experience for me. As expected, I received a short-term boost from the surgery, but I refused to attribute my well-being to the lavage. My father humored me: "So you don't think you're better because of the lavage, huh? Then what do you think helped you?"

I would self-righteously make up something about the potency of one of my medicines.

After the lavage and ten days of antibiotics, I returned home.

My mother spoke to Huang on my first night back, and when she finished with the telephone, she bore bad news: my doctor wanted me to spend another entire school year at home.

I cried wildly at the news, which promised to make me a freak. I had great faith in Huang, but I hoped she knew the sacrifice she asked of me. Again I fled to the future and its possibilities.

My young fifth-grade teacher lacked Trumbo's thoughtfulness and insight. She may have meant well when she joked about the intercom and reduced her class to giggles; she never noticed, however, that I didn't join in their laughter. When I paused in giving an answer, I would become the target of an absurd joke.

"Okay, Teresa, put the bottle down. We know what you're up to," the teacher would say. "Have you gone and gotten drunk on us again? I thought you were on the wagon."

While the fifth-graders laughed themselves silly, my mother would emerge from the kitchen in tears, having heard the exchange. Once I had to talk her out of trying to get the teacher fired. The comments never bothered me as much as they did my mother, but I'd roll my eyes at the stupid gray box.

More daring than I'd been during fourth grade, I visited school for several special occasions that year. When I attended a school play featuring most of my classmates, I felt frustrated about never being considered for even a non-speaking role. The class performed *1776*, and I thought I at least could have portrayed a silent delegate at the Constitutional Convention as well as anyone else. I asked the teacher when she had held the auditions, about which I'd never been told.

"Tuned-in Teresa"

"You didn't want a part, or anything, did you?" she asked in a tone that told me I would not have been cast anyway. I didn't know if I wanted a part, but I knew I felt hurt.

"Oh, no. I just wondered when everyone tried out for this, that's all."

Our parish newsletter attempted to use the cheery intercom arrangement for an upbeat feature story. I headlined as "Tuned-in Teresa." Next to the article, a picture showed me sitting in front of the box with one hand on the click button while the widow Goldilocks watched curiously from her bowl. I did not smile at the camera.

Welcome advice would come soon, however. While considering a move to Boston in the spring of 1980, my parents and I visited the Children's Hospital Medical Center there and met the renowned Dr. Harry Shwachman. Within minutes of meeting us, he spoke the words that first earned him my loyalty: "You should never have stayed home from school this long—we'll get you back there in the fall."

We didn't move to Boston but decided the six-hour drive to Children's would be worth it. He had more progressive things to say: "It's awfully hard to fit three treatments into a normal day; if you just do two sometimes, that's all right." He also said, "It's very important to increase your calorie intake; go ahead and start eating some of those high-fat foods you've been avoiding."

I found the dietary advice too good to be true. I could eat cake and ice cream at parties, which I could now attend. I could buy popcorn at movies. Best of all, I could eat chocolate.

So began a relationship that would make me an educated patient who sought to understand my medical care. From our earliest meeting, Shwachman explained every recommendation he made, although I asked few questions. Until then I had conformed nicely to the informal medical directive that patients should be passive and trusting. I had never cared to know the difference between drugs or the reason a new theory had beaten out its competitors.

Shwachman taught me to nurture a curiosity toward medical matters. At first I felt burdened with any new information; I wanted to let experts tell me only what I needed to know. But Shwachman helped me see that I needed to rely on my own knowledge and good judgment if I hoped to gain any measure of independence. I had wanted, been conditioned, to be a drone who obeyed without thinking. In refusing to let me be, Shwachman gave me self-reliance.

He also took care of Susan, who as a healthy, precocious four-year-old did not require the same amount of medical attention I did. Susan appeared to approve of Shwachman because she never slugged him as she might have otherwise.

Amicable but strong-willed, the aging Shwachman had been one of the greatest champions of CF patients. Just over seventy years old, he had spent more than thirty years fighting the disorder and couldn't bear to retire. Though he'd helped found the National Cystic Fibrosis Research Foundation in 1955, he often talked about how the modern Cystic Fibrosis Foundation had become a politicized big business he no longer recognized. His opinion came as disturbing, to say the least, to a family that had spent years raising money for the foundation.

In Schwachman's 1986 obituary the *Boston Globe* called him the "world's leading authority" on CF. Patients came to him from all over the world. His name fills CF literature, in part because he developed the Shwachman Score, a scale to rate the severity of a patient's illness. He singled out and named Shwachman's syndrome, a digestive disorder with some symptoms similar to those of CF. Shwachman worked hard at the

Teresa, Susan, and Dr. Harry Shwachman

violin, and always seemed to be preparing for a concert with the Newton Symphony 9 Orchestra, which he helped found. Textbooks, journals, and drug samples loaded down the shelves behind his desk, while pictures of patients and magic marker drawings covered his office walls.

He talked about his patients like a proud grandfather. The Jewish Shwachman, whose daughter lived in Tel Aviv, spoke most proudly about his Israeli patients. He often boasted about Les Fride, a young Israeli who helped found the International Association of CF Adults (IACFA) in the early 1980s. Shwachman kept copies of the IACFA newsletter on hand and first told me about the patient organization I would join later. Shwachman also felt proud of Olympic skater Scott Hamilton, whom he treated for Shwachman's syndrome.

Shwachman's bigger-than-life stature attracted envy, and doctors seemed either openly to admire him or secretly to despise him. He would not play political games and spent his last years in an outwardly imposed professional isolation for that reason.

He made the fight against cystic fibrosis his own yoke to bear, and it weighed heavily on him. Yet as much as he suffered, he found joy in so many things: when one of his patients won a beauty contest, he told the story so often I grew tired of it. More than anything else, Shwachman epitomized the kind of old-fashioned doctor who cared about little else besides the welfare of patients. So many crossroads would litter the medical field; so many arrows would direct doctors away from their patients. Competition, the keeping of secrets for publication, the race for titles—all would emerge as Shwachman watched in sad silence. Gradually, I came to understand these observations that so often made him sigh and hold his tongue before a young innocent.

When we left Shwachman's office that first day, his hospital and the entire city of Boston became for me a wonderland of new opportunities and a changed way of life. Shwachman had begun to revolutionize my world.

CHAPTER
❧ SIX

Shwachman recommended that I receive frequent courses of IV antibiotics, and I soon found myself spending two weeks at Children's every three to four months. There I grew accustomed to a tiny, twelve-bed, hospital ward called Division 39. Through its neutral decorations and the sportive manner of its staff, the ward deftly avoided all classification as a place for the very young. It still managed, however, to include one floor bathroom accessible to those three feet tall and under.

Young CF patients almost always stayed on Division 39 and sometimes as many as six of us would be there at the same time. Some patients clung to their parents or did not know enough about CF to allow for a straightforward conversation, but most of us became friends. We found among us a bond that stretched far beyond the few days we cohabitated. We understood each other the way no one outside our numbers could. We often communicated with facial expressions, warning each other from across a room to dodge a particular medical student or some other unwelcome visitor.

For many of us, the beginnings of cynicism had shaped our perspective, but we knew only that we shared certain assumptions. For example, we expected hospital budget cuts to hit close to home, and they did. We lost our IV team, which left us at the mercy of interns and residents. We lost some physical therapy coverage, which left us with fewer sessions of chest percussion. My father wrote a letter of complaint to the head of the hospital about the physical therapy, but we young patients regarded the cuts with resignation.

After daily rounds, we sometimes speculated about the politics between doctors. "They don't like her, do they?" we would note about a woman whose suggestions had been repeatedly ridiculed. We made it our business to observe as much as we could. We knew most doctors would never be fully candid with us; we could not even read our medical charts unless we fetched them when no interns or residents stood near enough to object. Nurses let us read the charts because they knew how we struggled to educate ourselves in this strange environment.

My friends and I actually felt relieved when we came across a new pulmonary fellow or resident who would ask his or her superior silly questions in front of us; more often we felt humbled by the mass of knowledge that so directly concerned us but of which we had so poor an understanding. Besides Shwachman, few doctors explained anything to us unless our parents stood within hearing distance.

Among this unnatural society of young CF patients groping for adulthood, I realized I would rarely find such friends with whom I could so readily express my fears and desires. I sensed it would be many long years before I could tell healthy friends my age everything I had to say. In this I grew apart from my young friends at home: I could not think of a way to convey what I had seen and felt on Division 39 to healthy peers finishing their last years in grade school.

Several of my admissions coincided with those of a tiny CF patient three years my junior. So Tracey Root and I became close friends despite the age difference between us. We built our friendship around laughter, both the amused variety and that of a sarcasm come early for our years. We endured so much absurdity together that we could only tolerate it by smiling.

When first we found ourselves roommates, Tracey and I took pleasure in the fact that doctors, nurses, and laboratory technicians repeatedly confused our identities. Because we appeared strikingly different, especially in size, we could not understand the mistake the first few times we received each other's mail or meals. Tracey's weight and bone development lagged behind her age, while I maintained a healthy weight. Busy medical professionals appeared to be too pressed for time to notice details like age, build, and hair color. Sometimes we let the mistake continue until a tourniquet had been tied around the wrong arm.

> May 29, 1982
> I am hereby starting a journal as I want someone somewhere to remember who Teresa Mullin was after I die. I have a constant threat of death hanging over my head because I was born with Cystic Fibrosis an inherited lung disease that is presently #1 on the Genetic Children's Killer Disease List. I am writing this to share my thoughts with my family as well as posterity after my death.

The first entry in Teresa's journal in 1982.
Even then, she was determined to tell her story.

Inevitably cheerful, at least to most observers, Tracey would often sing in her high voice; usually she parodied toy commercials or repeated her favorite top-forty song, "My baby takes the morning train . . ." Like any repeat visitor to a pediatric hospital, she could recite most of the dialogue to syndicated episodes of *The Brady Bunch.*

Most nights Tracey and I stayed awake and talked for hours after nurses arrived for the eleven o'clock shift; we discussed the day's events, staff members we did or didn't like, and our lives at home. One of our nurses made sure these talks took place with the lights out and the two of us in bed. When I heard her coming, I would whisper sharply to Tracey to "be asleep." The nurse often knew better and stayed to talk to her two restless charges. She liked to sing us the popular 1970s song, "They're Coming to Take Me Away," in which men in white suits escort the lyricist to a funny farm where life is always beautiful.

During the day, Tracey and I spent much of our free time before a pinball machine in the floor's activity center. When someone starts an IV in a hand vein, they will tape an arm board (often a rectangular piece of Styrofoam covered with a gauze bandage) to the hand to immobilize the fingers. Reduced hand movement may prevent the IV needle from poking out of the vein before its time. The boards complicate tasks such as writing, brushing one's teeth, and cutting up meat at dinnertime. Tracey and I prided ourselves on being the high pinball scorers despite the bulky arm boards. Instead of activating the flipper by hand on the IV side, we whacked it with a corner of the board.

The hospital tutor entered our room regularly, bringing Tracey's missed school assignments neatly written on construction paper pumpkins or cornucopias. Tearing into her books faithfully, even when I had buried my own in the back of the closet, Tracey seemed troubled by the prospect of repeating a grade. I told her several times, however, to work at a more relaxed pace, citing myself as a role model. As long as I could argue that I attended school in another state and I remained caught up with my work, thank you, I could avoid daily sessions with the tutor who chased after all my friends.

Tracey and I spent two consecutive Thanksgivings and two of her birthdays together. We twice voted the stretchable plastic pilgrim that came with the hospital's Thanksgiving dinner "Best Item on Tray."

Tracey became the happiest I ever saw her at one of her birthday parties, when most of the Division 39 staff crowded into the activity center to sing and watch her blow out candles on a hospital cake. Little Tracey sat at a small, round table in a room wallpapered with children's pictures of nondescript blobs, enjoying the party and thinking about the one that would be thrown for her later at home. Through her jubilation I saw for the first time an innocence that made me uncomfortable because it made her vulnerable. I mouthed the words to the happy birthday song, but I suddenly saw the party as an odd charade. I did not think Tracey could afford to remain a little girl.

I wanted to protect Tracey; I went so far as to discuss her case with the doctors we had in common. Couldn't they find a way to help her gain weight? I asked them. The information should officially have been privileged, but I wanted to know all the methods they had tried to help her gain weight. One of the doctors patiently listed all the failed attempts. When he said doctors could do little else for her, I did not believe him and quietly seethed.

After I outgrew Division 39 and began venturing up to the floor for older patients, I tried to persuade Tracey she should give the new floor a chance. We could both stay on Division 37 now, I told her. And I, for one, would find it a relief to quit making small talk with five-year-old roommates. No, Tracey said, she had found her niche; she knew Division 39 well.

The last time I saw Tracey, in the summer of 1984, our ways had clearly parted. I had just finished my grueling first year of high school. I had stayed on Division 37 several times and hardly knew any of the small children who frequented 39. That last time, I visited her room on movie night. Volunteer Bob Groden, known at Children's as the Movie Man, brought the video cassette recorder to the side of Tracey's bed instead of showing the film at the activity center as usual. Bob showed the movie Tracey had asked for, *The Muppet Movie,* forgoing the traditional vote among younger patients.

Tracey's mother and a friend sat beside her. Through the whole show she stayed leaning back against several pillows with her eyes closed. She opened them once to smile at me through the oxygen mask that took up most of her face. Her weak gesture made me bite my lip hard. I hated the little muppets laughing on screen for their happiness and nervously made about ten trips to the popcorn popper, just to have something to do. I could not decide whether to pretend to watch the movie or to lean over Tracey's bed in tears to try talking to her. I did not want to upset her, but she seemed to understand the moment.

When I did stand at the foot of her bed to talk to Tracey and her mother, I could not easily find words. How can you make small talk with someone you know is dying? Words, though perhaps all you have left to give, seem meaningless. Talking about plans for the future or your own health sounds callous. World events, sports teams, and the weather no longer affect the person you're addressing. What's left? Getting too serious means you all might break down into uncontrollable sobs. When you only have one chance to bid farewell to someone you loved like a sister, words form a barrier. I said only trivial things, commented about the pizza Tracey tried to eat.

Before I left the hospital a few days later, I went back to Division 39 to see her for a few minutes. I knew I would be more than three hundred miles away in Pennsylvania when she died. I tried to sound hopeful, talked about her getting better. Yet she knew as well as I did we would never see each other again. She held on for more than two months after I saw her, dying in late August, a battle-weary twelve-year-old.

CHAPTER
❈ SEVEN

Taken with the idea of having sisters as poster children, the Philadelphia chapter of the CF Foundation made Susan and me the official patient representatives for Eastern Pennsylvania, New Jersey, and Delaware in 1982. I had been a poster child in 1974, when I posed with Durham Mayor James Hawkins. I would adopt a more active role this time, however, as Susan and I began making appearances.

During my years in seventh and eighth grade, my mother patiently chauffeured the two of us to fund-raisers scattered throughout those three states. Susan and I came to enjoy the Foundation luncheons, where we met politicians and sports heroes whose names we would learn when Susan asked them to write in her autograph book. In our early days as poster children, Susan and I never spoke a word at the benefits we attended. A speaker would introduce us at the podium, the crowd would applaud, and then we took our seats.

At one such event, none of the speakers or anyone seated at the head table seemed to understand the cause for which they had undertaken to raise money. During the country club luncheon, the organizer's husband turned to my mother and asked in a conversational tone, "Just what kind of disease is CF, anyway?"

The keynote speaker, a local sportscaster, spoke mainly of his career, and talked of hair spray and helicopter travel. Discreetly,

I coughed loudly a few times to remind him and everyone else why we had gathered there. The women sat mesmerized by the handsome speaker, and if he'd said half a dozen words about CF, they would have remembered it. There would probably never be as good a chance to tell these people about CF, and this man stood coyly telling them he'd never thought of himself as a sex symbol but he guessed he had become one.

I stared at him hard, trying to catch his eye. I thought he might remember the cause when he saw the two "sick" little girls seated near the front of the dining room. Yet after the speech he left hurriedly, never having glanced in our direction.

Susan and Teresa, 1982 poster girls

"Oh, your daughters are so sweet," a woman said to my mother as we left, as though Susan and I could not hear them. "What's that called, that they have, again?"

My mother realized as a result of that luncheon that we needed to start educating people. She asked me if I'd be willing to give short speeches about CF, given the opportunity. I agreed reluctantly. Short science presentations in school had been the extent of my public speaking career. Once in biology, I'd lost points for addressing the blackboard during a presentation about an animal we'd been studying and its habitat. I'd drawn a diagram and stood staring at it until I finished talking, too nervous to turn and face my classmates. Now I agreed to tell hundreds of strangers all about my way of life because shyness never saved any lives and I thought maybe we could make a difference somehow.

At home my mother doggedly made phone call after phone call until she received a guarantee I'd get at least five minutes of the program the next time.

My mother helped me with the speeches in the beginning, and we labored over them. Then I got cocky and would still be composing in the car on the way to the benefit, scribbling notes on a napkin or tissue box.

"This is the way Lincoln did it," I'd say when Mom scolded me, alluding to the way the president drafted the Gettysburg Address en route to the battlefield.

On my first few outings, I spoke gravely about my medical routine and my determination to outlive statistics that said I wouldn't reach age twenty; I also delivered heartbreaking anecdotes about hospital friends. I practiced while standing before my mother with a soup spoon we used as a microphone.

"More eye contact," Mom would say when I'd look down at my notes for too long, "and try to slow down or they're not going to understand what you're saying."

When I first made an audience cry, I could not understand what had happened. I recited the known statistics: thirty thousand American patients; average life expectancy of twenty-one; and CF claimed a life every eight hours. I talked about my own life: the three daily treatments, the forty pills I took each day, the fact that I thought I would never be an athlete. I gave what I considered a pretty routine presentation—nothing I would have expected to make people cry—so the teary faces and stifled whimpers alarmed me. I looked to my mother, the only smiling woman in the room, for help. What had I done wrong? Adhering to my outline as much as possible, I began to insert comforting and optimistic words and phrases. I spoke louder and louder as the sobbing listeners grew noisier.

The afternoon unsettled me, but at home my mother told me I'd finally put the right amount of passion behind my words. She wanted, as I did, to raise as much money as possible for the cause and she knew tears indicated I had hit my mark.

While I gave speeches, Susan appeared at the functions as the shy but adorable little girl alongside me. Organizers would introduce her to the crowd while she sat quietly with my mother. At first I worried about speaking so bluntly about CF while six-year-old Susan listened. But my mother and I worked hard to emphasize the positive in conversations with her. Susan gradually came to understand the things she so often heard me say.

I rarely thought of healthy Susan as a CF patient, and fortunately her condition gave me little cause to do so. She would stay well and enter high school without ever having needed a single course of IV antibiotics. I took for granted the luxury of not needing to worry about her; so many CF siblings lived through parallel crises, but we never did. I saw my main responsibility to her as conveyer of all I had learned. For the most part we could just be sisters and give little thought to our mutual adversary.

Susan and I agreed that our brief meeting with Joan Rivers crowned our time as poster children. We met Rivers in a dressing room at the local Stabler Arena in April 1982. Neither Susan nor I had ever paid attention to Rivers or her unique brand of humor. When the CF Foundation arranged a meeting between Rivers, its honorary national chairperson, and the two of us, my mother needed to explain to Susan and me who Rivers was.

Cystic Fibrosis Picks Poster Duo

By BOB SHARPE
Globe-Times Staff Writer

Teresa Mullen is only 13 years old, but the Salisbury Township youngster has the vocabulary of a first-year medical student. Teresa and her sister Susan, 6, both suffer from cystic fibrosis, a disease for which there is no cure.

"It's an inherited lung disease that affects the lungs and pancreas and causes respiratory and digestive problems," said Teresa. "It can be very fatal. A lot of people don't realize the average life span of a child with cystic fibrosis is 20 years."

The Mullen sisters were chosen last week as 1982 cystic fibrosis poster children for eastern Pennsylvania, New Jersey and Delaware.

They met Thursday afternoon with Allentown Mayor Joseph Daddona, who proclaimed Sunday, May 2, as Cystic Fibrosis Bike-A-Thon Day. The 20-mile ride through Allentown, South Whitehall and Salisbury will raise money for cystic fibrosis research.

Teresa must devote three hours daily to medical and physical therapy, and take 44 pills a day that contain enzymes, antibiotics and vitamins. Her little sister spends two hours a day at similar therapy.

"I've gotten used to it, but I have to get up early to spend an hour on therapy before school, then when I get home from school and once more before I go to bed," said Teresa, a seventh-grader at St. Thomas More School in Allentown. Susan attends kindergarten at the same school.

In addition to daily therapy, Teresa is regularly hospitalized. "I have to go into the hospital for two weeks about every three months for IV therapy," Teresa said. The hospital treatment consists of concentrated doses of drugs.

This year is not the first time the sisters, daughters of Dr. Edward and Patricia Mullen of 2965 Fairfield Drive North, Salisbury, have been poster children. Susan was Lehigh Valley poster child two years ago and Teresa the same in North Carolina in 1974.

A genetic disease that is not contagious and whose cause is not known, cystic fibrosis has symptoms which appear at birth. The disease causes mucus to build inside lungs and hamper breathing. Intestinal organs fail to secrete enzymes which digest food. Excessive salt loss results in children risking heat exhaustion or dehydration.

"The extra mucus blocks the lungs and that's what eventually kills children," said Teresa. "Cystic kids have a hard time gaining weight; I'm a little underweight myself."

The chairman of the bike-a-thon, Jim Hallock, is pushing for 1,500 riders and hopes to raise at

least $75,000. Hallock, owner of Village Peddler bike shop in South Whitehall, has a special interest in the fundraising — his only daughter Jan died from cystic fibrosis 13 years ago at age 23.

Hallock said the mayor has promised not only to ride in the event, but to assemble a City Hall bike team.

Cedar Crest Plaza Shopping Center is both starting and finishing point for the fifth annual "Breath of Life Bike-A-Thon," which begins at 1 p.m. with registration from noon. Prizes may be won by riders who bring in $25 or more in sponsors and each participant receives a free cycling cap. For more information, Hallock asks interested persons to call 395-8288.

(Globe-Times Photo by Bob Sharpe)

Sisters Susan, Left, and Theresa Mullen of Salisbury Twp.

One of many newspaper articles

Several days before we met Rivers, I talked with my mother about what I would wear. I planned to pose in a turtleneck, pleated skirt, and corduroy blazer.

"I'm sorry, but they want you two to wear something frilly," my mother said.

"Frilly!" I shouted in disgust. My mother nodded. Frills, she had been told, would create the right look on camera—the fragile and vulnerable patients pleading for help.

"Gross," I decreed, and Mom shrugged.

After searching futilely in my closet for the required frills, my mother and I hunted for hours in a local shopping mall.

"You've got to be kidding," I said every time my mother held up what she considered a prospective outfit.

As the store began closing on the one night we had available to shop, we quickly conceded to a blouse with floral print, puffed-up shoulders, ruffled collar and bow, and a pink skirt that matched. We had decidedly filled our frill quota.

"Shoes! What are you going to do about shoes?" my mother panicked as we left the store.

"Sandals, Mom. No one's going to see my feet in the pictures."

My mother had an easier time with Susan, who merely opened her closet and picked out one of the pretty, ruffly dresses six-year-olds wear.

At the arena an official ushered my family into a small, lamplit room adjoining Rivers' private dressing room. We met her and quietly spoke with her for a few minutes. We told her our names, our ages, how we liked school; we asked about her tour, her daughter, and when she would return home.

Then an army of photographers and TV camera operators flooded into the room and started shooting away at Rivers, Susan, and me. The press moved in so fast it seemed I had only blinked once in the time it took for a low-key introduction to become a media event.

After a minute or two of talking to TV cameras and smiling for the flashbulbs, Rivers started laughing and leaned back in mimicry of the photographers contorting into awkward positions to capture small Susan and slightly taller Rivers in the same frame. Rivers knelt on the floor, wrapped her arms around us, and asked if she'd made it easier to photograph us together.

I had never looked into so many lenses at once before, and I tried to count them all but kept losing track.

"Over here," someone rallied for our attention and a good picture. "Look this way, girls."

Before the photo session had gotten underway, nine-year-old Ted had handed Rivers a bouquet of white roses and told her the flowers came from our family "in appreciation" for being honorary chairperson of the Foundation. Rivers, who had become involved with the Foundation because her godchild had CF, looked impressed with the friendly third-grader who had marched up to her and spoken confidently. Ted stood patiently aside with my parents while the cameras rolled. After several minutes of posing with Susan and me, Rivers stopped and motioned to Ted.

I'd worried sometimes about whether or not my little brother felt left out. He hadn't understood why our parents spent so much time giving Susan and me chest percussion. He'd cheerfully tagged along when we had to go to doctor appointments. It must have been difficult to watch his sisters receive so much attention, but Ted never complained.

Teresa, Joan Rivers, and Susan

"Now get some pictures of me with the boy," Rivers said. Though most of the cameras had been lowered and many lens caps replaced when Susan and I stepped away, Rivers gave Ted his own special moment. In another blink, the press left almost as quickly as they'd arrived. We left a minute later. Rivers had to prepare for her show. She impressed us in our few minutes with her as genuinely eager to help the cause.

Ted with Joan Rivers

Not all celebrities gave of their time selflessly; some seemed only to want the favorable publicity. My mother once took the three of us to Philadelphia so Susan could pose with a well-known baseball star. Young poster children and their families filled a small section of the stands, and we all sat in the hot sun waiting for each child's turn. The main incentive for children so young to endure camera lights was the promise of an autograph, so many sat holding baseballs and pens.

Ted and I had idolized many of the Phillies players and respected this one. For years Dad had taken us to games at Veteran's Stadium whenever possible. My brother and I regularly traded baseball cards between us, so we were looking forward to this day.

One at a time, children went to sit on the player's knee. Cameras rolled and he read introductions off cue cards. The baseball celebrity appeared to regard the children with distaste; he did not smile in many of the shots but managed a grimace of a smile for Susan's.

When the cameras were done rolling, he walked away without looking back. A couple of small children asked their mothers when he would give them their autographs. All the parents present had assumed the player would sign the twenty or so baseballs that would have been proffered him. Instead, a stadium official appeared and boomed out at us to remain seated until the player had left the area. I felt offended that I, along with the rest of the assembled children and parents, had been judged a security risk. I decided Ted could have all that player's cards if he wanted them.

If the baseball star merely acted out a role cast for him by a publicity agent, I did no better. True, I only wanted to help the cause, however possible. But I did not give enough thought to the business of being a poster child.

I should have realized, should have made the intuitive observation, that making myself appear pathetic to strangers served no purpose other than to raise funds. In the long run, I would hurt my fellow CF patients by perpetuating an image of us as frail and helpless. I made melodramatic statements to audiences and reporters; I looked sadly into cameras or else smiled a delicate smile. Instead of fighting for acceptance, I emphasized, on cue, the things that made my life different.

I find it most alarming that I never questioned this call to compromise myself. Society nudged me into a role I accepted eagerly. I could only make my dilemma heard if I adopted the pose expected of a sick child. With every penny raised through pity, I sold my dignity.

No child should be urged to appear pathetic. When I used to watch myself on television or read one of the articles, I felt troubled by the anchor's dramatic words or the reporter's sentimental lead. At its best, being a poster child subjects one to well-meaning condescension. Pity flung at a child leaves scars; I have struggled to leave behind my own. A society that needs poster children to direct people's attention where it must go has not become fully civilized. We should not need to stand at a comfortable distance from those less fortunate than ourselves and point self-righteous fingers in their direction.

The chronically ill have no recourse in the face of this treatment. I grew up with the impression that the U.S. Constitution applied less to me than to my friends because no one had guaranteed me and my kind the "life, liberty and pursuit of happiness." No one has ever urged that we be accorded the same respect as our healthy counterparts. The media, through its sensationalism, and the public, through its outpouring of pity, have oppressed what may be the last minority group to be recognized as deserving of some fundamental accommodations. Our circumstances should no longer be toyed with as gripping headline material or sound bites. Too many people treat us in ways that could be called racist or sexist if they regarded matters of race or gender. We have had no label for this condescension; in fact it has often been described as consciousness or awareness of our problems.

We have a responsibility to educate others about our conditions, but once we have transmitted this information, we should receive acceptance and help. We should not need to plead or reward. Naturally we will be grateful for assistance, but respect and adequate medical treatment should be our right. Unfortunately many of us have been taught to believe otherwise. And many years ago, as an eager poster child, I contributed to the problem.

CHAPTER ❧ EIGHT

When finally I returned to school in sixth grade, an occasion I had so long awaited, I barely knew the other students. They welcomed me back but had little time for the stranger in their midst. My two years at home with the intercom put an unbridgeable distance between us. I felt lost and frustrated as I struggled to make new friends among a once familiar crowd. Through six and seventh grade, I depended entirely on two or three friends.

New students who joined our sixth-grade class could not understand my status when all our teachers welcomed me back. Some students asked if I had moved away and now returned.

When I emerged from my intercom exile, I found that academics posed little challenge. At home, I had needed to work to compensate for visual aids; the struggle kept me interested in my school work. Back in the classroom, however, I barely needed to work for good grades. My success did not go unnoticed. Classmates tried to pressure me into providing them with answers during tests and quizzes. I avoided confrontations as best I could by pretending I didn't know answers or hadn't heard their questions.

Our class eventually voted for me to represent them in our school's version of "scholastic scrimmage." But academic recognition did not bring popularity. My classmates and I had increasingly less in common. Cliques had formed during my intercom years, and

I found myself unwelcome. I began hearing about parties to which I had not been invited.

At the same time, I found my classes unengaging. Our teachers rarely taught us anything we could not have learned from assignments. So I began to look for challenges outside the classroom. I worked hard to be taken seriously at a ballet studio where I had just returned; I had studied dance there for a year before the intercom, after having danced for two years in Durham. I'd taken piano lessons since third grade, including the intercom years when the teacher came to our house, and now I seemed to be improving. I joined the St. Thomas bell choir, which performed at Masses and helped me improve my sight reading. I sang alto in the school's choral group and helped edit and design our seventh-grade literary magazine. Poetry fascinated me, and I wrote lengthy poems for class instead of book reports whenever possible.

Ballet was always one of Teresa's loves.

I finally decided to leave the school I'd attended for six years, the choice made easier by the alienation I felt. I would attend a public school where I could enroll in "gifted" classes and learn a language. One day near the end of the school year, I told the group of girls I considered my friends that I would be transferring. None of them acted surprised; none of them questioned me. None of them, in fact, seemed to care in the least.

"Did you hear me?" I asked slowly, carefully. "Are you surprised?"

The only response I received came gruffly: "Well, Teresa, what do you want us to do?"

So after an anxious summer of anticipation, I began eighth grade at Raub Middle School. Raub, with its two thousand students in grades six, seven, and eight, came as a welcome change after attending a small parochial school of five hundred where my health gave me an unwanted celebrity. In addition, I found more to interest me at Raub than I had at St. Thomas. The small size of my class, which included about fifteen students, livened up discussions. I enjoyed Spanish classes. I played piano in the Raub orchestra and joined the band homeroom. I worked on the school's quarterly newsletter. At Raub I found the academic and social satisfaction that had eluded me at St. Thomas.

By the time I reached Raub, I had become excessively self-conscious about my health. At St. Thomas I could hide nothing: when I entered the hospital, the principal there would remember me during morning prayers over the loudspeaker. At Raub, I wanted anonymity so desperately that I never even named my medical problem in front of the class. I would call it my "cough" or "lung problem" only when a reference became absolutely necessary, such as when a teacher would inquire why I hadn't stayed home from school if I couldn't stop coughing.

In the fall, the few weeks I spent in an Allentown hospital first set me apart from my classmates. When friends came to visit, I explained CF to many of them for the first time. I tried to downplay the illness as much as I could from a hospital bed. I used diminutive adjectives as in "little lung problem" and said I would only be hospitalized for a few days. When the days turned into two full weeks as I knew they would, I acted surprised.

"I'm not sure why they're keeping me here," I would say to friends, after having glanced out the door to make certain no doctors or nurses stood within earshot. Meanwhile, my three closest friends at Raub asked me direct questions. They wanted to know if I felt frightened, if being in the hospital would help much, and when I would return. I gave them honest answers.

My class sent a card to the hospital, and I wondered how much my peers knew. I felt grateful that they didn't know enough to treat me differently. At Raub, I could let my four years as a pariah become part of a distant past.

CHAPTER ❧ NINE

In eighth grade I decided I should give serious thought to my future. Few of the CF patients I knew had remained healthy enough to attend college, and I felt apprehensive about my prospects. I determined, however, to make my own opportunities and to give my condition little regard. I would begin by attending the best secondary school I could.

For several weeks I researched high schools across the country. I looked for schools with high matriculation to top colleges, competitive student SAT scores, a high faculty-student ratio, and a broad curriculum. I also wanted to be sure I could continue with dance lessons and begin studying Russian. I had read that for every teacher of English in the Soviet Union, only one person studied Russian in the United States. As President Reagan escalated hostility between the two countries, I decided I at least wanted to learn the Soviets' language.

I carefully read education guides and began eliminating from a list of more than one hundred schools. Although I knew my family would have preferred that I live at home, I soon realized I could find some of the most challenging academic environments among the preparatory schools in New England. I showed my father the final list, and he recognized all five: Exeter, Andover, Hotchkiss, St. Paul's, and Choate.

I registered for the Secondary School Admission Test (SSAT), asked my father to schedule the five school interviews at times convenient for him, and set about composing essays and soliciting recommendations. My father agreed to drive me to the campuses for interviews, but he and my mother had no intention of letting me attend school away from home.

Along with my parents, my school guidance counselor, church pastor, and several family friends all urged me to attend school locally. They insisted I should stay home for my own good. What would I do, they all asked, if my health faltered while I lived on a campus several hundred miles from home? How could I possibly manage my daily medical routine on my own?

Time after time, I tried to convince everyone I had made an adult decision. I had considered the responsibilities of my medical care and felt fully qualified to sustain my routine. I would remain in close contact with my parents and would handle medical crises as they occurred. The idea's opponents continually called upon me to defend my new goal; many seemed unprepared to listen to what I had to say. I stopped seeking approval and wanted only to convince my parents to let me go.

Friends my age did not voice the same resistance as had their elders, but they could not understand what drew me to the schools. I finally stopped trying to explain.

I knew something I did not think the adults in my life could understand: If I stayed at home and found the easy path, I would lose the chance to develop the strength I needed. If I made this first concession to my health, the surrender might not end. The same protective arguments would apply later to college and to life on my own. I would face the world now or miss my chance.

To my parents and to a reporter who wanted to know, I said only that I wanted the prep school experience because I might grow too sick for college. I believed I would somehow attend college, but my parents' uncertainty gave them one more reason to send me to prep school. I tried to explain to them why I needed to face the challenge at hand, but fell short of communicating my thoughts.

Leaving behind my family would be difficult; the prospect almost unnerved me. I would miss my parents and Ted and Susan. Ted had entered fourth grade that fall and Susan had entered first. I especially wanted to be a mentor to Susan as she grew older; I had so much to tell her about our way of life. As painful as the separation would be, however, I needed to go.

In late fall, my parents and I took our five-campus tour. When we reached our first stop, the Hotchkiss School in Lakeville, Connecticut, the beautiful campus helped me imagine a new way of life. Snow and ice covered the grounds, foreshadowing a New England winter like the ones I would come to love despite their treachery. Hotchkiss held magic for me that day as a student guide showed us classrooms and dorms. I felt sure I could be like the students we passed if only my parents would let me.

Hot tea in the admissions office came as soothing before the interview. I wore one of the suits I used when being a poster child did not require me to look like a broken toy. I had never faced an important interview before but prepared myself by comparing it to a speech: if I spoke slowly and clearly I would sound calm no matter how I felt. While I waited, a receptionist reviewing my file came over to praise my SSAT score. "You did very well," she said a few times before returning to her desk. Armed with her compliment, I walked steadily into the interviewer's office when he called me.

Admissions officer Fritz Mark and I talked for a long time about my interests and about Hotchkiss. I enjoyed our talk as much as I could because I thought Mark might cut it short when I mentioned CF. I expected him to react the way everyone at home had. I had kept my "big surprise" off the preliminary applications. I considered it entirely possible that all five schools would refuse to let me attend, but I would do my best to gain admission.

The moment came when Mark wanted to know if I had any more questions or anything to add before we ended the interview.

"Well, there is one little thing," I said with manufactured nonchalance and a smile I hoped would mask my panic. "I have cystic fibrosis."

The five syllables never sounded so horrible to me. Involuntarily, I looked at the folded hands in my lap, as though hanging my head in guilt.

"I can leave now," I felt ready to say. "I'm sorry I took so much of your time. I just wanted to visit a place like this. I guess it would be sort of silly for me to want to come here, wouldn't it?"

Mark seemed not to have heard me. He looked too calm to have understood my announcement. I began repeating myself when he nodded and asked what my problem involved. I thought maybe he needed to act sympathetic and polite, but I told him.

At first I used the kind of language I did with classmates. I said I regarded my little lung problem as "unpredictable." Then I stopped and took a deep breath.

"It's pretty serious," I said, losing for the first time the half smile I had maintained for the past hour. I told him I did not believe in statistics but that numbers did not give me much time.

"Well, we'll certainly do everything we can to help you."

I could not believe my good fortune. Whatever happened to me come fall, I had been partially initiated into the ranks of productive, healthy people. If none of the schools accepted me, I had the confidence I needed to find another route.

Mark meant it when he offered help. Although I did not attend Hotchkiss, he corresponded with me for several years after our interview, writing me during his vacation once to tell me about a big CF fund-raiser somewhere in the Midwest.

As my parents and I progressed on our tour, I could only hope they felt as mesmerized as I did. Phillips Exeter Academy stood out for its quaint brick-and-ivy campus and its incredible facilities. When we missed getting a full tour there, the director of admissions, history instructor John Herney, showed my parents and me the academy's library archives. Through ancient newspapers and documents, Herney led us through some of the climaxes of American history. After the impressive tour, I could sense my parents giving way to my prep school plans.

Later in the gym complex, I pressed my luck with the two of them.

"Look at this," I said about the two ice rinks and pools and all kinds of playing courts. "This is amazing. Don't you want your daughter to go to school here?"

I didn't get a yes response, but I suspected I might gain their reluctant approval by the time I needed to tell the schools my plans.

The wait for decision letters seemed endless. Fortunately, one of the schools called my parents early to tell them I'd been accepted. By the time of the phone call, my parents knew how much the acceptance meant to me. They buried their misgivings and celebrated. After dinner that night we ate cake reading "Go Hotchkiss!" in a dining room decorated with streamers of the school's blue and white colors.

The five acceptances came in mid-March. I stayed home from school the day they came to await the mail carrier. With five schools to choose from, I felt sure I could make the proper medical arrangements at one of them.

My parents and I failed at first to find a physical therapist near enough to any of the campuses to hire for my treatments. Only Choate Rosemary Hall had ever graduated a CF patient, and the student, we learned, never needed the same amount of treatment I did.

Meanwhile the doctor at Andover told my father I would be overwhelmed by the strenuous workload there.

"The seniors here can spend up to eight hours per night on homework," she told him, a figure my experience elsewhere would validate. "I think that might be too much for your daughter."

I chose Exeter over second-choice Hotchkiss because of its more diverse curriculum. To my great relief, officials at Exeter began making plans for my care. The school located a physical therapist willing to rearrange her schedule to visit campus and treat me. In April my parents and I met with Exeter's dean of students, the school physician, and several members of the infirmary staff.

So began an institutional experiment. We sat in a small waiting room at the infirmary, negotiating how I would lead my day-to-day life at the academy. I studied the faces in the room, trying to read and remember them at the same time. No one with a chronic illness had ever attended Exeter. One of the nurses called me a trailblazer during that first meeting, but I just wanted to be a normal student.

We agreed I should live near the medical building. The officials in the room decreed that Lamont Hall, a dormitory that once served as an annex to the old infirmary, would serve well as a base for me. Only a few dozen feet would separate me from readily available medical care.

My physical therapist, Roxane VanAmburgh, would treat me in a room on the third floor of the infirmary. This arrangement would give us access to a hospital-style bed, which tilted easily for drainage positions, and allow me to keep my medical care apart from dorm life. I did not realize the three daily trips to the infirmary, lasting half an hour each, would do more to remind myself and others of my illness than it would to help me lead a normal life. I did not know enough to propose that the chest percussion take place in my dorm room.

I thought I could protect my fragile dream by being agreeable. So I nodded assent to everything proposed that morning.

I did not think to look to Shwachman for support when I applied to the schools, yet he emerged as a staunch backer when Mom told him my plan. Ironically, he had treated me through days of flickering prospects and gloomy predictions.

Once during my Division 39 days, he had recommended that I have one of my lungs removed. For several days surgeons flurried about my bed while I tried to bury my mind in the trivial. I had learned you should never anticipate in a hospital because it does no good. When the verdict came in, I found it disconcerting but pushed it from my mind: although either lung would be a perfect candidate for removal, neither could support me by itself.

More recently, unbeknownst to me, Shwachman told my parents about a year before I applied to the schools that only a tracheotomy could keep me alive much longer. The operation would have involved surgically inserting a tube in my throat to suction fluid from my airways. With the procedure, my doctor felt he could almost guarantee I would live for several months; without it, he could make no promises.

"There's a new procedure they're starting to do more often," my mother had tested me calmly while sitting at the foot of my hospital bed one afternoon. My father stood quietly beside her while she explained. Then I recoiled.

"That sounds dreadful! Please don't ever make me do that!" They did not, but they did not expect to send me to boarding school, either.

At the end of what seemed to me a very long summer, my parents and I loaded the station wagon and drove the eight hours to Exeter. The next morning we queued to register in a hot and sunny quadrangle. The crowd waited quietly, sedately, as a cloud of familial expectation floated high above. My presence there threw tradition on its ear, but I knew only that I felt strangely defiant. I had every right to be on this campus, and that thought thundered comfortingly in my head.

My parents and I met Roxane for the first time at a well-attended planning session at the infirmary. Before meeting me, Rox called a Boston CF doctor to ask about my condition.

"Pretty bad," assessed the doctor, who did not take care of me but knew my case. "She won't last long at Exeter."

Determined to do everything she could for me, Roxane didn't complain when she learned I wanted to receive three sessions of chest percussion each day instead of one, as she had expected. She could only arrange two visits on weekdays but loyally came three times daily on Saturdays and Sundays. A student volunteer organization helped me find people to perform the third treatment during the week, and occasionally Roxane could recruit other therapists to replace her. For most of my time at Exeter, however, we spent more than eight hours together each week. Roxane would be the first person I spoke to each morning and the last at night.

A very outgoing woman around the age of fifty, Roxane struck me right away as someone who took great pleasure in life. I would learn that she divided her two closets into "work clothes" and "play clothes." In conversation she could instantly express her impression of a choice vacation spot or an extravagant car. She and her husband, Henry, a broadcasting expert, worked hard for their fun.

Rox stood a few inches taller than my five feet four inches and had brown wavy hair and brown eyes. Impressively practical, she often would play the realist to my daydreamer in our conversations.

She said she remembered the way I came to that first infirmary conference, unsmiling and unnaturally grim for my years. She did not hear me laugh for several weeks and could not keep a conversation going with me for a few months. I did not take lightly the serious burden of preserving my health.

Roxane never shook me by the shoulders as I would be tempted to do to someone like I was then, but she became one of the best influences I could have had. As I changed over my years there, she helped me see who I had been. She and Henry remain close friends of mine. Working with me tried her nerves at first, but she kept her humor. She wanted to help the frail little girl who barely smiled when they met.

Our first big infirmary meeting kept me from much of the orientation activity. While others joined in games on the playing fields, I began my acquaintance with the infirmary. My parents then nicely outfitted my dorm room, complete with a refrigerator for snacks. We struggled through the tasks of rearranging the furniture and folding under the carpet remnant we had brought for the floor.

When my parents returned to an empty car and prepared for the return trip, I did not want them to leave. As they pulled out of the infirmary drive and the one-way lane

Teresa's little sister Susan with Roxane VanAmburgh

in front, I forced myself to stand fast. Independence asked a high price.

As school began, I wanted so much to be like everyone else. Unfortunately, my adviser soon announced my condition at a dorm meeting. At least I did not tell anyone how much difficulty I had at a required orientation swim test. I had been too stubborn to call for help, but I barely stayed afloat through the length of an Olympic-sized pool and back. Halfway across I had ceased to be able to breathe. I gasped and forced myself to keep going. When I finally staggered out of the pool, having passed the test, I felt sure I'd caused one of my lungs to collapse. I wondered how I would explain a self-induced pneumothorax at age fourteen. When the girl who accompanied me commented on how easy the test had been, I agreed for her benefit, although I could barely speak.

Teresa on her first day at Exeter

Fortunately, I fared slightly better outside the swimming pool. I found classes as challenging as I expected, and I worked hard. I took courses in math, Greek history, religion, Russian, and English. I soon appreciated the academy's Harkness Table system, which places about twelve students around an oval table. Teachers initiate conversation but let students speak to each other. We questioned each other, defended our positions, argued, and occasionally raised our voices in the competition to speak. We never raised our hands, rarely took notes, and always came prepared for class. The teacher would intervene if we followed a ridiculous path of debate, if someone soft-spoken could not enter the discussion, or if we all missed the point. If lost, we received hints, but no teacher ever told us anything. Sometimes they grilled us in Socratic fashion until we could scarcely defend our premises. Everyone spoke during class because the Harkness system provided too small a system for hiding.

Our classes met four or five times a week. In the humanities courses, teachers assigned about fifty pages of paperback reading for each class. For first-year students, or preps, the routine came as grueling even to those who came from schools with annual gift drives. "Follow the syllabus," one instructor told us unsympathetically, and none of us questioned the strange new word until he left the room.

To me those first weeks as a prep meant obeying my alarm clock at all cost and following a strict schedule that gave me just enough time for my course work and writing home when I could. I missed my family, but I had found the place I needed to be.

CHAPTER
❧ TEN

In my mind, little made me different from my schoolmates. I did not cough often but used cough drops when I needed them. I missed no appointments or assignments and never asked for special treatment. My misfit years at St. Thomas had left me excessively shy in my approach to some social settings, so I avoided encounters that would have made me feel awkward. I headed back to the dorm a few hours early on Saturday nights to adhere to a strict regimen of chest percussion. When a handsome classmate tried to flirt with me outside of class, I acted oblivious to his overtures. I had accepted the responsibilities that came with CF, and I did not feel sorry for myself. I did not realize, however, that in some ways I had isolated myself from the community. I felt I needed to be serious and undistracted to continue balancing health and academics. And I had been without the company of peers for so long that solitude seemed natural to me.

The first outward sign that I did not fit the Exeter mold came when my adviser called a special meeting early in fall. Students in rooms adjacent or near to mine complained they could not sleep at night because of my cough. All our infirmary planning meetings brilliantly had overlooked the fact that the school built Lamont, a onetime infirmary annex, with the thinnest walls of any dorm on campus.

I did not know what to say to the small gathering of students, especially because I could think of no solution. They all kept telling me I should not take their complaints personally. By that time in the semester, two or three new Lamont residents had dropped out of school, prompting an elaborate parade of room-swapping. A basement room big enough to serve as an emergency triple stood far enough away from all other rooms that no one would hear me cough there. All at the meeting urged me to move there, and students who had complained to my adviser helped me carry my things downstairs. I had liked the first room, which drew in morning sunlight. My parents felt disappointed that I needed to move after they helped me arrange everything.

More reality would invade my new haven. I entered the infirmary one November afternoon to hear the news in a rush: a Children's doctor had called to say the oxygen level in my arterial blood sample had plunged lower than ever before. Based on the results, the doctor had arranged for me to enter Children's the next morning. We had no need for consultation. The poor results definitely showed I belonged in a hospital. In front of the nurses and some students, I tried to take the stunning news well.

As so often happened, I had not noticed my compromised condition until the hospital tests gave their evidence. Just to get through a day, I had to put breathing difficulties or tell-tale chest pain completely out of mind. When I had the tests taken at Children's a few days earlier, I had been unable to satisfy doctors with my responses to their questions.

"How are you feeling?" one would ask.

"Same as always, I think."

"Well, how's your energy level been?"

"I think it's been good. I mean, I've done everything I needed to do."

"Well, how's your breathing? Is it any more difficult than usual?"

"Seems all right. No, I don't think it's more difficult."

"Well, Terri, you're the expert on how you feel," a doctor would say in a frustrated plea for feedback. "Do you think you're doing better or worse?"

"I don't know; I never think about it. I'm sorry, I just don't know."

When chest pain came, I would wish it away and note it on my mental calendar of the two or three months between doctor visits. Sometimes I could feel the sharp pain I knew to be the attachment of a damaged section of lung to my chest wall. At its worst, the pain would linger for three or four days and seem aided by a ninja arsenal with each inward breath of mine; more often the pain would flare once for a few minutes only to disappear for many months. I experienced all the typical shortness of breath of any CF patient, but noticed it mainly when my gasping attracted strange looks or comments. I would envision the top of a flight of stairs and climb it without paying mind to any breathing difficulty.

During hospital visits, I dutifully reported any symptoms or difficulties I noticed, treating the interval between doctor appointments like sentry duty. Still, I relied more heavily than most patients on the concrete assessment of laboratory tests. I always felt silly when asked by a doctor how I felt; I could rarely be helpful and never successfully conveyed my discomfort with such subjective questions. I wanted an authority better than my own vague observations and recollections to determine all courses of action. I usually would not let myself feel the least bit sick until tests heralded decreased lung function or imbalances in my blood. With the news on paper, I would concur that perhaps the preceding few weeks had found me with less energy. I had not entered denial; I just constantly needed to adapt to my condition and the tasks at hand. Except when I faced a dramatic deterioration, I found it a morose pastime to think about how I felt at any given time.

So on that grim day at Exeter, I underwent my customary ritual of shock and disbelief which followed each discouraging lab pronouncement.

That same day my English assignment required me to sit on the bank of the Exeter River for fifty minutes so I could record my observations there. Though several other students shared the same assignment, most had already completed it and I could find no one willing to accompany me.

I stepped out of the infirmary back into a day whose overcast skies became a darker shade to me. I could not judge how anyone at home or in Boston would react to this new decline in my health and supposed I might be expected to leave Exeter. As I walked toward the river, I stared hard through the walls of mist at every building, every tree. Exeter became a forbidding place where I might be welcomed but could not stay. I could not guess whether this would be my last trip across campus or if I would return after a few weeks in the hospital. I walked slowly and drew in every sight, as though memorizing the view might make it mine. The paths and playing fields stayed empty through my vigil. I felt glad not to pass anyone because Exeter decorum required a greeting, and I wore too many tears to utter a simple hello.

The walk tired me, and I gasped impatiently for breath. At the riverbank I dropped my notebook and crumpled to the grass. I attacked my notebook and tried to clear my mind. As I wrote a few mindless sentences about the colors of leaves, I tried hard to keep tears from hitting the page. I didn't notice the rain until the lines of the loose-leaf paper became a blue puddle. Then I tossed away the notebook and pen in frustration.

I could not stop crying. I knew people would tell me coming to Exeter had been a mistake. I could only hope none of them would have the power to make me leave. If I did not make it through Exeter, I wondered, would anyone remember I tried? Would they know how much I wanted to be a part of the place? Would they know I had pushed hard toward another way of life?

The weight of a thousand failures crushed my shoulders as I wondered how many CF patients ever came to feel as disenfranchised as I did then. I felt angry at a world oblivious to our efforts; we would be some of the best contributors to society if first, society would give us medical help. I wanted to help change a world in which already I could barely function. How should, or could, any of us proceed? Birch trees in pairs and threesomes looked askance as I waited for their answers.

On the phone later, my parents wanted to know what had happened. Hadn't I been eating well, sleeping enough, remembering all my medication? I grew defensive.

"Of course I take care of myself! What are you saying? I think I deserve more credit than that."

I spent most of the next month at Children's. I realized immediately I would not be able to tackle all my schoolwork, but my instructors did not. I had left them all hastily written notes which I stuffed into their post boxes. Two of my teachers visited me during my hospital stay; one of them stopped by on Thanksgiving when he came to town to see relatives.

Yet no amount of support could keep me caught up in my classes. I spent hours each day working on the abbreviated assignments my teachers designed for me. One teacher suggested taping the classes I missed, so soon I obtained recordings of all my Russian, religion, and history classes.

Two or three new tapes arrived each day as teachers sent off the cassettes with Boston-bound students or faculty. Quickly I became backlogged. I stayed in a room with three other patients, and the constant noise generated by the television, telephone, visitors, doctors, and other staff made it impossible to hear the recorder. Headsets and small cassette players had not yet become popular or they might have solved this problem.

On several occasions I carried my tape collection to a clean, spacious supply closet down the hall from my room. I rolled a wheelchair into the tiny space between shelves of tissue boxes and basins and pulled down the shade of the door window. My nurses knew where to find me and told callers they could reach me later. A surprised janitor once walked in during a lively discussion of Elie Wiesel's *Night*. He looked at me curiously, stayed to hear a few words about Nazi concentration camps, then backed out the door with his broom. Soon the closet became my office, and I spent all my free time there trying to sort out my schoolwork. When a card came from a classmate telling me to "enjoy my vacation," I ripped it into tiny pieces.

Three and a half weeks later, I left the hospital after my longest stay ever. No one at Children's had targeted Exeter as a cause of my problems, and I had worked hard to keep prep school out of all conversations with doctors.

I arrived back at Exeter in time for the pre-holiday hype. Classmates welcomed me back with only a little awkwardness. Teachers had explained my absence, and I could see the great care that went into not saying the wrong thing. Everywhere students counted down the days until winter break, but I wished I could stay at Exeter and try once more to belong there.

CHAPTER
❂ ELEVEN

During my stay at Children's, Exeter admissions officer Rheua Stakely, who had taken a special interest in my case, proposed to the faculty that I should skip a year of the regular curriculum. She said that because of my illness I should be allowed to combine prep year with tenth grade, or lower year. I knew nothing of her proposal until the faculty voted to approve it. I may never know who said what to precipitate this strange breach of tradition, nor whether the faculty acted out of pity. With high mid-semester marks I had proven myself a good student, but I never expected to skip a year and become what was termed a lower.

My adviser, Francesca Freccero, a young English teacher spending her first and only year at Exeter before she would leave for law school, called me at Children's with the bewildering announcement: "How would you like to be a lower next semester?"

I asked her a dozen questions about how and why this promotion had come about and how it would be implemented, before I said I would seize the opportunity. I could not imagine the Exeter faculty holding a vote about my status, and I found the whole situation a curious one. Yet I could think of no reason to refuse the chance to graduate early.

As I left Children's, and then left Exeter for home, the announcement put added pressure on me. I had fallen behind in my schoolwork and could only assume the promotion hinged on my graceful completion of the semester. Throughout winter break I struggled to catch up with my course work. In January I eagerly returned to school for our test period called "hell week."

Soon after I returned, my parents called to tell me of the birth of my second sister, Elizabeth. They described the beautiful baby to me, but I would have to wait a few weeks to see her. The addition to our household made me regret the distance between my family and me. I could speak to Ted and Susan on the telephone, but I would not have so easy a time communicating with the baby. I would have liked to have been at home for Elizabeth's early years, but I knew someday I would tell her why I had gone away to Exeter. My family soon gave me a show of support by outfitting Elizabeth in a tiny Exeter sweatshirt. Mother sent pictures of my new little sister in the mail.

When the second semester began at the end of January, I needed to explain CF to a new batch of teachers who had been told nothing about me.

"That's some cough," one teacher repeated through several Russian history classes until he asked for an explanation.

"Oh, I have a chronic lung problem," I said as nonchalantly as I could before my classmates. The teacher acted as though my cough interrupted his class and he wanted to know when it would stop. So I added, "I'm sorry, but I'll be coughing like this all semester." When other students began groaning at the prospect of listening to my cough for a whole semester, I sat shocked and could only manage a fake laugh. *Forget them*, I told myself, *you belong.*

In February, I left for Children's, where my mother and Elizabeth would stay with me while I received a planned course of antibiotics. Through this preventative measure, my doctors and I hoped to avoid such a draining bout with infection as I had faced in the fall. I confidently told friends, faculty, my ballet and piano teachers, and the editors of the school paper for which I'd been writing that I would be gone two weeks or less.

I felt so sure of my plans that I asked the editors of the weekly *Exonian* to let me cover an upcoming speech. Anti-nuclear activist Helen Caldicott would be visiting in late February, and I hoped for the chance to interview her. I had been attending meetings of Exeter's Committee for Nuclear Awareness, but no one at the *Exonian* knew anything about conflicts of interest. If we had, we would barely have been able to put out a paper at the small school.

Shwachman had worked with Caldicott during her training at Children's when she studied CF. She rarely used this part of her background except on such occasions as once when I would hear her say, during an otherwise cogent speech, that nuclear disarmament would eliminate bad elements in the earth, which caused problems like cystic fibrosis. I believed in the cause at hand, that the Seabrook nuclear power plant posed a threat to an area for which its owners had not developed a thorough evacuation plan. Nonetheless I wanted to stand and shout that CF patients required something besides disarmament in the way of help.

During rounds one morning at Children's, Shwachman, aware of my upcoming assignment, suddenly called Caldicott and handed me the phone. As he did so before I had eaten breakfast, or for that matter opened my eyes, I did not take kindly to his gesture at first.

"Uh, hi," I said to the activist as I cast Shwachman a displeased look. "I'm looking forward to hearing you speak at Exeter in a few days; as a matter of fact, I'm covering your speech for the school paper."

She said something about giving her a good review and I laughed politely. I had not woken up enough to carry on a

The Exonian

The Oldest Preparatory School Paper in America

coherent conversation, let alone try to interview her, so the call ended shortly.

A few days later, my mother drove Elizabeth and me to Caldicott's speech at Exeter. There the activist made all her customary statements about the dangers of the nuclear arms race, then answered my questions. Our conversation after the speech went strangely: I wanted to confirm the numbers of some of the warheads she had mentioned, and she wanted to know whether any of the CF patients she knew from Children's remained alive.

Then Mom and I took Elizabeth to visit Lamont, where a dozen of my dormmates competed to hold her and make her smile. I fetched some necessities from my room, and we returned to Children's. We received an unceremonious greeting on Division 37.

"Guess who died while you were gone."

The comment came from a young patient as my mother and I walked down the hall. We could guess: a twenty-one-year-old CF

DR. HELEN CALDICOTT, an active proponent of a universal nuclear freeze, spoke last Friday in the Assembly Hall. She criticized President Reagan's policy on nuclear weapons.

Caldicott Demands Electoral Activism
by Terri Mullin

On Friday, February 24, Dr. Helen Caldicott, President Emeritus of Physicians for Social Responsibility and founder of Woman's Action for Nuclear Disarmament (WAND), presented a lecture entitled "We, the People . . . The Hope of Ending the Arms Race" at the Academy.

Mrs. Barbara James, faculty advisor to Students for Nuclear Disarmament, welcomed Dr. Caldicott, hailing her as one of the many who had accepted the challenge of working to save the planet from nuclear destruction. Mrs. James concluded, "Paul Jacobs, who was a reporter and covered the nuclear testing in Nevada, who died of cancer from radiation, used to quote the Talmud frequently. He said, 'It is not encumbent for thee to complete the task, but neither art thou free to desist from thy part in it.'"

Senior Philippe Selendy, co-president of Students for Nuclear Disarmament, presented Dr. Caldicott, listing her successful campaign against atmospheric testing of nuclear weapons by France in the Pacific Ocean, her book, Nuclear Madness — What You Can Do, which came out in 1978, and her work on Physicians for Social Responsibility as just a few of her many accomplishments.

Caldicott began, "This is the most important year in the history of your life. If we don't elect a president and a Senate and Congress who are forever by unilateral disarmament, the world will end. The world will end. And the reason I say that is that President Reagan, who doesn't understand most of the stuff, plans to build 17,000 more bombs and they're the sort of bombs that make nuclear war a certainty."

See CALDICOTT on pg. 5

Teresa's Exonian *article*

patient had been struggling for several days. I had not known him well but remembered him celebrating his most recent birthday. "I never thought I'd make it this far," he had said. A nurse jumped from behind the front desk to lead the young herald, stricken he did not provoke much of a reaction from us, back to his room. Mother and I could only sigh at the news; during the years we had been going to Children's, we had lost so many young friends and acquaintances that tragedy heaped on tragedy had lost some of its meaning for us.

The next few days, I filled much of my time by working on the Caldicott article. The night before my deadline, I inefficiently stayed up all night, listening to a tape of the speech. In the division's activity room, I wrote a dreadful article that the paper staff needed to rewrite later. At 5:30 I walked back to where my three roommates had slept since midnight. My nurse, who brought me a blanket when I grew chilly in the activity center, never made me feel irresponsible. In the hospital, even the slightest of tasks associated with the outside world carries enormous importance. I wanted the article to be perfect.

The staff nurses let me sleep the next day, but a group of student nurses made their rounds with an instructor about two hours after I had gone to bed.

"Is it true you stayed up all night? That's what they said in report," said a student who woke me up to start a conversation.

"Sorry, but I really need to sleep today."

"Oh, that's all right," she said and then, to the great amusement of one of my roommates, woke me once each hour to ask if I needed anything.

"If I need anything," I said the fourth or fifth time, "I promise, I'll call." When the student left, I looked for something to throw at my roommate, "Biz" Crowley, who would not stop laughing.

Elizabeth Crowley, an Emmanuel College student from New York, would sling a knapsack over her shoulder and leave the hospital to attend lectures. I admired her emotional toughness because it gave her strength to cope with the insanity of the hospital world. Biz could not have weighed more than one hundred pounds and carried the trace of a New York accent. She did her best to make me socialize with other patients, but brought me floor gossip when I found excuses to stay in our room.

A natural comic, Biz never let anyone take themselves too seriously. Doctors usually ask in rounds if they can solve any problems for a patient. Most often the question receives a negative response.

"Well, you know, there is a very serious raspberry sherbet shortage around here," she would answer solemnly.

I'd never spent Valentine's Day or my February 19 birthday in the hospital before. Biz and I passed the time by watching most of the Winter Olympics. We soon became the floor authorities. Doctors and nurses, too busy for television, would stop by our room for updates. We rooted hardest for Scott Hamilton, who took the gold medal in the ice skating competition, because of his battle with Shwachman's syndrome.

My entire family arrived in town for my fifteenth birthday, and they brought me roses that morning. I put on a smile for them, but I felt sick and went to sleep as soon as they left. I didn't wake up until five o'clock that evening. I showered and dressed and pretended to feel decent so my mother could lure me to the activity center for a surprise party.

The admission dragged on for almost a month while my test results did not improve. Doctors began telling me I would get no better and might as well leave. I asked if I shouldn't stay long enough to determine whether an infection I had developed posed a threat. The doctor who discharged me said it would go away by itself, so I left for Exeter. I knew I could still salvage the semester.

Fatigue and dizzy spells thwarted my first attempts to hit the books after I returned to Lamont. I convinced myself I only suffered from the typical post-hospitalization symptoms of exhaustion after inactivity and dehydration after relying on IV fluids to keep me hydrated. So I put these difficulties out of mind and worked slowly but steadily between naps. I did not attend classes because I had missed too much material to follow class discussions; I believed however, that I would be able to join the discussions in a short time.

I met with teachers to determine how much academic ground I had lost. The meetings did not bring the encouragement for which I had hoped. When I spoke to my Russian history teacher, I referred to one of the main course books only to forget its title. The teacher looked frightened by my lapse and ended the session abruptly, saying we would meet again "when you feel better."

When I visited my math teacher in his classroom the next morning, I did not have the energy to sit up. While I rested my head on the table in the center of the room, the teacher enthusiastically told me his plan for me to make up the work. We thought I could catch up, and we would have kept thinking it except after twenty minutes, I jumped up to stand over his trash can. A violent cough triggered a gagging reflex that caused me to vomit. My teacher calmly rose to empty the trash.

"Okay, you stay here. I'll be right back. No problem." He spoke carefully as one who has just realized the guest in the living room is the escaped convict on the six o'clock news.

When I left a few minutes later, he watched wide-eyed and seemed prepared to follow me. I figured I looked pretty sick.

Several minutes later I wandered into my Russian teacher's classroom. I couldn't find him, but a French teacher with whom I had taken dance classes had borrowed his room to teach a class. She asked if I would be performing in the school's dance show later that spring. I said I hoped so but admitted I'd had a rough last few weeks. She said she knew I could do it.

After several minutes I decided to leave a note for my teacher. Ambitiously I found paper and pencil only to realize I fell just short of being coherent enough to write a message. I put my head on the table in a now familiar posture and tried to think until Rheua Stakely and my photography teacher frantically burst into the room.

"We've been looking all over for you!"

When asked, they said they had no particular reason for seeking me out; they had just heard about the trash can incident and felt concerned about me. No more than fifteen minutes had passed since I left my math teacher. Everyone kept acting strangely, coming out with dramatic lines that seemed inappropriate. I began to feel that maybe I had joined the cast of a low-budget movie and no one had told me. My Russian teacher arrived a few minutes later, but before I could say much, Stakely hurriedly escorted me to the infirmary.

There I spent the next twenty-four hours throwing up. I soon wrestled with a nurse who would not tell me my temperature. She tried to lie as she first read the mercury, but when I started to grab the thermometer, she told me it registered 106 degrees Fahrenheit. I could not help but be fascinated in the detached way of a perennial hospital patient.

"Shouldn't I be hallucinating?" I asked the nurse, referring to my high temperature. She seemed too shaken to respond. All day, nurses and friends took turns putting wet washcloths on my forehead and helping me sip ice water from a straw. I remained alert and felt somewhat in awe of the few students, mostly Lamont seniors, who came to the scene. I knew I might have avoided participating in such a drama if our roles were reversed.

When I spoke to my parents on the telephone, I tried not to sound sick, but a nurse already had spoken to them in a voice too low for me to hear. Dad said he would meet me at Children's in the morning. I had grown maddeningly tired of the place but sanely agreed to let Stakely drive me there.

When I stopped by my room before I left Lamont the next morning, I ended up sitting in a senior's room. Soon half a dozen of my dormmates had gathered in the room and focused their full attention on me. I huddled in a rocking chair with a blanket wrapped round myself and told them I would not be gone long. The sight of me undoubtedly contradicted every word I said. I saw the unease in their stares and tried to still it with my own confident banter. When they would not be reassured, I wondered if I should begin to worry. Still, I irrationally refused to pack clothes for an overnight stay.

Glaring at the highway, I said fewer than ten words to Stakely during the trip. A bulky yellow infirmary blanket kept out the chill of the March morning as I pulled it tightly around myself. The silence in the car and the bare trees lining Route 95 South seemed sinister.

Shwachman had recently entered into a more formal retirement than the one he had been in when we began seeing him, so my father and I met with a doctor whom we did not know well. When this doctor insisted I be admitted for at least two weeks, I cried for the first time in front of a doctor. I had seen what happened to patients who cried: they never received candid advice or direct answers from doctors. Medical people wore expressionless masks when treating them, and every test, every procedure became "just routine." I cried nonetheless.

"You're becoming a familiar face around here," a nurse said as I walked onto Division 37.

"I know and I hate it," I snapped. While waiting for the bedspace to be prepared, I grimaced at the artificial light and stuffy air of the corridor. I felt trapped.

Doctors spent the first week of my admission trying to discover what made my temperature climb. Because no one questioned my pulmonary condition, thought to be as good as when I had left, I received no IV medication. I became a novelty, one of those rare baffling cases with which to challenge medical students or interns. The parade of guessing faces began.

After a week a doctor who knew me well emerged from the melee to order pulmonary tests. The results, stunning all but the doctor who called for them, showed my lungs to be in terrible shape.

Quickly I became the focus of more attention than I had ever received in a hospital. Doctors who usually walked briskly past my room began to come to a full stop and read my chart. Like a group of flustered magicians fumbling in their bags for that elusive white rabbit, the doctors began making suggestions every time they saw me.

"Have you ever used oxygen?"

"What do you think about mist tents?"

"There's a new drug on the market called———"

The impulsiveness of their proposals made the doctors seem desperate. They had reached a threshold past which they ceased to be experts. Their fallibility terrified me; I had never seen doctors hold such little control over a situation.

I felt old, older than the inopportune bike-a-thon newscast I heard as a nine-year-old had made me. I had seen through to the inside of the medical world and I preferred the mystique. I realized I had Shwachman to thank for giving me confidence in my own knowledge and judgment, poor as it would sometimes be. I had myself to count on or else I might have despaired.

I began to act on whatever suggestions came my way. The use of supplemental oxygen, inhaled with a face mask or nasal prongs, had always seemed to me like a last resort. I wanted my own two lungs to do all the work and get all the credit for the breathing I did. I knew that regular oxygen use should be continued once started, and I didn't want to feel dependent on a machine for the rest of my life. But at this juncture I agreed to breathe out of a tank.

The one night I spent in a mist tent, a huge humidifier with plastic walls, nearly drove my roommate and me crazy. Its hissing noise belonged with the sound editor of a monster movie. Dr. Richard Fox had made the suggestion every day for a week and I finally agreed to a one-night trial.

When the respiratory therapist arrived to assemble the tent, he apologized.

"Hey, I'm sorry," he said, before I had spoken. "I swear I had nothing to do with this." This remark, coming from someone unaware of my reluctance, did not seem a promising start.

Nurses handed me towels underneath the plastic walls of the tent, which covered me down to my thighs. Despite the towels I felt like I had agreed to spend the night in a washing machine. Just a few years earlier, most CF patients had spent every night inside similar tents. Later the tents had been discovered to be a breeding ground for infection. Coming from Fox, the suggestion had been a daring one as the tents had been out of fashion for quite some time.

The noise kept my roommate and me awake hours later than usual. I thought it amusing that my feet stuck out the bottom of

the tent, and as the evening dragged on, I serenaded my unfortunate neighbor with songs about feet.

Soggy, irritable, and not very well rested the next day, I had
trouble answering questions about the tent. I could not discern
any benefits from the one-night trial and declined to use it again.

Having exhausted the peripheral IV sites in my hands and
arms, doctors finally inserted a large catheter into one of my
jugular veins. Besides causing neck pain and keeping me up at
night trying to find a comfortable sleeping position, the new line
made showers impossible and baths very difficult. In a hospital
like Children's where patients dress in the morning and wear blue
jeans all day, I made a dramatic concession when I began
wearing hospital gowns. I did so partly because the IV made
changing difficult and partly because I had begun feeling sick.

I stayed in bed most of that admission and usually needed a
wheelchair to travel down the hall. My outgoing roommate, Anne
Marie Nunnari, spent most of her time in other patients' rooms. I
often felt left out and bombarded my roommate with questions.
"Where are you going? When will you be back? Why don't you stay
here for a little while?" Because she knew me from other admissions
and realized how sick I had become, Anne Marie tolerated my jeal-
ousy and spent time in our room trying to cheer me up.

Anne Marie and I probably had little in common besides CF.
We had an age gap of almost ten years between us. We both
became jaded utilitarians in the hospital and our hospital selves
got on well. Much of the time we spent together found one of us
too sick for small talk so I knew little about Anne Marie's interests. I knew only that she professed to like the music of Laura
Branigan at a time when I wanted to listen to the Talking Heads
and David Bowie.

She wore her straight, dark hair so long it seemed to belong in
the 1960s, and she saw the world through thin-rimmed glasses.

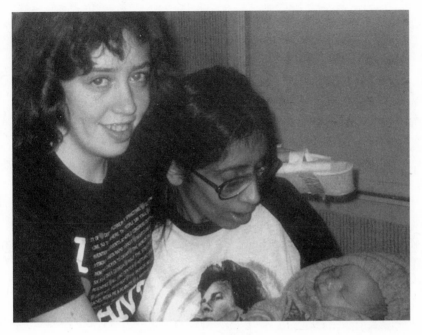

Teresa, Anne Marie, and Elizabeth

Her raspy voice and impassive nature made her a character on the division. Few happenings could rile or surprise her. As a hospital veteran she had grown set in her ways and could often be heard disagreeing diplomatically with her doctors.

When I became sick and stranded in my room that March, the two of us found all the distractions we could. Once we blew soap bubbles out of our small window until we filled the sky above a parking lot next to the hospital. People stepping in and out of cars began looking up, trying to interpret the cloud of bubbles hovering over them. For a few minutes, we took turns blowing the bubbles fast enough to keep the sky full. The car drivers kept flashing puzzled expressions skyward and we relished the confusion we caused with so little effort. No one appeared to notice that the bubbles kept flying out of a seventh-story hospital window. I laughed my first spirited laugh since leaving Exeter in February.

The phone rang after a few minutes of our bubble antics. One of the nurses called from the front desk and asked us to stop. She told us the mother of an infant in a room down the hall had complained about our activity. She said the noise of the bubbles hitting the child's window had frightened it. We hung up the phone and felt guilty for a full five seconds.

"Bubbles," Anne Marie said, suddenly enlightened, "don't make noise."

We angrily marched to the nurses' station to confront the overprotective mother. The nurse who had placed the call sat laughing behind the front desk. She said the baby's mother had not visited the floor for several days.

"Then how could she have . . ." I started to ask, but Anne Marie began pulling me back down the hall in time.

"And you thought we'd fall for that?" Anne Marie called over her shoulder, muttering under her breath.

Although I felt well acquainted with Anne Marie, I evidently knew little of her musings. I debated points with doctors but rarely challenged their advice, so I reacted with great surprise one night to see Anne Marie open her closet and start piling all her clothes into a brown paper bag.

"What are you doing over there?"

"Packing."

"You've got to be kidding! Where are you going this late at night?"

"Home!"

"How can they discharge you during the night shift? Is anyone around to write orders?"

"They're not. I'm just leaving."

"What? Well, does your doctor know?"

"'Course not."

As I watched sleepily, my roommate left against medical advice. Days after her departure I began to feel the same restlessness that had made her decide to leave. After six cumulative weeks in the hospital, I needed to escape. The endless experimenting with my treatment had yielded no success.

"I know I'm not ready, but I have to leave this place," I told my mother. I sensed that the doctors who had all but given up on me would be willing to send me home. I believed I would be able to fight best once away from the hospital.

Anne Marie lived into her late twenties. I did not see her often, but we had a strong warmth between us. I would learn of her death from a doctor who chatted about hospital news as he prepared to draw arterial blood from my wrist. I never felt his needle; instead, I mourned for a rebel.

CHAPTER
✿ TWELVE

After the pulmonary doctors agreed to let me continue IV therapy at home, my parents and I began planning the trip back to Allentown. We knew the seven-hour car ride would have overwhelmed me, so my father arranged for a friend's company plane to fly my mother, Elizabeth, and me home.

One morning late in March, I rolled out of my hospital bed and stepped into blue sweat pants and a pair of dockside shoes that had received little wear since early February. I had brought no street clothes to the hospital. I pulled on a large turtleneck to hide the IV in my neck, and the winter coat I wore on top hung loosely on my thin frame. I had become a pathetic scarecrow.

As I bid other patients farewell, they could not hide their surprise at seeing me leave in such condition. I could barely stand long enough to enter their rooms, and propped myself up on chairs, bedside tables, or the edges of their beds as I spoke to them.

At Logan Airport, my mother struggled to balance Elizabeth over one shoulder and two oxygen tanks over the other.

"Can you manage?" I kept asking, but we both knew I could barely walk, let alone help her.

We waited in the terminal long enough to wish we had taken a commercial flight. We could not turn on the oxygen around all the people smoking in the airport. As the smoky haze above our cluster of airport seats choked me and prevented use of the tanks, I nearly burst into angry tears. But sobbing would have required more breath than I could draw right then, so I fought for control.

We could not rush the pilot because our passage on the private plane had come as a favor. It became so hard for me to breathe that I thought I might faint and warned my mother of the possibility.

As soon as we boarded, my mother handed me the nasal prongs and switched on one of the tanks. Our exhaustion kept us silent during the flight.

In a little more than an hour, we landed in snowy Allentown, where my father and grandfather shouldered the tanks and led us to the car. After seeing Ted, Susan, and my grandmother at home, I started toward the stairs leading to my bedroom. I lifted one foot to the first step while I leaned on my mother and the railing. The top of the stairs seemed farther away than ever before and peering up at it made me dizzy. My mother saw me wavering and knew what to do.

"I'll throw a sheet on the sofa bed in the family room," she said quickly and helped me back down.

My IV remained intact one week, during which my parents gave me the antibiotic azlocillin. Earlier that year I had never heard of the drug before, but we had reached the time for experimentation. After I had been home for a few days, azlocillin began leaking out of the site around the catheter. My parents and I wrapped towels around my neck, but I still kept waking up in puddles of foul-smelling azlocillin. Finally we made a trip to the local emergency room, where an anesthesiologist sutured the site to reduce the leakage. The IV could not be saved, however, and many attempts to replace it proved futile. My veins had become virtually inaccessible. Oral antibiotics would have to do, and we hoped I would be able to keep them down.

Meanwhile, friends at Exeter had not forgotten me. Cards arrived daily from classmates and teachers, and my family read them all to me. When my dormmates called, I tried to become alert enough to speak to them without frightening anyone.

"It's Lamont," my mother would say, holding the phone long enough for me to take a deep breath and compose myself. My world had narrowed to a smaller sphere than any of them could imagine: it included the sofa bed, oxygen mask, and food my mother brought me. Talking to friends about teachers, tests, assembly speakers, and snowy New Hampshire seemed meaningless. One morning I noticed a calendar hanging on a wall in our breakfast room. I had lost all sense of time so I studied the calendar to determine the date and day of the week. After deciding it must be April 1, I recalled the practical jokes my family traditionally played on April Fool's Day—tricks like serving newspaper sandwiches and filling the sugar bowl with salt. My presence silenced the laughter that year because I had grown too sick to tease.

Coughing triggered more and more vomiting as April trudged along. Keeping down a few sips of water became an accomplishment. Family friends sent over cakes and cookies, not realizing I drank a glass of milk for my big meal of the day. I lost more than twenty-five pounds in a month.

On Easter Sunday we held Elizabeth's christening in our living room, with Ted and me as godparents. I could not sit up to greet the relatives that began arriving Friday night, so they all kept leaning over and gravely kissing my cheek. Some aunts and uncles hid their surprise at my changed appearance better than others, but all acted as though saying good-bye.

That morning my mother helped me pull on a pretty nightgown she thought looked like a dress. I sat up on the couch for the half-hour ceremony, for which our pastor came to the house.

He would have christened Elizabeth in church except for my condition. I struggled to concentrate on the service, throughout which I wanted to lie down. Ted held Elizabeth most of the time, because I could not hold her by myself for long.

I removed my oxygen mask for pictures, and the family photographers went crazy. If I had any doubt these people thought they would never see me again, it disappeared in the flashbulb fury.

The oxygen level in my blood continued to fall. I removed the mask before blood tests, so we could get an accurate reading. Once when I forgot to take off the mask, the results showed the oxygen content in my blood had fallen to 40 percent of normal, too low to tell I had been breathing supplemental oxygen.

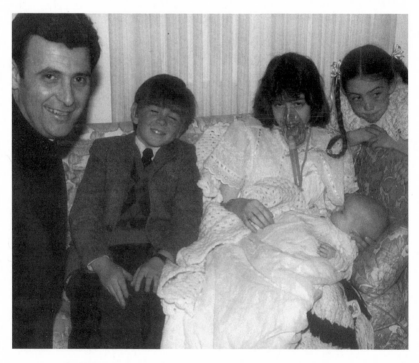

Elizabeth's christening: (left to right) Monsignor John P. Murphy, Ted, Teresa with baby Elizabeth Mary Mullin, and Susan

I lost more and more strength and finally could stay awake for only a few minutes each day. Gradually I grew resigned to the thought of dying, and I kept telling myself I had led a pretty full life. And whether I had or not, I thought, I would be relieved if I could stop fighting.

I kept remembering one of the last classes I attended during the fall semester. In religion class we read John Gunther's *Death Be Not Proud.* As we entered the classroom to discuss the book, the teacher pulled me aside. Expecting to hear something about work I needed to make up from my time in the hospital, I did not respond immediately to his words.

"It's fine with me if you would rather not stay for this class, Terri. I know this discussion may be hard for you."

After a minute I understood. Essays of mine, reflecting society's directive that I be accepting and serene about my lot in life, had talked placidly about living with a short life expectancy. When I wrote those essays, I thought I had learned to cope, but I had not even learned to fight. I politely shrugged off his concern and walked past him into the classroom.

The teacher asked two very provocative questions of us that day.

"Would you withdraw from the Academy if you knew you had five years to live?"

After a few moments of chatter, the class reached a negative consensus. In five years, someone said, research could provide an escape hatch. The students said they would not sacrifice an Exeter education if they stood a chance of recovering.

Even as my classmates spoke such words, I could tell the situation seemed unreal to them. They could not imagine having a future limited to five years. To friends of mine struggling in the hospital for one more day, five years would have been an eternity. I remained silent.

"Would you withdraw if you had five months to live?"

To everyone else in the room, five months seemed so short that they laughed at the absurdity of the question. With only five months left, they said, naturally one would return home to die. The scenario seemed less real to them than the other. Their concept of time as an inexhaustible resource roused me to speak.

"Wait a minute," I said slowly, looking around the table. "Five months is a long time." I realized instantly I should have maintained my silence. Nervous chuckles told me my classmates wanted to believe I spoke with sarcasm. My teacher looked as though he might cry. I did not elaborate.

Three months later, after a priest came to hear me confess my sins for what he thought would be the last time, I thought fleetingly about the class. I wondered if anyone would remember what I had said.

One afternoon a flower basket of red and white, Exeter colors, arrived from Roxane.

"Now is the time to rally," the card said. "Exeter awaits you."

When the message came I hung suspended between two gates. The obvious, the comfortable, the seemingly natural act would have been to surrender. I felt mature enough to die peacefully. Yet in the back of my consciousness, something troubled me. Something about my face-off with the illness suddenly seemed wrong and unfair and unnecessary.

I realized I should rebel against the process at work. In cystic fibrosis we faced a simple and primitive adversary. Those who died from a problem science should have controlled long ago bore the ultimate degradation. Few people had made our struggle a priority; among those who had, few understood how we wanted them to focus their full attention on the development of a control. We sought only a means of interrupting the colonization of bacteria in our lungs; researchers could provide this through an agent to thin secretions or an effective antibiotic to kill the infections.

My friends and I faced death not for a cause or a belief but because we had been eclipsed during the age of technology. People viewed us as inevitable casualties in an era of space exploration and sophisticated war props.

In the bed at home, I suddenly knew I could not let go nor ever again be the same naive and passive patient I had been.

To fight I would need a goal. I grabbed onto the image of Sylvester Stallone, as boxer Rocky Balboa, jumping up and down on the steps of the Philadelphia Art Museum. I kept picturing myself climbing the Academy Building steps in Exeter's quadrangle.

Late in April I summoned the breath to tell my mother, in spurts, "I'm going . . . back to . . . Exeter." She must have been startled. She and my father had told Ted and Susan I probably wouldn't live much longer than a few days or weeks. My announcement came with no forewarning.

"Okay. When?" she said matter-of-factly, the way she knew I wanted her to sound.

"As soon as . . . you can . . . drive me."

"All right, but don't you think you should go back to Children's first?"

I tried to convey the urgency of the matter.

"Not . . . to stay."

My mother held her questions because she could see how the conversation winded me. She insisted I sit up and eat dinner with the family before the trip.

"You're not ready to go back until you can sit at the dinner table," she said.

Within a day or two, not sure I could pull it off, I sat to eat a meal with my parents, grandparents, Ted, and Susan. During the dinner conversation, I did a lot of nodding and shaking my head because I could not manage long-winded replies to my family's questions. After three or four bites, more than I had taken at one time since the beginning of April, I stopped eating. In response to everyone urging me to eat more, I could only shake my head and push away the plate.

After calling one of the deans to say I would be coming back, my mother warned me: "I'm not sure they'll be ready for you by the time we get there."

Ready for me? I had not thought any preparation other than my own would be necessary.

At Children's I met with Dr. Richard Fox, whom my parents and I asked to follow my case. Fox impressed me as the most resourceful doctor I had met. While other doctors proceeded cautiously, hesitant to make an unpopular suggestion, Fox bombarded me with experiments like the mist tent.

"I'm surprised your daughter wants me to be her doctor," he told my parents. "I think I gave her a harder time than anyone else."

Fox, an easygoing doctor who completed his pulmonary fellowship at Children's, spoke with the subtle, vowel-flattening accent unique to Minnesota. He and his wife grew up in the Twin Cities area. Perhaps because Fox had experimented in a few fields before entering medicine and had spent time in college contemplating a career in business, he brought a special pragmatism and sense of wonder to his work. As Shwachman had done, Fox gave thorough explanations when I asked questions. In fact, both doctors often taxed my shallow background in science when they lapsed into jargon or drew complex diagrams to illustrate their theories.

When I grew sick that spring, Fox became the first person to see me who did not look afraid. He did not treat me like the gasping, gaunt patient I had become. He acted like I had every reason to want to return to Exeter.

The dilemmas facing Fox would have been a stumper for medical students: the patient needs to boost her oxygen level and put on thirty pounds in a hurry, but she can't keep any food or pills down, doesn't want to enter the hospital, and is going somewhere where she can't manage an IV. Ha! It's a trick, the students would say; no patient could be so unreasonable.

Fortunately for me, Fox stayed current in his reading. He had just seen an article in the British medical journal *Nature* about the use of IV antibiotics as inhalants. Although I would later hear that doctors across town at Massachusetts General Hospital had been using this technique for years, no one spread the news. The staff at Children's still considered the method highly unorthodox in the spring of 1984.

I would start inhaling tobramycin in aerosol form three times a day. Fox could offer no guarantee, but I asked for none. Even if I returned to Children's for IV antibiotics, the drugs had made little difference during my prolonged stay a few weeks earlier. I could have received IV nutrients, but it seemed that nothing could control the vomiting that robbed me of my strength. So Fox and I made a doomsday deal to see if the aerosol would work.

We kept the plan a secret. We knew other patients should not be tempted to try the technique unless it proved harmless and perhaps helpful in my case. We did not want other doctors to regard Fox as an irresponsible maverick when, if in fact, he had found what may have been the only option I had left. And most important, we did not want a pharmacy to challenge the prescription of tobramycin for inhalation. So to everyone who asked, I had returned to a course of IV tobramycin.

"Yes, we have plenty of syringes, thank you," Mom would tell the pharmacy. "No, we don't need any more IV tubing."

I visited Division 37 after seeing Fox. When a nurse caught sight of me, she immediately helped me to a chair and rushed to the kitchen to bring me something to drink. Too surprised to protest, I sat by the nurses' station wondering why the busy nurse showed me so much attention. I kept forgetting what I looked like.

"I'm going back to Exeter," I explained coolly to everyone who asked.

Though the nurses seemed glad to hear it, they all openly expressed their surprise. I had been so sick before, they said.

I tried to hide my build under a bulky sweater and jacket, but the floor's activity coordinator, Evelyn, noticed the difference. As I headed away from the division to the elevators down the hall, I heard an observation not meant for my ears.

"She looks like she's lost a lot of weight, doesn't she?"

The folks at Exeter had not yet prepared for my return, so my mother and I spent the night in Boston. In the evening we attended a skating exhibition to which Evelyn had invited us. Scott Hamilton highlighted the program, and he would make a special presentation to Shwachman. A large group from Children's came to applaud both heroes.

There I saw Biz Crowley, thin as always but looking strong.

"Things are really going well for me now," Biz said, thrusting her hands into the pockets of khaki pants she wore with a sweater and blue corduroy blazer. She spoke about college in a way that encouraged me. She focused on the mundane but implied I would be facing the same trials one day. Naturally, she cut the conversation short before it grew sentimental; she never tolerated emotionalism pertaining to CF. She wisely seemed to believe that despair constituted acceptance.

Eight months later she died. Never before had I known someone with CF to attend college. Many CF patients attend college, but at that time I knew none of them because I had drawn my friends from people I met in hospitals.

Having seen my role model looking better than ever, I headed back to Exeter in the morning.

CHAPTER
❀ THIRTEEN

When we returned to Exeter on a balmy May morning, I had missed watching fall turn to winter, then winter to spring. Exeter's spring always came late, and my mother and I reached a campus full of sun lovers celebrating the dawn of the season. No more would they sprint between buildings; now they covered lawns everywhere to negotiate their tans.

Inside the infirmary a nurse ceremoniously led my mother and me to a small, square room with sky blue walls. In it friends had hung posters and get well signs. The room, located next to the second-floor nurses' station, contained standard infirmary furniture: bed, bedside table, night stand, and locker. A large wooden dresser, chairs near the bed for visitors, and a machine to concentrate oxygen from the room's air so I could breathe it made noticeable additions.

Through the room's two windows I could see the spacious infirmary lawn, complete with "do not walk" signs and frisbee-throwing violators. Down a small hill to the left I could see the entrance to the school post office. I found myself squinting down at students hurrying to pick up their mail, hoping I might recognize someone. Across the street, to the right of the science building opposite the infirmary, I saw students climbing stairs to the Academy Building. Seeing them rush to class made me feel a small part of Exeter again, despite being stranded in the infirmary.

My parents took turns staying with me and sleeping on the third floor of the infirmary. I had become so dependent on them during the last several weeks that their being at school seemed natural, although my family had to make sacrifices for this arrangement. In Mother's absence, my grandparents took care of Ted, Susan, and, for part of the time, Elizabeth. My father took vacation time to stay with me.

When I came to the infirmary, I descended on a group of nurses who most often treated headaches and sore ankles. Students who had pulled all-nighters sometimes went to the infirmary to complain of stomach aches or other pains; usually the understanding nurses would ask few questions and give the student a medical excuse from classes so he or she could sleep. The infirmary nurses referred most serious matters to Exeter Hospital, and I represented a change in the building's atmosphere. My presence charged the nurses with responsibility, if only symbolic, for a very sick patient. I brought tension to the tiny ward on the second floor. At first when they came to take vital signs or ask how I felt, the nurses entered my room solemnly and seemed burdened with worry.

Through them I could tell when the tobramycin began to work.

"You looked awful when you got here," they said after a few days.

Almost no one outside the infirmary could appreciate the highlights of my gradual recovery. I spent more and more time awake until I kept almost normal hours. Back on a regular meal schedule, I could tolerate small amounts of food. I could carry on coherent conversations and sit up for long periods of time. I could even take off the oxygen mask on occasion. My family became ecstatic over each little event.

My presence on campus served little purpose but to remind me to keep fighting. Though I felt busy and productive during the last four weeks of classes, I earned no real grades for my work. My teachers knew the importance of humoring me: after two and a half months of shelving the books, I needed to be a student again.

Teachers helped me feel responsible, but everyone knew I could not function in nearly the same capacity as before. I needed a ride to attend classes or drop off articles at the *Exonian* office. Interviews that would have seemed trivial in the fall turned into major undertakings. Someone else typed my articles for me. The helplessness I felt all spring did not go away, but at least I had begun to combat it.

My 8:00 A.M. English class met four times a week and remained the only class with which I could keep pace. Other classes depended too much on the work of the past ten weeks; I had to drop photography and Russian history.

Attending English class made me agonizingly self-conscious. A well-meaning faculty member with only a partial understanding of CF had visited the class one day to explain my problem to the students. I could only guess what the students had been told, and I knew none well enough to ask. When I arrived for my first class in May, no one except the teacher met my eyes.

My teacher and the eleven other students had sent a card in April, signed by all, reading, "You're still a part of this class, Terri." When I returned, however, I could not hope to freely join an English class bonded together by Harkness Table meetings. After ten weeks of discussions, the students knew each other. I had no natural place in their debates about poetry or plays. I sat quietly through most of the classes, prepared for discussion but unwilling to interrupt the cadence of debate with the awkwardness of a comment from the stranger. When I did speak, I prompted long pauses while no one wanted to engage me; the faces at the table, meanwhile, unnerved me with the discomfort in their glances.

I fared better among the students I knew well from Russian class. Dispatched by our teacher, volunteers from the class stopped by the infirmary every few days to tutor me. Though the sessions seemed like an important first step toward progress, I had not recovered enough to be able to concentrate for long periods

Sisters Teresa and Susan

of time. I never knew how to explain this to the tutors, who must have wondered why they needed to keep repeating things.

My math teacher, John Warren, visited each day to ask how I felt. Apart from my parents, he became one of my biggest confidants that spring. When I spoke to him about my frustrations, I often found myself crying. For his trigonometry course, Warren let me work on specially made tapes and worksheets at my own pace and said I probably would be able to enroll in Exeter's next level of math in the fall.

Another faculty member visited regularly. Tim Pettus, whose algebra course I had taken in the fall, came by every few days with his two-year-old son, Stephen, on his shoulders.

Stephen would cry out and point to "Carrie's room," as he and his father approached the steps to the infirmary. I would hear his small voice and wave from the window.

"No, Stephen, can you say 'Terri'?" Pettus would ask.

Pettus's wife also brought Stephen over several times and occasionally brought food for me.

Fascinated with "Carrie's mask," through which I inhaled oxygen, Stephen always asked about it.

"It gives Terri clean air to breathe," Pettus would explain, not quite accurately.

One day I pulled out an unused mask and gave it to Stephen to keep. Still on his father's shoulders, he left the infirmary showing off the mask that looked just like Carrie's.

While some other faculty members made brief appearances, only a few students came to visit. I kept myself occupied with assignments and the business of recovery and might not have thought much of the sparse traffic into my room except that it upset my mother. She wanted to know why I had been forgotten by the majority of my peers. I told her not to worry, that I would see everyone when I recovered and we might all feel more comfortable that way.

The real reason some students stayed away never occurred to me. I knew a few faculty members had met with students in Lamont to discuss my condition. These meetings made me uneasy. Throughout grade school, I had never been pleased with the results when someone told my peers about my health in my absence. When I could not control what people said to them, students might be led to develop permanent false impressions.

I learned more about the Lamont discussions during the next school year. I could not develop friendships with certain people and pleaded with a more receptive dormmate to help me understand the distance wedged between us. Her disclosure shocked me: not only had I been depicted as pathetic and beyond hope at the meetings, but at least one faculty member tried to make my dormmates feel guilty that they had not shown me more attention. The intervening faculty member made me

an object of pity and a source of guilt to girls who might otherwise have been my friends. I tried and failed for the next two
years to redress the associations of guilt the students made
during my spring in the infirmary.

A small core of student visitors kept me from wanting for
support. In Lamont I had gotten to know a clique of seniors and
third-year students called uppers. Many of these girls came to
the infirmary when they could. Also, three of the volunteers
who had done my chest percussion in the fall lived in a dorm
near the infirmary; they made a point of stopping by often to
make me smile.

On one occasion a volunteer and her roommate sprang up
the infirmary steps to visit me while in the midst of a water pistol
duel. Another time the three girls invited me to a birthday luau,
my first party in months. My mother drove me to the student
center for the party, and one of the girls loaned me a green and
orange shirt with palm trees and tigers. They sent me back to the
infirmary loaded down with plates of coconut and pineapple.

In my cheerless and preoccupied state, I could not have been
much fun to visit, but at least I had realized I needed to change.
Although I had few events in my own life to discuss, I tried to
keep conversations going about my friends' activities. When
people visited, I had to remind myself to smile and to be less stiff
when I laughed. My ordeal had changed me—taught me I
needed to find more pleasure in a day—but I would need several
months before new behavior would come naturally.

The peculiar seemed ordinary in the infirmary that spring, so
when flowers began arriving from an anonymous source, I did
not think it strange. Bouquets of bright spring flowers came every

day for a week until I had monopolized all the infirmary vases. By this time, visitors pressed for an explanation.

"What do you mean you don't know where these things are coming from? Someone's blowing a fortune on you."

I had asked the nurses to help me find the sender, but the head nurse said she knew but would not tell. Finally she told me two boys who had heard me mentioned during chapel service sent the flowers as encouragement.

Once I returned to my room to find an elaborate computer-made "get well" banner strung across the wall opposite my bed. I suspected the flower-senders and made a nurse, who had seen one of them, page through the student directory until she identified him. Preps Mike Zorn and Thi Thumasathit finally introduced themselves and came by to visit a few times. They represented the best in Exeter's student body: they had not known me but gave a local florist a lot of business just to tell me to hang in there.

I spent much of my time that spring with other infirmary patients. I grew particularly close to Penny Britell, a lower who had lived next door to me in the fall. Back then I spent hours lounging on her bed and depleting her store of animal crackers, or listening to her play guitar. Our conversations usually began with her explaining the always-meaningful lyrics of whatever music she had listened to on a given day and led to deciding whether her shoes matched her outfit.

Penny had officially entered the infirmary for a bad cold but actually came there to rest and sort out the death of a friend. Now the two of us used the sun parlor down the hall from our rooms in much the same way we had the Lamont common room. We brought meals there and took turns controlling the television. Penny attracted more company than I did, and the two of us and her guest-of-the-hour would sit in the sunny room to chat.

During late-night conferences in the sun parlor, we usually sent my mother to find a suitable snack. We became loyal patrons of every fast-food restaurant in town.

In my mother's thoughtfulness, she always asked other patients and the nurses on duty if she could bring them some food.

"If they don't have peppermint stick, then what flavor do you want?" she would ask, and dutifully memorize long lists of preferences. Sometimes these people would join Penny, my mother, and me. Our gatherings over snacks came to represent important social time for me.

Before I left for the summer, a prep staying a few nights to rest an injured ankle made me realize how removed from Exeter's rigorous academics I had become. Once after a teacher visited him, the prep lamented about missing two math classes.

"I've fallen so far behind," he said earnestly. "I hope I'll be able to make up all the work."

I sat on the parlor couch and stared at his tanned face, too overwhelmed to speak. I had not let myself think in terms of the three hundred classes I missed.

"Oh, I think you can do it," I managed to say.

Then he asked what brought me to the infirmary.

"A little lung problem," I told him, and he nodded absently.

Days later, the prep did not believe Penny when she mentioned the length of time I had been gone.

At one point we thought that in order for me to attend the Academy in the fall, our whole family would need to live nearby. This idea came from my mother, who stood willing to move the family so I could get through school. We did not know then whether I would ever again be strong enough to be completely independent. We had seen so many other CF patients make repeated concessions to the disorder; we tried to dispassionately prepare ourselves for the possibility that my condition would not improve. Mother knew that unless I recovered dramatically from the condition I was in that spring, I would have a difficult time resuming my studies in the fall. Once they moved to the town of Exeter, my family could offer me the support to help me finish.

During a sunny afternoon in mid-May, my mother, Susan, who was visiting, and I toured a beautiful home on Pine Street, just a few blocks from campus, with the real estate agent and owner. We talked about what the new lifestyle would be like: Ted and Susan could walk to school and take lessons from a piano teacher who lived across the street. My mother looked forward to the cordial atmosphere of rural New England where the shopkeepers know your name and ask about your family. I would become a day student, and my Exeter classmates could take study breaks at our house. My family would appreciate the twenty-minute drive to Hampton Beach after living inland for so long.

My father briefly considered giving up his stable Allentown practice. As it happened, however, Exeter's eleven thousand residents did not particularly need a new urologist. Ironically, the need to pay my medical bills and tuition prevented him from considering the change to a lower-paying job for long, so if we decided to move, he would have to stay in Allentown and drive eight hours to visit us on weekends and vacations. My mother offered to return to work and hire a nurse to take care of me when I needed it. Her earnings, though, would not have been enough to supplement my father's income in a new job. Because Susan and I incurred so many medical expenses, which insurance covered only partially, we depended on my father's income. At Children's, some of my less fortunate friends could barely afford the care they needed.

The owner of the house on Pine Street rejected our offer.

"You offered a good price for this area," I told my parents. "He'll want it in a few weeks, you wait and see."

Meanwhile, we looked at other houses. Nurses told us about a faculty member who planned to move during the summer. No "For Sale" sign hung on the property yet, but we drove past the house several times and tried to picture its inside.

Unimpressed with the available homes, we discussed the move daily. Eventually we decided it would not be practical. The fact that my family considered the move so seriously and for so many days meant that they knew Exeter meant more to me than almost anything else. When we finally decided to abandon the idea, I felt relieved. I did not want my family to change their whole lifestyle for me. I determined to gain back my independence in time for the fall.

The day we left Exeter for the summer, the real estate agent called the infirmary and spoke to my mother. Mom had been packing our station wagon in the tiny infirmary parking lot. The agent told her the owner had accepted our offer. She thanked him and declined the deal.

CHAPTER ❈ FOURTEEN

When I rode home with my mother at the end of May, I left earlier than planned. I had expected to stay in town to see many of my friends graduate. However, the head nurse of the infirmary showed for the first time that she felt threatened by my presence. She ordered me to return home in a move that foreshadowed the one-sided nature of many of our future dealings.

First she said she did not have the staff to take care of me through graduation. I silently objected because, although I did not feel well and needed assistance to walk long distances, I could certainly maintain my own medical regimen by myself. The nurses had been supportive helpers but knew little about cystic fibrosis.

I understood, however, that the nurse did not want me present in a short-staffed building because we might encounter a crisis unprepared. For this reason I had made alternate plans. While my mother went home for a few days to be with the other children, I would stay in the home of friends from the local Catholic church. My mother and I knew well that CF brought long-term difficulties more often than sudden crises. My mother wanted me to stay to see my friends graduate and my would-be hosts felt comfortable with the situation.

I told the head nurse I did not intend to trouble the infirmary staff by lingering. I would stay with friends.

No, she said, I absolutely should not stay in town. If I did, she pointed out, my mother would have to drive back to Exeter to get me.

I told her my family already had grown accustomed to frequent long car trips and my mother said she didn't mind.

"Yes, but I think your mother's been through enough during these past few months," she said.

She stopped me short so I could not respond. I wondered how this woman, who barely knew my mother, could judge what would be best for her welfare. I wondered if she meant I had been responsible in some way for the difficult times we all had endured. I wondered why she cared so much whether I left town.

After a few moments, I answered calmly and politely that my family had made these plans and we all felt happy with them. I told her she would not need to worry about anything; in fact, I would leave the infirmary sooner than scheduled.

"No, T, I think it's best if you go home." She delivered every word forcefully, even the "T" meant to keep a staged familiarity in the conversation.

Next she spoke with a nuance that thundered in the space between us. She said something about planning and the future and working things out.

She watched my face and made no reaction to the way my jaw dropped. When she saw that I understood, she looked pleased.

I began to cry because I could not believe the threat.

"Don't worry, T," she said. "I know you're going to live to graduate, and I'm going to be there to see it." Then she reached over and wrapped her arms around me in a robotic hug.

When she left I could only cry some more. She should have had no hold on me. Whether I stayed in town or not did not concern her. Yet she had tested her authority and implied that things might not work out for me at Exeter if I did not agree with her will. I wanted to refuse her outright and keep myself from being manipulated.

She knew my weakness, however: a bureaucracy like the Academy's, which owed me nothing so early in my career there, would heed any advice that came from the nurse who ran the infirmary. If I should suddenly be found too sick to safely continue my studies—a scenario that would surprise few people after the rocky spring—the school would probably tell my parents and me it would be in my best interest to attend school elsewhere. I knew (and she proved me right) that her apparent resentment of me could only intensify over time. She could make my years at Exeter very difficult. I considered finding an ally among the administration, but did not know enough about the nurse's role at the school to risk criticizing her. I thought about transferring schools except that I had missed all the appropriate application deadlines. And things might be worse at another school. Besides, I decided that if I left I would be letting the nurse win. I would have to stay and learn how to play these politics.

Warren, the math teacher, came to visit after my conversation with the nurse. In tones I kept low, despite a voice made high-pitched by so much crying, I told him the story. He agreed I could do little. I made him promise not to repeat the story because I would feel safer that way.

When I told the girls from Lamont and the three chest percussion volunteers that I could not attend their graduation, I felt terrible. Some of the girls asked why; after all, I had been planning to stay for a long time. I did not want to make trouble, so I blamed it on transportation problems. I said an early good-bye to all the graduates.

I had little respect for myself after handling the situation that way. I cannot guess how the nurse would have reacted had I challenged her. Perhaps she would not have made me leave, but I could not be sure then. The nurse kept her hold on me throughout my Exeter years, although when a senior, I managed to loosen her grip.

In college I read *Black Boy*, the first volume of author Richard Wright's autobiography. By then I felt I knew some of what Wright and other African Americans trying to work in the post–Civil War South had endured. I would never liken a rich culture and heritage to an illness and know the analogy to be flawed; I mean only to compare our treatment at the hands of people who chose to hold us back. Naturally I could only empathize with part of Wright's experience, but through Wright I felt I suddenly knew why I had obeyed the nurse. I could not be blamed for my deferential behavior, although I finally could see it as the yoke of discrimination. When Wright painted portraits of the people who had mistreated him, their words and mannerisms often struck me as eerily familiar. Some reminded me of the nurse, others of brief exchanges that had never before seemed odd to me. I had accepted my lot in the same way as did some of Wright's acquaintances who did not listen when he told them to seize back their dignity. He wrote:

> I began to marvel at how smoothly the black boys acted out the roles that the white race had mapped out for them. Most of them were not conscious of living a special, separate, stunted way of life. Yet I knew that in some period of their growing up—a period that they had no doubt forgotten—there had been developed in them a delicate, sensitive controlling mechanism that shut off their minds and emotions from all that the white race had said was taboo. Although they lived in an America where in theory there existed equality of opportunity, they knew unerringly what to aspire to and what not to aspire to.

Some of us with chronic illness may face certain obstacles in school or the workplace not experienced by our healthy counterparts. In teachers' or employers' minds lingers the possibility that our health might one day jeopardize a project or a deadline. We should be encouraged, however, to fight our limitations, not live by them. Whenever people say or imply that by excluding us, sheltering us, or choosing a course of action for us they act in our best interest, they must be shown this is wrong. No one knows what lies in our best interest as well as our doctors and ourselves. Discrimination under the guise of protection should not be tolerated.

American society habitually sets the chronically ill apart from everyone else. People think us unable to judge what is best for us, unable to fulfill obligations, unable to be put to the test, and unaware of how sick we are. They think decisions, commitments, jobs, should be taken out of our sincere but incapable hands. This country raises us to be meek. We have grown up watching sad-eyed poster children and listening to the media dismiss our futures as hopeless. We have learned not to talk about ourselves when we make new friends. Like so many of today's disadvantaged groups, we find that no one wants to think about us.

I am not a socialist, but I do think we have much to learn from the products of socialism in Western Europe. When the government funds medical research directly, there is less need for a humiliating fund-raising apparatus. When the government funds medical care, people can receive treatment without worrying about impossible payments. Republican capitalism has worked to make those of us with serious chronic illness a group most Americans wish to not consider. I do not feel good about being part of one more cause in a time of so much worldwide need. I do not wish us to distract people from environmentalism or the fight for an egalitarian world. Yet we remain here needing help, help that seems unlikely to come to us from a country that has too many other items to fill the agenda.

My European friends with CF carry their heads high. One of them tells me her Swedish friends actually envy her because CF has given her cause to travel so much and meet so many people. In relationships, at school, and at work, these Europeans do not fear for their footing as much as I have known patients to do in this country.

We need to begin at the beginning and teach children to seek greatness. We need to show them, and it must be made true, that everything possible is being done to give them an equal chance with their peers. We need for people to stop patronizing others and tearing them down.

We have a long way to go.

CHAPTER
❖ FIFTEEN

Maintaining a soup diet and walking the infirmary halls had not meant I'd fully recovered, and after leaving school, I went straight to Children's. I found Division 37 crowded because summer vacation had just started and, ever the academic strategists, most patients waited until vacation to schedule their admissions.

My first roommate, a mother and full-time worker in her thirties, had not spent much time at Children's. She came from among that minority of CF patients who do not face pulmonary difficulty until they reach adulthood. She recounted a story of a few years earlier when she had been healthy and delighted to become pregnant.

Most women with CF have been made well aware that sharing oxygen with an infant is likely to jeopardize the health of a mother with CF. Our doctors have repeatedly cautioned us to avoid pregnancy, and many of us have been deeply saddened by the knowledge that it would be unwise for us ever to conceive children. The issue remains emotionally charged and many women choose to have children anyway.

When my roommate learned of her pregnancy, she had been a patient of Shwachman's. In what I consider a classic example of his hard-line approach to patient care, Shwachman responded to the news in a way meant to jolt my roommate into realism. She had been euphoric about the pregnancy, and I can only assume that Shwachman gently tried to point out the risks to her before he went for the dramatic approach.

"Do you want to die?" he asked her. He recommended she have an abortion. She would not think of it. When I met her at Children's, she was one of the only patients to have a small son come to visit her. Most men with cystic fibrosis are sterile.

My roommate spent most of her time talking on the telephone and watching soap operas while I sincerely tried to hit the books. When my knapsack full of math and Russian books hung idly on a wall hook, we made conversation. I could only respond to her stories and insights without sharing mine. My experience of the previous four months did not seem ripe for retelling. This young mother, whose pregnancy thrust her into steady decline, died several months after I met her.

My next roommate, a bank employee with CF in her late twenties, kept a bear named Freddy by her bedside. Like the mother, she worked full-time and had made few visits to Children's. She liked to fall asleep around ten o'clock, early enough to interfere with Division 37 nightlife.

Derrick Bolling, an outgoing CF patient my age, decided the banker needed to loosen up a bit. One night he forced her to sit up and watch videos with us. Derrick had paid me similar late-night visits before, but this time he found me with a roommate obsessive about her beauty sleep.

Having just learned the words to "When Doves Cry," Derrick and I sang along with Prince, much to the initial distress of my roommate. She did not crack a smile until Derrick started dancing around the room, making sure not to tip his IV pole.

Division 37 patients regularly sent out for pizza. The real veterans could not only direct you to the particular spots on closet doors and bedside tables where they had carved telephone numbers of pizza places, but they could recall which fast-food services would deliver to the Children's emergency room late at night. We reverted to this route after the main entrance closed for the evening.

Once during that admission, another patient and I carried the pizza box past rows of tired and waiting parents in the ER. They glared at us because we looked happy and healthy while they waited to hear if their children would be all right. The simplest of errands led us through the most bizarre of routes. It made me think about how hard other patients and I were trying to lead normal lives and the extent to which we had stopped noticing the strangeness of the hospital environment.

After about ten days, I left Children's with an IV, hoping it would fare better than the last. At home, after attending the first meeting of a summer theater program, with my IV bandaged to look like an injury, I realized I had become too inhibited to feel comfortable on a stage. Acutely aware of my gauntness and ever-present cough, I could not concentrate during improvisational exercises.

The summer before I had enjoyed myself in the chorus of the group's production of *Hello, Dolly*. But I no longer had the energy or enthusiasm to perform, so I dropped out of the program.

Teresa in costume for Hello, Dolly

Not wanting to remain completely inactive, I called up the dance studio where I studied before Exeter. Instructor Marie Schneck, who first met me as an uncoordinated but eager eight-year-old, welcomed me back into her summer ballet classes. I had not seen Marie since the summer before, when we wondered together what Exeter's dance program would be like. At home, she told me, I likely would have been admitted to the Lehigh Valley Ballet Guild. I had given up that chance by going away to Exeter.

When I talked to Marie this time, neither one of us knew how much dancing I could endure. She said I could stop as early in the classes as I liked and sit to watch the other dancers.

Most of my former classmates had joined the Guild by now, and their dancing had improved dramatically since I left. Now I could compete only with myself, struggling to remain standing and in motion for the ninety-minute sessions.

Dancing in Marie's hot, unairconditioned studio, working on balance and positioning after four months of barely moving, took more willpower than any other physical activity I had ever undertaken. Each day I hoped not to faint. I knew efforts like this marked my best hope at regaining strength.

One of Marie's assistant teachers had been a principal dancer with the Pittsburgh Ballet, and some of the combinations she called out to us seemed impossible until I had finished them. At the end of every lesson I felt relieved I had not collapsed in front of everyone. I told classmates only that they could not catch my cough.

A dancer who joined up late in summer stopped dancing and stared when he first heard me cough.

"Hey, are you all right?" he asked incredulously, looking panicked. Dancers do not cough the way I did. I told him not to worry, but he never got close enough to talk to me again.

Also that summer I continued in my role as an aging poster child. By that time the task had grown mechanical. I could not play for sympathy and still sound dignified, so I tried not to think about the pleas I extended. I had burned out and could barely write phrases that hid my exasperation with the healthy world. I worked to hide all trace of bitterness.

I needed to write a letter to the contestants of a beauty pageant benefitting the CF Foundation. I spent a week trying to achieve the right tone in the brief letter. My longhand would be copied and specially printed for all the contestants. I wrote in a nice even hand that I thought transmitted the proper vulnerability.

I had only one speech to compose that summer. For their annual fund drive that year, the state branch of the Future Business Leaders of America chose to raise money for the Foundation through a program they called project life. FBLA member Bill Knepper, a seventeen-year-old CF patient, would join me to talk about the project at the organization's Pennsylvania state leadership conference in August.

In preparation for the FBLA conference, I pulled out old speech notes and struggled to assemble fresh material. I knew that we needed to educate people about CF, but I had begun to find my turns at the podium distasteful. I had spent too much time as a carnival freak and had seen no results for my effort. I knew well that most times I spoke to kindhearted people, but no audience could make the forum a noble one. I fought these musings because they interfered with my assignment.

Fortunately I still had whole passages of speech memorized and could give myself a two-word cue on an index card to automatically spout three or four minutes' worth of phrases. Begging for help all the time had grown boring as well as degrading, and I did not want to listen to myself anymore.

One afternoon in July, Bill Knepper and I sat on my family's back porch discussing our plans for the speeches. Bill felt understandably nervous about speaking before friends who knew him only as FBLA's state treasurer and remained unaware he had CF. A relatively healthy basketball player, Bill had been one of the lucky among us.

We both knew Bill would have a difficult time addressing familiar faces. Tainted enough by now to go right for the tears, I taught Bill some of the catch-phrases I used in speeches. For example, Bill did not know how he should refer to people who had CF.

"Oh, call us 'victims,'" I said, using a word I have since disavowed. "That always makes people listen."

Susan came with me to be introduced, and Mom and Ted rode to Hershey, Pennsylvania, with us. Until I entered the big auditorium on campus, I had expected to appear at a luncheon, where people divide their attention between dessert and the speaker. I tried to look enthusiastic as I shook the hands of the FBLA officers and realized for the first time that I would have to hold the attention of four hundred teenagers who did not have pieces of cake in front of them.

When I started, the words moved along by themselves. Suddenly, however, I began worrying about the speed of my breathing. I could fit only four or five words between breaths and knew my increased respirations made me sound nervous. I had not noticed myself breathing so rapidly, but the microphone and speaker system betrayed my every inhalation.

Since the last time I returned home from Children's, I had been telling myself I had recovered from the spring. I ignored all breathing difficulties. Mid-speech I realized I could no longer pretend to be better; I would have to fight harder.

After the Hershey speech, Ted, who kept a stopwatch handy for just such occasions, timed my ovation at an undistinguished eighteen seconds. Finally it had become time to hang up the old index cards.

CHAPTER
❧ SIXTEEN

Back sometime in March, while I fought my mystery infection at Children's, a childhood friend of my mother's called our house to ask about me. My grandmother, who had once been the woman's Girl Scout leader, took the call. Normally I would not have received a detailed account of this conversation because we could not keep track of all the wishers-well that spring. Yet this call warranted attention.

Usually when I had seen the woman who called, she had acted self-absorbed and immature. Of course, she had been acting then, portraying Erica Kane on the ABC soap opera *All My Children*. Susan Lucci told Grandmother she hoped I would be able to visit her at the studio in July. She knew my mother would be in town then for their twentieth reunion at Garden City High School. Grandmother said she thought I would like to visit her if I could.

Puzzling over the timely call, I later learned that a mutual friend of the actress and my mother had spread the news that I had fallen seriously ill. I found the invitation a novel reaction to word of my condition; when I received it, I had only a remote chance of ever accepting.

Grandmother managed to record the conversation on our answering machine and played it for me after I returned home. At the time I found it strange to hear someone assume I would be alive in July. Lucci had extended a very nice invitation, but I thought it had come too late. I wondered if she would take my family around the studio without me.

Even when my condition worsened, we never declined her invitation. In July, after I had begun my recovery, my family and I traveled to New York for Mother's reunion. She saw Lucci there and they firmed up plans for our visit. So my father battled New York traffic one morning to get to the ABC studio on the Avenue of the Americas. While riding into the city from a friend's house in the suburbs, I realized the coughing fits I had experienced all weekend would become an awkward disturbance on a quiet set. I used half a dozen cough drops during the thirty-minute ride but did not grow any quieter.

In front of the studio we walked past an army of fans waiting to glimpse their favorite performers and firing questions at us about how we planned to gain access to the building. A fierce-looking security guard blocked our path inside while a desk clerk called Lucci. My mother's dark-haired, petite schoolmate soon emerged, wearing a black evening gown that would have looked out of place this early in the day anywhere but here. I would have been taller than Lucci, who stands about five feet, except that she wore spike heels. She met us all with unassuming graciousness. I felt silly at first because I knew I no longer looked sick, despite a lingering frailty. I wondered whether she thought her friend had exaggerated my condition. I wanted to talk to her; she had been kind enough to call our home when she knew so little about me. Yet I kept finding that I could not decide how best to tell a busy actress about the struggle of mine that made her call so welcome.

First, Lucci led us down a hall to the wardrobe area. She showed us a rack with most of the day's costumes. To show us her own outfits, she let us peer into the locked costume office storing the most valuable clothes, Erica's included.

She pointed to two sombreros and Mexican costumes and said, "There's a scene coming up on the show where Mike asks me to run away to Mexico with him. I'll let you judge for yourselves. Do I go?" We laughed.

When Lucci asked a question requiring a response, something about how I felt that day, I burrowed the cough drop into my cheek in squirrel-like fashion. Keeping my answer to one or two syllables, I quickly crunched up and swallowed the lozenge.

Predictably, with my last suppressant gone, my cough gained volume and frequency. When we stopped to watch two performers rehearsing, I wondered if they could still hear each other over the noise I made. I braced myself for the temperamental director, whom Lucci said we caught on an off day, to turn and scream at me. I held my breath and wished more than anything I could disappear. My kindergarten fantasies about singing or acting before large crowds never included the cough.

The actors continued with their lines, and the director and crew kept their eyes trained on them, still watching even if they could no longer hear. Having prepared myself for a hostile reaction, I admired their professionalism. If they had been taping instead of rehearsing, they would have been forced to start again.

Years of soap watching in hospitals made me familiar with the cast and sets we saw that day. During stays at St. Christopher's in Philadelphia, strolls down the hall between one and two in the afternoon had produced *All My Children* in stereo; every available television followed the day's events in Pine Valley. I began to associate the show's theme song, played in part before commercial breaks, with the hospital; it became one of few comforting sounds among a cacophony of ominous machines and voices raised in alarm.

I did not follow plots or learn names until nurses and therapists at Children's began asking what Erica had been doing while they tended to the baby down the hall or some paperwork. They expected me to know. I found the same thing my few times in Allentown hospitals: everyone talked about soaps all day long, knowing, I suppose, they had found a neutral conversation topic.

Another patient explained the mania to me this way: "When you're stuck in here for weeks at a time, you can't let yourself think too much." Patients do not usually ask other patients about test results. That subject remains delicate even among the closest of friends. Nurses and therapists know better than to ask patients questions that will prompt introspection. Many hospital conversations weave delicately and leave much unsaid.

Yet anyone can initiate a moral debate over the way soap opera characters treat each other.

Discomfort kept me from saying much to Lucci that day. Coughing fits have a way of sending the most ready-to-be-articulated thoughts too far for retrieval. So, I likely seemed awed by my surroundings.

When we entered the makeup room, a beautiful young actress in bathrobe and slippers complimented little Susan and me on our dresses. I thanked her but did not add to the conversation because I continued to hold my breath to keep from coughing. My two years at Raub and Exeter had given me occasion to practice the imperceptible breathing technique, which sometimes suppressed the cough.

Elizabeth, in her cuteness, attracted several performers who approached and admired her as we walked through the studio. One actress, whose character later became gun-happy and turned a wedding into a shootout, held my little sister for several minutes until our host gently asked us to continue on our tour.

Next, Lucci brought us into a lounge, where she said performers sat sipping coffee and watching *Good Morning America* while they waited for the director's call. Then after seeing the sound room and a few rooms of monitors, we arrived at Lucci's dressing room at the end of the tour. Pictures drawn by her small children adorned the walls of the small room our host shared with Erica's mother.

I thanked Lucci before we left and quietly sought words to end the awkwardness I had created with my silence. I found none. I felt incapable of bridging our different realms of experience with any small comment; I had glimpsed her way of life but could provide no glimpse of mine.

As we tried to leave the building a few minutes later, a jealous fan stood in our way.

"Who do you know?" she asked.

"One of the cast. Sorry." I shrugged, not quite sure how to help her.

"They know an actor," she told her friends who had appropriated the sidewalk. Apparently they had been staking out the building for some time. The dejected group watched us get into our nearby car, then sat back down on the pavement for an afternoon of celebrity seeking.

A few years later, when she visited our area, Lucci taped a simple and dignified publicity spot about CF with my sister Susan. We felt grateful for her time and interest. Unfortunately, the CF Foundation said, for reasons it could not specify, that the spot did not fit in with its campaign.

CHAPTER ✸ SEVENTEEN

Toward summer's end, I let the Academy dean's office know I would be returning to Exeter. I made the disheartening discovery that school officials had not reserved a place for me in the class. I could still go back to school, but I had been decidedly unexpected. I found the reactions of people other than the deans more heartening.

"Your letter came today," Roxane wrote in response to the news I would see her in September. "You are a wonder."

"So glad to receive your letter," my Exeter dance teacher wrote. "Very excited about your dancing again."

Friends from Lamont and the three graduates who had helped with chest percussion probed cautiously in their letters. They knew I would return if at all possible. Some went beyond the question at hand and asked if I would return as a lower or upper.

"What do you have scheduled for next year? Are you going to be an upper?"

"Say, are you going back? Let me know."

"What are your upcoming plans? I suspect it's a touchy subject, so my curiosity can be subdued if you'd prefer it that way."

I responded triumphantly that I'd be returning to Exeter as an upper. I would maintain my promoted status despite the missed semester. Even as a lower I would have struggled in the classroom after my absence; nonetheless, I chose to stay with the class I had joined. My letters back to friends bore great optimism because I could not have imagined how difficult the coming year would be.

A letter from my new adviser, a strong-willed language teacher who often had shown well-intentioned but patronizing concern for me during my first year, hinted at the way I would spend the next several months. He wrote: ". . . I do recommend room 5, 6, or 7 [in Lamont] as a 'day room.' I am sure the infirmary will love to have you for your evening 'rub' [my chest percussion] and keep you overnight. So, that would be the best of both worlds."

I had no desire to have the infirmary "keep me overnight." Although we had not discussed my living arrangement before, I assumed I would continue to live in Lamont. I made no immediate objection to my adviser's proposal because I did not want to press my luck. But I hoped I would find an opportunity to convince him and everyone else I belonged with other students.

My adviser said something about my being safer in the infirmary, in case I needed medical assistance during the night. I found his concern frustrating because it implied I did not have the judgment to be independent. I had never before needed help at night and had always had time to foresee crises.

In the spring the adviser had raised the issue of my oxygen concentrator, which he incorrectly called a fire hazard. I tried to explain then that the machine distilled oxygen from room air. If I had kept several tanks of pure oxygen in my room, and if girls had been allowed to smoke anywhere in the dorm except a tiny, isolated room reserved for this purpose, then perhaps we might have run a risk. In his letter, my adviser did not raise his fire hazard concern, but I suspected he remained unconvinced by my assurances.

According to the plan, I would be a regular dorm dweller until nine o'clock, when I would make the obligatory upper check-in with an infirmary nurse instead of a Lamont adviser.

In late August the dean of students approved my adviser's plan. In a grave bureaucratic oversight, no one remembered to consult the head nurse of the infirmary. Shortly before my arrival on campus, someone mentioned the plan to the nurse, who grew indignant. To her, my presence seemed to represent the end of her order and control of the infirmary. I would have happily let her alone if I could have.

She could not refuse to give me a room when the administration required it of her. So she agreed to let me stay there and made a few visible political gestures, such as assigning me a large room and buying curtains for it, yet it felt perfectly clear to Roxane and me, as well as other nurses, that she did not approve. She did not say so plainly; instead, she filled conversations with parenthetical references to my bothersome presence. I believe she blamed me for my move to the infirmary, as if I had chosen to live there. I would come to dread her saccharine show of regard for me; she did not want friendship, only control.

After my long summer of waiting to go back, returning to Exeter proved a letdown. My mother helped me carry suitcases, cardboard boxes full of medicine and books, a small refrigerator, and my oxygen concentrator through the infirmary's back door to a large room at the end of the second-floor hall. As we walked back and forth, our voices echoed in the empty building. We spoke briefly to the nurse on duty but encountered no one else. Without any neighbors to greet, I felt a loneliness I had not known since my intercom years.

The infirmary staff had made the room look reasonably inviting. They moved one of the beds out of a room meant to be a double, brought in a desk, gave the walls a fresh coat of standard issue ivory paint, and covered the brown linoleum floor with a thin, rust-colored, industrial-type carpet. Three huge windows gave the room an airiness far removed from the dark room I had kept in Lamont's basement.

After unloading the car, Mother and I dined at a restaurant down the road from campus. There I met up with a girl from Lamont and her parents. We talked about the status of the returning dorm: room locations, wild haircuts, and girls who had withdrawn from the Academy during the summer.

"Where are you living?" she asked. "I didn't see you before."

"Yeah, well, I've got this room in the infirmary. They want me to live there for now. But I'll be in the dorm as much as possible."

"Have you seen Kelly yet?" she asked.

"Not yet."

"Well, have you seen . . ."

"Haven't seen anyone yet. We just finished unpacking."

"Well, come on over," she said.

I wanted so much to believe I could overcome the distance the infirmary would impose between us. Over dinner I told my mother I would make the arrangement work until I could move elsewhere. I did most of the talking that night and assumed the eight-hour drive had tired my mother. Later she told me she had sat there thinking about how lonely I might become.

During my first days back, when I most needed to see familiar faces, my classmates made comments that almost unnerved me.

"Terri, I didn't think you'd be back."

"Oh, hi. I didn't think . . . Um, so how was your summer?"

I heard the words countless times; I knew the sentiment behind them to be harmless despite my discomfort.

"Well, I am back," I would say, disappointed no one had greater confidence in me.

I found it difficult to explain myself to new Lamont residents, who kept saying they hoped I would feel better soon and leave the infirmary. I took their get-well wishes with simple thanks as we rushed past each other on the paths.

At our first dorm meeting, my adviser clarified things beyond all doubt: "Terri's kind of special, okay? She's got cystic fibrosis. She'll be in room 105, but she's going to sleep next door."

My face turned a dark scarlet as preps and lowers turned to mark the special student, much as they would the dorm's fire exits.

Meanwhile my mother and the head nurse sparred within two days of my arrival. Mom called me the night she drove home to tell me she arrived safely. She phoned again early the next morning to tell me of the death of a young aunt of mine, who had battled cancer for several years. As the nurse saw it, my mother had made one call too many.

"We have to put a stop to this," the nurse said. She scolded Mother for tying up infirmary phone lines. After that I called home regularly on an outside line because the nurse would not allow Mother to call except in cases of emergency.

The head nurse met with me soon after I moved into the building to establish what she called ground rules. I would be treated independently except that I would not be allowed to have a lock on my door. We would argue about the lock continuously, especially after the many times it appeared that someone had been in my room without permission and the occasional times I found something missing. The infirmary did not want to be liable if anything happened to me behind the confines of a locked door. I asked many times that I be allowed to lock the door only in my absence, to keep strangers out of my room, but the nurse denied me my lock.

The infirmary staff needed to make great sacrifices to enable me to live there, the nurse told me in our conference, and she did not want me taking advantage of the situation. Only now do I wonder what she possibly could have meant: she implied I was in an enviable position, able, if I wanted, to grab at all the advantages of life in the infirmary, none of which I could identify. She felt obligated to govern my presence there out of fairness to other Academy students. I sought to be independent, and ultimately to return to a dorm, yet seemed to remain in her eyes a threat and burden to the infirmary staff. I learned quickly to bury my incredulity at her remarks.

"You're keeping up your end of the bargain, T," she said often after our first talk. I smiled blandly when she said this, never caring to know what bargain she meant.

Only once did I venture into room 105, which my adviser called my day room. I needed to pick up my laundry bag with sheets, pillowcases, and forms to send to the school laundry.

"This room sure looks empty," said a girl who stepped inside to talk to me. I agreed. I had already hung all my posters in my infirmary room, and did not have enough sheets to make up an additional bed. I needed access to my books and papers at night and in the morning, so the desk and shelf in room 105 would remain empty. My clothes had to stay in the infirmary too, unless I planned to race to the dorm in my bathrobe.

My adviser initially proposed reopening an underground tunnel that had connected Lamont and the infirmary before being sealed years earlier. Legend held that dorm residents had regularly raided the infirmary's drug supply until administrators bricked up the passage. Such a passage would have allowed me to spend most of my time in the dorm. My adviser talked about the passage several times but apparently never pursued the idea beyond our conversations.

I realized I would never use the day room. Most socializing took place after check-in anyway, and a day room would not make me a part of things at night. And when I visited the dorm, I would hardly want to spend time in the tiny, barren room to which I had been assigned. I would go to see others in their rooms.

Beyond my own use for such a room, I had to consider the dorm's overcrowding. Some preps and lowers had crowded into emergency triples in the basement. I could not keep the key to an empty room while others lacked adequate space. Someone moved into the room within hours of my relinquishing it.

Everyone in Lamont knew they could visit me in my infirmary room. Yet the few times people came over there, the strange setting inhibited all of us. I lived in a hospital room with nice curtains. When the girls sat in the stiff chairs, they looked, and perhaps felt, as though they had come to visit a sick friend.

Although my adviser remained adverse to my returning to Lamont, I resolved that somehow I would find my way into a dorm. I would change his mind or forge another plan. I could stand for nothing less.

When I returned that fall, I faced a lonely struggle to recover from the spring. Although I still tired easily, I forced myself to maintain the schedule expected of me. I rarely missed class, and during four dance sessions a week, I suppressed my urge to sit down. I studied in the infirmary but spent as much free time as possible elsewhere. I threw myself into extracurriculars: the *Exonian*, the Committee for Nuclear Awareness, dancing, piano, and a Catholic student group I helped start. Although I had genuine interest in all the activities, I needed them for another reason: they provided escape while I sought a way out of the infirmary.

At the same time that I busied myself with distractions, I had the beginnings of several realizations. I reacted with delayed fear to my recent struggle with the illness and began to regard everything around me as fragile and tentative. The trial brought with spring had stolen upon me, and I had never seen it head-on. Where could I look now for stability, for permanence, or might these things always elude me? For the first few months of school, I waited for an understanding I expected to be forthcoming. I asked myself questions as I walked to classes or climbed the small infirmary hill: *Why me? Why anyone? What can be done?* and *How can the world be roused to help us?* At times my need for answers made me scoff at seemingly shallow academic assignments to which I nonetheless devoted my time.

Finally, I learned to stop asking the questions that would drown me if I let them. I could only worry about my own little space in the universe. And that space needed tidying.

That fall I found I could look at myself and see my past as though I scrutinized another person. I resolved to change the two major traits I found unseemly: my extraordinary shyness in social settings and my overriding solemnity. Roxane and I spoke of the behavioral changes I wanted to make, and we both knew they would pose a challenge. Smiles and laughter still did not come easily for me, but I began reminding myself to punctuate conversations with them. Rox and I look back on that year as a transitional one, by the end of which I could dispense with internal reminders to take myself less seriously.

While I experienced my own complicated reverie about the spring, my classmates avoided all reference to my absence. One-fourth of the year's calendar had been ripped away, gone to all of us.

"Were you here for that?" students would ask cautiously after mentioning an assembly or other event I missed. "I guess you weren't." Then they would change the subject. No one ever asked about my time away or its effect on my psyche, and I never felt comfortable enough to talk about it.

Only new students asked questions about CF, and this they did awkwardly.

"Terri, can I ask you something? . . . Well, this is really personal, but . . . I hope you won't mind. . . . Well, that problem you have . . . How serious is it?"

They seemed to be seeking assurances that they did not need to worry about me, and these I tried to give them.

As I began classes, my teachers of math, English, and American history showed they had been briefed about the past year. None of them reacted to my cough, and all asked how I felt several times, although I never spoke to them about my health. In October, when I told them I would be leaving for Children's, they all remained expressionless as though awaiting the announcement. I never asked how much they knew or who had spoken to them.

My Russian teacher, Charles Deardorff, taught me throughout my three years at Exeter. He remembered my auspicious beginnings there and offered more encouragement than most teachers. When he needed to decide in early fall whether I should start over with Russian or continue with my class, he generously placed me in the second-year course. He allowed me to receive a pass/fail grade, a practice rare at Exeter except for post-graduate students. In three and a half months of missed classes, I had fallen so far behind that I worked almost as hard to pass as others did for their coveted Exeter As.

"What does that mean?" someone asked once when he saw a big red P at the top of my corrected test. I started to stammer an explanation, then thankfully grew silent as our lesson began.

Deardorff's preparation for my hospital stay demonstrated the relaxed attitude he developed while teaching me. My teachers of

English and American history talked about papers I would miss and sent an armload of books to the hospital with me. My math teacher rushed to the infirmary with a stack of worksheets. I knew I could accomplish almost nothing at Children's and felt grateful to my Russian teacher who said offhandedly, "Try to take a look at the next two chapters while you're gone."

In addition to evidently briefing my teachers, the school administration made helpful, if unnecessary, special arrangements for my classes. None of them met during the first period, which began at eight o'clock. Extra time in the morning kept me from being rushed after my first aerosol, my chest percussion, and my tobramycin aerosol, all of which occupied ninety minutes. The deans also ensured that my new teachers had first-floor classrooms. Although I now realize I need to get all the exercise I can, at the time I felt relieved to avoid the stairs that tired me and left me breathless.

Each day for our class, Deardorff borrowed a first-floor classroom and abandoned his own third-floor room. My classmates did not understand.

"This room is so small. Hey, why are we down here anyway? His room's on the third floor. Why aren't we up there?" someone asked before class. He looked to students on either side of him for explanation.

I almost spoke up but could think of nothing to say. The girl on his left answered almost immediately.

"So Terri can . . ." She saw me sitting at table's end and broke off mid-sentence.

So Terri can what? I wondered. How had she planned to finish the sentence?

The boy nodded slowly in a painfully long moment of realization, and I wondered again if I should speak. The five or six others at the table stopped talking. After a moment, one of them noticed my discomfort and launched another topic; I managed to grin with thanks when he looked over at me a minute later.

For friends through this time, I could count a handful of girls in Lamont, the students I sat with in the dining hall, and the people I knew through extracurriculars. I had no close friends except for Roxane and one of the infirmary nurses. Ironically, this period of isolation helped me begin to overcome my shyness. I had no choice but to introduce myself in the dining hall and to start conversations with people I barely knew. I grew so exasperated with infirmary life that I became increasingly uninhibited in social settings; I could no longer afford to keep to myself. I did manage to initiate a few friendships that would blossom by senior year. For the most part, however, my efforts went without success.

My relief came once a week when a family from the nearby church picked me up for Sunday Mass. After the service

Back home in Pennsylvania, Elizabeth and Tim filled their days drawing pictures and "writing" letters to Teresa. The day this photo was taken, they collected and mailed a huge box of colorful leaves from the front yard at home.

we always went to the church basement for coffee and dough-nuts. I spent more time each Sunday talking to the family's daughter, who attended a local high school, than I spent with any of my classmates.

I looked forward to Sunday mornings, when I rushed to be ready for nine o'clock Mass and then ran to the Coty family's car with hair barely dry. After church I would draw in the comforting basement scene of so many gathered families for as long as possible. The parishioners at St. Michael's had won me over the previous fall when I saw them giving every spare cent to surprise their pastor with a trip to Rome. Among this unpre-tentious community of soft-spoken New Englanders, I could glimpse that stability, that serenity, for which I longed. I knew I needed to remain at Exeter even while the infirmary made me miserable; this contact with a patient and inviting outside world helped me endure.

CHAPTER
❧ EIGHTEEN

I became fast friends with Susan McLeod, an infirmary nurse whom Roxane and I called "Sunny" because the name just seemed to fit. Sunny joined the infirmary staff during the summer as a part-time nurse. Indirectly I created a full-time opening for her.

At the first staff meeting of the year, the infirmary nurses discussed my move into the building. One of the nurses objected to the arrangement, saying she did not think it would be safe to have me spreading infections to other patients. The other nurses explained that cystic fibrosis infections could not be transmitted to healthy people; the bacteria could only thrive in our lungs as a result of the special conditions established by the CF gene. The answer apparently did not satisfy the nurse, who then resigned unexpectedly. The head nurse would never have told us any of this, but Roxane and I had our spies throughout the building.

With Sunny working regular shifts, I gained a friend and confidant who saw my loneliness and helped me understand it myself. "This is no good," she would say often, shaking her head. "You should be with other kids."

"Yeah, tell me about it," I most often replied.

A wife and mother in her early thirties, Sunny came to the infirmary job fresh from experience in perhaps the most demanding of medical settings, the emergency room of a local hospital. She stood about my height, with curly blond hair just shy of ponytail length. Sometimes she seemed more like a coach, clipboard in hand and pen behind her ear, than a nurse. When students came in looking for excuses from class, Sunny would be tough but fair. She remembered her high school days well and empathized with her patients. Her ER background gave her the versatility to soothe one minute and cope with a crisis the next.

Sunny had worked with CF patients a few years earlier, and she comprehended my situation better than anyone else at the Academy. Only with Roxane could I lapse as easily into medical jargon or cynical pronouncements about new theories.

In Sunny, I found someone to whom I could candidly describe my days. Sunny often tended to several patients during an afternoon, but if I met her in the hall, I could simply roll my eyes and she would understand. In the evening, after other nurses and other patients had left, we would sit downstairs and make sarcastic sense of the day's events. Sometimes Sunny talked about her husband, Randy, or her two children or about the other nursing jobs she had held. More often, however, I told her about academic or medical headaches, slights big or small, and the unpleasant nature of infirmary life. She offered perspective and advice. I quizzed her about her own experience. And we always found a way to laugh at ourselves. Usually we grew quite animated.

"I can't *believe* it!" I would yell about some new source of frustration.

"Terri, you gotta *do* something!" she would yell back.

During her shift, Sunny had to tend to paperwork and maintenance tasks, and sometimes our talks had to be postponed while she helped a late-night infirmary visitor. Many nights, however, no one came through the infirmary door. With the building to ourselves, except for an occasional upstairs patient or two, Sunny and I felt free to raise our voices; we even gained some small satisfaction from it.

Early in the fall, the two of us discovered we shared a love for science fiction. Sometimes on weekends she brought her video cassette recorder to the infirmary and we watched select episodes of *Star Trek*. We would analyze characters and plot, and Sunny would fill me in on the trivial background details of the series she knew so well. We never clashed except on Friday evenings, when the program *V* aired at the same time as *Star Trek* reruns.

"Come on, Sunny, wouldn't it be more exciting to watch an episode you've never seen before, hear dialogue you don't have memorized?"

But she never saw it that way, and the two of us would stalk off to our separate rooms: she pulled rank and used the large set in the dispensary and I used the small one in a waiting room. If a patient entered in need of Sunny's attention, I would rush to commandeer the dispensary set.

Late in the fall, the head nurse spent a few nights in the infirmary while she overcame an ailment. One evening she heard me calling Sunny's name. The head nurse then lectured Sunny and reprimanded her with such severity for failing to keep a professional distance in our relationship that Roxane and I feared for her job. Sunny received a warning about our friendship; the head nurse implied Sunny would go through some sort of probationary period until the nurse approved of the distance between us.

Next morning the head nurse, all smiles, called me into a staff room and made a big speech. She spoke slowly in thick condescension, with syllables uttered so carefully she sounded like children's TV host Mr. Rogers. I almost laughed.

"Peo-ple in the in-fir-ma-ry are called 'Miss' or 'Mrs.' Do you un-der-stand?"

She talked about respect and authority, but I tuned out before she got very far. The nurses I knew at five different hospitals all expected patients to call them by their first names. Although most elderly patients prefer that surnames be exchanged, nurses and patients are rightfully friends in the fight.

Sunny and I could not have been more incredulous and bewildered by the head nurse's reaction. I still feared the nurse as much as I did when I missed graduation, and the two of us made a pact to appear to humor her.

The warning given Sunny added a strange drama to our friendship: for the rest of the year we spent much of our time darting in and out of infirmary rooms to check for the presence of the head nurse or of one of the nurses we called her lieutenants. The lieutenants all seemed nice except for the way they kept a watchful eye out to ensure that I performed the head nurse's bidding. Around the lieutenants, Sunny had to mouth the words "Mrs. McLeod" before I spoke to her, because I kept forgetting. Of course, Sunny and I remained as close as ever and found plenty of secret time for conversations and for *Star Trek*.

During spring break of that year, Sunny met me at Children's, where I underwent a routine course of antibiotics. From there the two of us went to a science-fiction convention in downtown Boston. For Sunny, the *Star Trek* series she loved served as a draw to the convention. I had a deeper love for science fiction that stemmed from early childhood. Right after our move to Allentown, I had written a play, complete with a few simple songs, about a young girl who escaped her planet during a war, only to look at the stars and wonder what became of her family and her people. I even had costumes and props but could not find any other eight-year-olds to perform in my play. Then at age nine, I was supposed to keep a journal for my third-grade teacher. Instead I used the notebook to write about a young girl and her grandfather as they scurried about in their shuttle, between all manner of unpopulated planets. I wanted criticism, so while I stayed in Allentown Hospital for a few weeks that year, I made all the student nurses read my "journal."

My fascination with such an unorthodox genre comes from a cynicism that has hope at its outer edges. I was born into a country loudly lauding itself for sending astronauts to the moon, yet so early in my life, I would see technology fall short. As a small child, I decided the Nixon White House and then that of Ford must not know about cystic fibrosis or they would be helping us instead of spending so much money on machines. In so much of popular science fiction, I could view societies that had settled mundane health issues and moved on to other important work. I wanted to see alternatives, even if imaginary, to our society of the present. I have found the genre to be very popular among my hospital friends.

Sunny and I went crazy at the convention, spending every last nickel on books and magazines. We were children in a toy store, pulling each other this way and that. We netted a few first-edition *Star Trek* books and a few script outlines for future projects. That night at my room in Children's, we sat quietly reading our purchases for a long time. Sunny had to get a good dose of *Star Trek* before she could start her trip home.

It's probably not surprising that, with my interest in science fiction, I once had a dream like this.

"Wait, everyone, wait if you please," a harried figure begged. *"I have one small item to add to the agenda. It will only take a moment."*

The committee members grumbled, but none made a move to leave the chamber. The session had been a long one, and all ten of them had planets to rule back home. Still, their weapons expert deserved a chance to speak.

"Thank you. As you've already been told, our last scouting mission to other systems uncovered several forms of life which seem likely to pose a future threat to us. You all know the dangers of failing to act before our rivals grow powerful. Clearly, we remain in an early planning stage, but my staff and I are planning a little experiment. Gor here is coordinating the project, and I will now turn the speaker's privilege over to him."

A figure who had been standing silent in a dark corner throughout the meeting now slowly strode into the light.

"I thank the committee for its attention. Our plan is to insert a deadly genetic packet into the life cycle of the young race of humans. We will monitor the creatures as a small segment of their population fall prey to our weapon. If the genetic combination produces the effects we want, we may reproduce it elsewhere. Genetic tampering is unlikely to be detected, and thus we consider it the perfect weapon."

Gor yielded to a committee member who indicated on her desk-front panel that she waited with a question.

"Excuse me," she said, "but just what are the desired effects of your weapon?"

The scientist grinned, eager to tell of the genius of his plan.

"A question easily answered, my lady. A human's most vital organ is the heart, so we have found a way to deactivate it. The gene packet will create a condition in which the human body will simultaneously shut down its own respiratory, digestive, and reproductive systems. Respiration will be impaired by an internally created substance that will block breathing passages and ultimately cause a recipient's lungs to stop functioning. Nourishment will be rejected by the body, robbing it of its

strength to fight. Males will be incapable of producing offspring, and females will perish if they try."

"But sir, why bother with such a slow-acting weapon? Once they develop the technology to aid recipients, the kind of decay you're talking about could take at least one-fourth of a normal human life span."

"Because, my lady, of the frustrating course of the condition we have created. It will quickly destroy morale among recipients, and without that, they are lost. They will enter intermittent stages of apparent recovery, only to have their hopes dashed. Suffering in a society hurts a people's fighting spirit. If a whole race of our enemies succumbed to this condition, we would be protected."

Gor was buoyed by the attentive faces. He decided to press his luck and say some things he had not discussed with the weapons expert. He felt sure he could keep the committee interested, and better, impress them.

"There is an added feature," he began. "Naturally, this is only speculative, but we believe that instead of combating the relatively simple symptoms, target populations will invest their time and resources into trying to identify the genetic defect. While they do this, the condition itself will ravage the population."

Then he turned to another waiting questioner.

"How will the condition be spread if recipients have no children?"

"Sir," Gor responded coolly, beginning to think his plan would secure him a high post in Weapons, "there will be a sizeable carrier population in the experiment. These unsuspecting carriers will transmit the genes we have designed, and many of them will bear offspring with the condition. Among our sample, we estimate that one in twenty-five hundred humans will be a recipient."

The committee members had no more questions, and Gor wondered fleetingly if he had been overconfident. He dismissed the *thought of reminding them, as planned, that this was only a trial. He cleared his throat, then launched back into the presentation.*

"You will all receive a thorough report on the weapon," he said hastily. "We believe it really does have an impressive array of effects: weight problems will make recipients gaunt and unattractive to their race; an unstoppable choking reflex will make them social outcasts; they will lose large amounts of the mineral salt in their perspiration, making them . . ."

"Pardon, sir, but we are politicians here, not scientists," interrupted the chair of the committee. "We trust you have tended to details. Thank you for your presentation. Meeting adjourned, everyone."

There was the melodic hum of computer panels, a bustle of robes as members hurried out of the chamber, and then the room fell silent.

CHAPTER
❂ NINETEEN

When my stamina waned in late October of my infirmary year, I headed to Children's for a course of antibiotics. Although I did not like the idea of leaving school for any length of time, I planned to be gone for only two weeks. Although I knew none of the roommates who passed through my two-bed room, a few old friends stayed nearby. Each night I gathered with Suzy Ahlman, Brian "Tex" Teixeira, and Mark Nims, three CF patients close to me in age. The four of us watched late-night movies; debated the merits of Mark's favorite rock group, Van Halen (whose posters covered the walls near his bed and who had evidently inspired him to pierce one ear); and found other fun and safe topics of conversation.

In the room shared by Tex and Mark, we formed a jaded little society of hospital critics. Our knowledge and intensity may have surprised most doctors if they had heard. When we discussed antibiotics, for example, we grew quite technical. We all knew the names of the various bacteria in our lungs and knew which antibiotics might be best for use against them. We knew how long most antibiotics had been available on the open market, and we knew which ones still needed approval from the Food and Drug Administration. We knew which antibiotics cost more than others. We made it our business to know which doctors had assigned which patients which drugs. Among ourselves we went so far as to analyze the preferences of doctors whose recommendations appeared to have produced few positive results. In the end, however, we felt that antibiotic use became an almost subjective science; we had learned through so many painful years of loss that none of the antibiotics available to us could truly be considered effective against cystic fibrosis.

We knew well the side effects of all the drugs. Three of us spoke loudly and with defined lip movements so that Tex, deaf in one ear from prolonged use of IV tobramycin, could hear with his good ear or read our lips. Ironically, the three of us all continued to receive IV tobramycin, the antibiotic most powerful against the common bacteria *Pseudomonas aeruginosa*. While on tobramycin we tried to remember to have our hearing and also our liver function checked often, because naturally we worried more about these irreversible side effects than doctors did. We had no choice, however, but to use the strongest drug available. The watch for effects from this and other drugs became one more thing we all kept in our minds.

Despite the adult nature of most of our conversations, our meetings occasionally degenerated into chaos. While I had given up on childhood, Mark, Tex and Suzy continued to make a valiant effort at it. I never took part in two of the most popular forms of hospital recreation: using giant syringes to squirt water out the window at passersby or through the elevator doors as they closed between squirter and prey. Similarly, I did not join my friends when they engaged in what they called Pancrease fights. These occurred when two parties began hurling handfuls of our pancreatic enzymes at each other. We all kept containers of Pancrease near our beds because we needed to take the enzyme before we could eat anything. The little capsules made excellent missiles, but the waste always bothered me.

Halloween approached during our time in the hospital, and Tex and Mark remained secretive about their plans for costumes. So did Suzy and I, but only because we had no plans.

"You'll see," she kept saying, when pressed to reveal what our disguises would be.

A few days before the thirty-first, Suzy and I had an urgent conference in her room. She chose to appear as Cleopatra, but I still had no ideas.

"She looks like a Raggedy Ann," Suzy's mother finally said, after concentrating on my face. I decided not to think about whether or not I should consider that a compliment. Suzy and her mother spent the next several minutes persuading me to dress as the beloved rag doll.

Suzy would make her toga out of a hospital sheet, but we both puzzled over what I could wear that would resemble a jumper.

"We'll steal you a scrub from the bin downstairs," Suzy decided, referring to one of the blue scrub dresses worn by women doctors and nurses in certain parts of the hospital. The scrubs always remained in short supply on the floor because many doctors and nurses and even some patients wanted to wear them whenever they became available.

During the next few days, I assembled my outfit: red yarn wig made by a hospital volunteer, blue hospital slippers, red tights and blue and gray striped socks on loan from a nurse. I would cut an apron out of a sheet and wear it over the scrub dress.

October 30 came so quickly it caught us unprepared for one of the biggest events of the hospital social calendar. That night Suzy and I spread out our sheets on the floor of the Division 37 activity center to design one standard toga and a rag doll apron. Suzy kept taking breaks to work on the wig she made out of darkly colored yarn. So many nurses came in offering to help with the apron that Suzy and I concluded that someone at the front desk was spreading ill-founded rumors about my incompetence as a seamstress. Later that night we decided to fetch the scrub and gathered a group to escort us through the uncharted territory of the hospital basement. Suzy, Mark, Tex, and a younger patient named Craig came with me. First we checked at a second-floor bin to make sure we could not find the scrubs there and avoid the basement entirely. As expected, we found that the scrubs had all disappeared from the bin. We got back into the elevator and descended to a floor some of us had never seen, and which we knew to be off limits to us.

Halloween 1984

Suzy, Mark, and Tex had deemed Craig an overall handicap to the expedition. They warned that his loud and silly ways might attract unwanted attention in the basement. I jumped to Craig's defense, however, because I could see he wanted to come with us. I remembered the days at St. Chris's when I had been traumatized by the all-important teenagers and would not be guilty of a similar affront.

When we started prowling around the deserted basement, having first ascertained that no guards could see us, my IV pole made me nervous. I had been the only one of us unable to be disconnected from the IV tubing before we left the seventh floor, and now my pole made me the most detectable one of the group. I also held up progress because one of the wheels at the base of the pole did not move very well and we had to creep along because of it.

For several minutes we searched for the correct bin among a warehouse of medical supplies. Our quest took us farther and farther away from the elevator, and we lost our planned excuse that we had stepped off on the wrong floor by accident. We passed carts and crates loaded with hospital trappings and emerged from the main room to a place where small rooms broke off of it. The longer we spent there the more I dreaded the almost inevitable confrontation with the guards. We made a conspicuous bunch— there could be no doubt.

After we wandered for what seemed an intolerably long period of time, Suzy quietly indicated that she had found the right bin. She began running through the grocery list the nurses had given us.

"OK, Diane wanted a small, right?"

"Here, Mark, see if I have enough mediums."

None of us noticed that Craig did not follow us into the dimly lit room.

We heard a stifled scream that made us all lose our cool. Four of us stood close and looked frantically about for Craig.

Then he called out to us, apparently forgetting the need for caution.

"Bodies! Hey, you guys," he shouted as he ran up to us. "There's bodies in there. Gross!"

We all turned with disgust to our young accomplice.

"Wrong, Craig," Tex sighed impatiently. "Pathology is on the second floor."

"Well, there's still bodies in there."

Someone needed to prove him wrong, so Suzy entered the room into which Craig pointed. She began laughing so hard she could not speak for a moment. When she did, her words came as a reprimand.

"It's linen, Craig."

"But why's it covered up?"

"Because it's sterile."

Craig needed to open a bag to see.

We fell silent as we realized Craig's outburst summoned one of the guards we had managed to avoid for so long. A young but grim-faced man strode toward us.

"What are we gonna tell him?" someone whispered. I had no idea and braced for a confrontation.

Still tense, four of us watched in surprise as Mark grinned and walked right up to the guard.

"What's he pulling?" Craig wanted to know.

We saw the guard smile, and we all relaxed. Mark knew the guard, who worked part-time as a hospital messenger. The guard had met Mark on his travels through the hospital. The guard herded us up and took us back to the floor, generously neglecting to confiscate our scrubs. To be discreet, we waited until after our escort left before we began distributing our booty to the nurses.

Tex, who spent more time at Children's than any other CF patient, survived for about two years after that Halloween. He knew much more about the hospital and its employees than the rest of us, and this background earned him a spot on the planning board for a new hospital building at Children's. Most CF patients at Children's knew of him or could call him their friend. Although we all knew that during the few months of the year he spent outside the hospital, he liked to drive around town and "cruise for chicks," we also knew that he began to feel more comfortable and more wanted inside the hospital than out. During his last years, he found little motivation for his own schoolwork, and yet he always lauded my success. He bragged about me as the brain of the floor and told everyone I had skipped a year. He seemed such a fixture at Children's, such a content and functioning individual, that I never expected him to die. At the cemetery his mother hugged me and said, "He always admired your smarts." For him, and for so many others, I wish there could have been another way.

Mark lived for about another five years. News of his death truly stunned me because more than any of the rest of us, Mark acted as though he never once belonged in a hospital. He seemed destined to be one of the "survivors" who lived far beyond the given life expectancy. For many years I saw the two of us as alike in that way—for all the horrors we watched at Children's, we managed to keep ourselves from becoming participants in the drama. Like Tex, Mark noted my academic dedication and took to calling me "Brain," as in "Hey, Brain, did they get that IV in?" I never got to know him well, partly because we both kept so busy and partly because I thought there would be time later for that.

Suzy survived for the next five and a half years. Every time I met her after that, I found her plans in disarray. She did not finish high school and spoke to me of plans for a high school equivalency test. She wanted to be a beautician, like her mother, but dropped out of beauty school after a while. A regrettable distance grew between us. Suzy's quick wit made her an entertaining companion, and we had great fun together. Yet I learned with her, as with a few others, that my college career loomed large as a parter of ways. I had something she never would, and I could do nothing to fix the imbalance. I could not give her an experience similar to my own, so I took my only option as friend and gave her the space she required. I wanted to see her find happiness. Suzy, one of the most beautiful patients among us, left behind a fiance I never met.

The day after our basement conquest, Mark turned up as a ninja and Tex a pirate, while most hospital workers wore costumes. Craig went home that day. Suzy made a wonderfully flirtatious Cleopatra. And, of course, I made an excellent Raggedy Ann, dressed in the last vestiges of my girlish innocence.

CHAPTER
❧ TWENTY

Since my first days at Exeter, faculty members had urged me to tell my classmates about cystic fibrosis during one of our mandatory school gatherings. I finally agreed to speak to the assembly, mainly because I still maintained the same naive faith that had made me a poster child. I believed that the more people knew about CF the better and that perhaps I would reach a future scientist or philanthropist who would someday change our lot. It did not occur to me that I would be permanently segregating myself from the healthy students with whom I attended school.

I spent much of upper fall considering how I might best address my classmates during the speech scheduled for December. During chest percussion, I brainstormed with Roxane, who agreed with me that I needed to be as nonchalant about my own health as possible. I combed through all the literature about CF I could find, hoping to locate a source to quote in my speech. Roxane and I marveled, however, at the morbidity pervading everything printed about the disorder.

In Frank Deford's 1983 book, *Alex: The Life of a Child*, the sportswriter focused on the helplessness and fragility of his daughter who died from CF at age eight. Although my family and I have great respect for Deford and the work he has done to teach the public about cystic fibrosis, I felt alienated by a book that focused more on Alex's death than her life. Instead of celebrating the short life of a fighter and calling for stepped-up medical progress, Deford cloaked Alex's story with a father's grief. I wanted to learn from Alex, not pity her, but when I read the book aloud to Roxane during percussion, I could not last more than a page with dry eyes. None of my hospital friends felt comfortable with the book, either; many at Children's asked their families not to read it.

I realized observers had spoken for the chronically ill for far too long; we needed to find our own voice. I decided that eventually I would tell my own part of the story as best I could. In the meantime, however, I struggled to write the perfect speech.

When the day finally arrived, my adviser introduced me to the assembly by saying I had dreamed of standing at the podium since arriving at Exeter. He managed, in a few short seconds, to make me feel cast as the fortunate beneficiary of the community's charity. My adviser patronized me in front of everyone, but I could not have said then why I suddenly felt humiliated.

Quickly I pushed his words away and launched into the best speech I had ever given. The poster child years left me with a poise and a discipline that controlled my every syllable. I looked directly into peoples' eyes and with the aid of a tight outline told them about cystic fibrosis and research trends and about my own experience and that of my friends from the hospital. I used eighteen minutes of one of the three weekly twenty-five-minute periods usually reserved for leaders of student organizations, junior government officials, or presidents of small colleges.

Unfortunately, although I delivered the speech well, my remarks did not extend beyond the uncritical scope I retained as a poster child. I provided facts without analysis and implied that research would soon provide medical answers for cystic fibrosis patients. I told anecdotes about life in the infirmary but did not tell my peers I wanted so much to get out of there. I never considered using the forum to force the administration to give me lodging in a dorm. I made light of as much as I could and joked about such things as my massive cough drop consumption. I did not say I used so many cough drops because other students would not tolerate my cough.

Mom and Susan drove to town for the assembly. At the end of the speech, Susan surprised me with a bouquet of roses while the students and a few attending faculty members stood clapping for almost a minute. Friends from Lamont hugged me, and I felt simple triumph.

Ralph Waldo Emerson said, "The years teach much which the days never know." Although I supposed initially that my speech would rid me of the questions and awkward interactions that had continually confronted me at Exeter, I realize now I expected too much from a group of teenagers. At first the barrier I had raised made itself known in the dining halls, where other students labeled me amongst themselves "that girl who lives in the infirmary."

Later I could sense the distance between me and others in intangible ways, such as the way certain cliques kept their distance from me. By senior year I had become outgoing enough to make friends easily; yet I still faced a different reception than most students. My difficulty at Exeter taught me that, at college, I should tell only friends about CF.

Teresa at Lamont after her Exeter speech

The assembly did not generate exclusively damaging results. I received about a dozen notes from faculty members who offered me their respect and support. These endorsements seemed to validate my presence at Exeter; they lessened my fears that the head infirmary nurse or my adviser could singlehandedly make me leave. Unfortunately, most notes came from faculty members who acted as advisers in boys' dorms or who lived off campus, so I could not ask any of them to help spearhead my move to a dorm.

Undeniably, I created for myself the same notoriety that I had been so pleased to escape when I attended Raub. Others pressed me to the task, and I had not yet learned to resist. A yearbook story about our graduating class noted me not for my work on the *Exonian* or the Committee for Nuclear Awareness or my dancing or anything else, but for my life in the infirmary.

CHAPTER ❧ TWENTY-ONE

Through the fall I coped as best I could with daily life in the infirmary. Each morning I rushed past the waiting area filled with familiar faces and tried to avoid being noticed by the students who flocked there for excuses to sleep. When I had more time, I took the elevator downstairs, slipped out the back door, and walked around the building so no one would see me. If anyone spotted me, the detour made it look as though I had come from Lamont.

The daily indignities began to grate on my nerves.

Once before I dressed for class, a nurse rushed into my room with unpleasant news: "There's a gas leak in the kitchen and we're evacuating the building."

In full view of everyone on their way to eight o'clock classes, I walked over to Lamont in my bathrobe.

"Why aren't you dressed, Terri?" Girls rushed down the walk but turned to squint at me in my robe.

"Gas leak in the infirmary," I said helplessly to all who asked.

When I continued to plead for permission to have a lock, the head nurse advanced an interesting logic in response.

"You're not a resident of the infirmary. You're our guest."

"So, where do I reside?"

"Well, officially, you're a part of the dorm."

"But I don't have a room there anymore."

"Well, that's not our fault."

Roxane and I often joked about my lack of a place of residence.

"Instead of the man without a country, you're the girl without a bedroom," Rox said.

Roxane and I found all our conversations with the infirmary staff to contain increasing amounts of absurdity. If Sunny could get away with it, she poked her head in during evening treatments, and the three of us laughed quietly about new rules or practices, such as the dictum allowing all nurses to enter my room at will. Among us we understood that I had no choice but to cling to my sense of humor, and we did fancy ourselves amused by the situation.

Meanwhile, my living arrangement startled or confused students who did not live in Lamont.

"What's wrong with you?" an acquaintance once asked as he saw me heading to the infirmary. I said as nonchalantly as possible that I lived in the building.

Another time I heard two girls whispering in the waiting area: "That girl's here all the time. I swear, it's like she lives here or something."

After my first month in the infirmary, I had told Roxane and my family I would find a way to move into a dormitory when the second semester began in January. I knew it might take time to argue my case with deans and faculty; they had arranged my room in the infirmary with my "welfare" and that of my dormmates in mind. The strategy sessions began in earnest when I returned from Children's. Rox helped me plan how I would systematically break out of the infirmary once and for all: I would begin by gradually winning over my adviser. She had great optimism.

For the next few months, I spent more and more time at the student center and visiting other dormitories. At nine each night, I cheerfully checked into a quiet, usually empty medical building and talked with the nurse on duty for a few minutes. I smiled when friends told about late-night conferences, crowding around television sets after hours to watch David Letterman, and study sessions over coffee and popcorn (both made with ever-illicit hot plates). I did not doubt that I would be part of it all again soon.

In the week before Christmas break, Lamont included me in their "Angel" lottery, which assigned each girl to secretly give gifts and perform good deeds for a dormmate. My "mortal" knew my identity immediately; the candy and decorations she received only appeared in the afternoon. Any angel living in the dorm, she said later, would likely have left surprises at other times as well.

At ten o'clock, the night before break began, I walked over to the Lamont Christmas party. Before I left, a nurse told me I would not be able to stay very long.

"But it's Christmas! And I'm only going next door."

While a departing Roxane looked on, unsure whether to intervene or not, the nurse insisted I return by a certain time. She said something about the infirmary protocol, prompting Roxane and I to exchange aggravated glances; there could be no protocol in a situation with no remote precedent. After the party, I would simply return to my room and read or go to sleep. What did it matter to this nurse whether I stayed at the party past the change in her shift?

I left for the party, still hoping I could negotiate my curfew over the phone.

I enjoyed the party until the nurse called after my allotted time had passed. I took the call in my adviser's study. The call drew me away from a room full of girls opening Angel presents. I pleaded on the phone, to no avail. The nurse said that if I refused to come back right then that future outings would be in jeopardy. We had made a deal, she said. I knew discipline awaited the rebel. I asked my adviser to intervene, but he refused.

"Well, I've got to get back. I'll see you guys. Have a great break, everyone."

A photo of the family at Christmas

I went back to the self-righteous lieutenant nurse, back to the institutional room in which I did not officially reside. I sat on the bed in which I did not officially sleep night after night and fought to keep calm. I cried until I no longer felt the pain of being left out of the dorm life. Then I made myself concentrate on the problem, its causes, and the potential solutions. I stayed up half the night considering my status from every angle. I wondered how much I could contest the infirmary arrangement before the Academy would ask me to leave. I wondered at what point I should refuse to be manipulated and leave the Academy on my own. I thought long and hard about the reasons I had decided to attend Exeter; I could still see them through this haze of discontent, but they were fading.

I decided that night that my entire dilemma hinged on issues of respect, my own for myself and the regard others had for me. I realized I should think enough of myself to stand up to discrimination and I should believe in the act of protest even if it landed me far away from Exeter. I should care only for the opinions of those who did not judge my health to be the characteristic that defined my identity.

That Christmas with my family, I could talk of little else but my plans to move to a dorm. I practiced the speeches that would win over first my adviser, then the infirmary staff, then the deans, and possibly the adviser of a new dorm. After I returned to school, I would have three weeks before the new semester began. I felt almost sure I could find a room vacated by one of the many seniors who planned to graduate early.

The day after Christmas, I entered Children's to fit in ten days of antibiotics before the break ended. Halfway through the admission, my father joined me in Boston. We spent a bleak New Year's Eve by Division 37's front desk with one other patient and a nurse. My roommate, and most other patients, dejectedly went to sleep early. At midnight the other patient banged his noisemaker on a table in sarcastic celebration as the crowd on the radio edged into hysteria. My father put a party hat on my head, but I removed it and threw it at him.

The banging noisemaker would be my most vivid memory of the other patient. He was a quiet young man, a friend of Anne Marie's, and I had tried unsuccessfully to get to know him. More than CF weighted his shoulders down, but I would never hear him talk about his troubles.

I heard the news at home sometime later. He had leaped out of a Division 37 window.

A shadowy vision returned to me when I learned of the tragedy. I remembered rooming with Anne Marie on Division 39 years earlier. The sad young man and one of his friends came to see her. The two visitors stood up on her window sill, raised the blinds, and looked out the window. Screaming nurses rushed into the room. The two of them laughed and held out for a while before they stepped down. I was about twelve and thought it all must be a joke. I thought they had been looking at the view.

None of us ever talked about the suicide. We had all been stunned enough initially to ask for an explanation, for details. None of us would stay in that room again. The division staff saw to it that one-timers, those with a virus or healing limb, stayed there instead.

Children's has since moved its patients to a new hospital building. In the new building the windows are thick, and you can't open them.

At the end of winter break, my father and I returned to campus a day or two before the masses. Dad would help me move my bulky load, which included the oxygen concentrator and most of my school books, back into my room.

We saw that my adviser was home, and before we began unpacking, we took the opportunity to visit him in his house, which adjoined Lamont. While Dad stayed with me at Children's, I had briefed him well: my happiness depended on getting out of the infirmary. I knew I could find the space on campus to house me, so if my adviser continued to feel uncomfortable, I would take the step and go elsewhere. I certainly considered my position a reasonable one; after all I would not be asking for special treatment but rather to be treated fairly.

I read my adviser well enough to know that anything I could say to him would gain more credence if it came from my father. He never seemed to take the convictions and decisions of his young female charges very seriously. Fortunately, I had a father on hand to help my case. I spent much of my time at Children's telling Dad what I wanted him to say to my adviser.

When the big meeting commenced, Dad and I sat in my adviser's living room adhering as best we could to the informal script I had composed for us.

I said that I could endure the rest of the semester in the infirmary but that, come February, I would need to live in a dorm again. I could no longer bear the isolation the infirmary imposed. I apologized for not giving my adviser more than a month's notice, but I noted for his benefit that I had been trying to "give the arrangement a chance."

"And it's just not working out," I said.

"Oh, I think it's working out very well," my adviser said.

I had expected him to resist the move but not to speak to me as though I did not own my thoughts. I tried again, hoping that perhaps he had misunderstood me.

"Well, actually, no, it's not working out. It's driving me crazy."

"Oh, no. It's been a very good fall for you."

I lapsed into defeated silence and looked to Dad for help.

"Well, Teresa has given this a lot of thought, and I think she's really unhappy living there," Dad said.

But we had both met an immovable opponent. My adviser gave no reasons for keeping me out of Lamont and continued to act as though he had not heard us describe my wishes. He acted as though he knew better than my father or me what would be in my best interest.

My father and I began taking turns trying to break through to him.

Dad recited all the reasons I had given him why my residence in a dorm would be completely safe and without risk. Because my adviser had always been wary of the concentrator, Dad explained once again that the machine was not a fire hazard. Dad also explained, as prompted, that my health had stabilized and that I would almost definitely not face any medical crises for the rest of the year.

My adviser did not even treat these points as though they had been raised. He persisted in the role of the quiet, all-knowing mentor who would only be thinking of me when he kept me out of a dorm.

I went to the reserve strategy: I said that I would understand if my adviser felt uneasy about my being in Lamont and would be entirely willing to move to another dorm. In fact, I said, I knew of several openings where graduating seniors would be leaving spaces behind. I said that my adviser could stay out of it if he wished, and I would approach the other advisers alone and ask if they would allow the move. Privately I supposed that if I rid my adviser of all responsibility, he would be pleased.

"Terri," he said slowly. "No one else is going to want you."

He described me as a burden and said I was lucky to have him as an adviser. He implied that he had explored the possibility of my moving elsewhere with some of his colleagues and that I had no avenue to pursue. I stared at him and tried to guess which faculty members had consented to my continued stay in the infirmary. He could not have spoken to all of them; there had to be others I could approach on my own.

Dad and I politely made clear that we disagreed with my adviser, and then we left. As we unloaded my things into the infirmary, I felt even more dejected than when I had first moved in with my mother's help. My adviser showed up to help us move things, but we thanked him and said we had almost finished. I suddenly saw his gesture as a symbolic one: he wanted me well settled in the medical building.

Though stranded for the moment, and in need of a new strategy, I felt more compelled than ever to find a route out of the infirmary.

CHAPTER
TWENTY-TWO

I filled upper year with activities that helped me replace the self-esteem the infirmary drained from me. In December, I auditioned to be a dancer in a large production of *Godspell.* I even forced myself to undergo a singing audition as well, although nerves threw my voice off-key when I had a large group of spectators.

The dancing audition brought me the first real satisfaction I had felt in months. I worked harder than most of the forty dancers there because I had more of a reason to care than they did. When we did our combination in groups of five, I kicked higher and vamped more than the others alongside me. I could tell I made an impression. Afterward I left the audition with two of the best dancers in the school, and as I stopped in front of the infirmary, they both complimented me.

"You looked really good back there, Terri."

"Yeah, you were one of the best."

I thanked them and returned the praise. I turned away quickly because I had begun to cry. I reached a personal milestone with that audition. I had received attention for something other than my health, something, in fact, that I had done despite the natural obstacle before me. I had spent months trying to distance myself from my well-known condition; I hoped I had found a beginning.

A New York choreographer brought to campus for the show picked half of the dancers who auditioned. After winter break we began six weeks of rehearsal for *Godspell*. We danced for thirteen hours each week, and I never stopped once. Our choreographer pushed us to the limits of our endurance, and many times I kept moving although I had not caught my breath. I vowed I would not let myself be sidelined during the production. The choreographer noticed my cough, but I usually tamed it with cough drops.

"Are you going to be all right there, sweetheart?" he asked.

"Yeah. I'm pretty sure I'll be able to stay quiet during the show." I answered quickly and with apprehension. I worried he might cut me from the troupe.

"Oh, I'm not worried about that. How are you feeling?"

I had been poised to say I would recover by show time and beg to stay. The choreographer's compassion caught me off guard, and at first I could not answer the simple question. Because of the constancy of my medical problems, I could never remember that the average person generated concern when he or she fell sick.

"Uh . . . fine. . . . I'm fine. It's just . . . a little lung problem. Nothing to worry about. Really." I tried to smile endearingly.

I waited anxiously for more questions, but none came. After that he ignored my cough except to occasionally insist on sending me to the water fountain.

Our rehearsals became a wonderful time for me. I knew some of the eighteen dancers from the campus dance program, and we all formed a camaraderie that helped us work well as a group. As we rehearsed, our crazy choreographer told us stories about his Broadway experiences and confessed candidly that he had grown quite sick of *Godspell*. He had apparently come to Exeter as a favor to the head of the drama department. Sometimes he filled rehearsal conversation with trade gossip, wasted on us but fascinating nonetheless.

Nothing helped my state of mind that year so much as the show. Although I eventually gave a stiff and preoccupied performance because I thought too much about my dancing, I had at least proven to myself that I could function as part of a troupe. The huge cast included eighty singers and actors in addition to us, and most saw the show as a chance to have fun with others in the theater community. I could not help but regard the experience differently both because I had fewer friends there than anyone else and because the show remained a serious testing ground for me.

My family came to town to watch the show and help me celebrate my sixteenth birthday. I had

Teresa in Godspell

made great strides from a year earlier when my birthday found me limited to a hospital bed.

Later when I wanted exercise during spring break at Children's, I took my visiting father out to the chilly garden and made him sit on a bench while I performed my entire repertoire of dances from the show. I made sure no one but Dad could see me. It took some planning to stage turns and high kicks without pulling over the IV pole. My shivering audience kept telling me to return indoors or at least put on a sweater. I refused his suggestions until I quit abruptly after stepping on an earthworm in the damp garden grass.

After *Godspell*, I stayed involved in the theater when my dance teacher made me assistant director of her annual Dance Concert. Through March and April, I spent several hours a week critiquing dances, counting costumes and props, taking roll at rehearsals, and compiling the program. I had found another way to belong and another way to avoid the infirmary. *Godspell* truly had been a beginning.

Through the fall I wrote weekly *Exonian* articles and joined the new editorial board in February. I almost received no title at all: the seniors appointing the board did not remember the work I had done as a prep and nearly left me off the new masthead. I had one ally within the board, however, who reminded them I had worked hard for the paper before and after my long absence. I joined the staff as an associate editor in charge of a page of campus news briefs. I kept long hours with the rest of the editors and helped proofread and paste up several pages of the paper.

My work at the *Exonian* office provided me with the closest thing I had to a group of friends. True, everyone else left the office at night to go back to dorms or family and kept their social lives far removed from our room in the student center. Yet our work made us all friends for the moment, passing time and handling stress as a unit. Our editorial staff spent Tuesday, Wednesday, and Thursday nights at the paper office, as well as hectic Friday mornings before our Friday noon deadline. We met to assign stories on Friday evenings (rendered regular nights of the week by Saturday morning classes), and we lunched with our faculty adviser on Saturdays.

Nights at the *Exonian* helped me bear the prospect of returning to the infirmary. Sunny and Roxane would ask about my time at the paper, and I always had stories for them. As I had with *Godspell*, I took the whole experience too seriously because I needed more from it than anyone else. I sought to have input in all major decisions, and I quietly took offense when staff jokesters said the same disparaging things to me that they did to everyone. Fortunately, the offbeat characters surrounding me often pulled me into their merriment. During pizza parties or popcorn fights, I could not help but be a part of things. Similarly, I grew accustomed, as did we all, to our paste-up expert skateboarding recklessly around the room and to our layout editor trying to drown out our radio with his guitar. Many staff members had strange ways of amusing themselves while we waited for runners to bring back copy from the *Exeter News-Letter,* which typeset our articles. Often someone would march down to the campus radio station in the basement and refuse to leave until the disc jockey played a bizarre request.

Our marathon sessions the night before press run brought the whole staff into the office, and in these gatherings I had my only source of campus gossip. We clustered around two light tables and guarded our X-Acto knives, which someone kept stealing for target practice at the ceiling. We fought over the blue editing pens and rulers. We had a reliable manual waxer except that our paste-up editor sometimes liked to remove the wax so he could chew it.

At first I made an uncomfortable and conservative profile among this group, but prolonged exposure to the others helped me relax. Rarely did anyone mention the infirmary to me, except once when an editor wanted me to snoop around for birth control statistics. I declined, explaining sheepishly that if we printed anything, I would be at the mercy of the tyrannical head nurse.

With a few staffers I reached the threshold of genuine friendship. Executive Editor Margaret Riley and I spent increasing amounts of time in friendly conversation. Meg instinctively found a way to make me feel comfortable, and I began to show my sarcastic sense of humor during paper nights. I remained inhibited throughout the spring, but her efforts to include me helped reduce my insecurities.

In Meg I had finally found someone whose friendship did not depend on my being healthy and cheerful all the time. She took her cues from me and ignored CF entirely unless I wanted to talk about something. But she did not shy away from my lifestyle. When I entered Children's a few weeks after school let out, she and her mother drove to Boston from their home in New Hampshire to see me. Meg bravely met me on Division 37 although hospitals made her ill and she had recently passed out in one. The three of us spent a fun day in Boston tempered by the unspoken hope that in a year Meg and I would be refining plans for a fall at Harvard.

Most important, Meg brought the laughter of childhood back into my life that spring. We did silly things and made silly faces, and I learned a new kind of laugh that had no sadness hidden in it. For me, our friendship developed none too soon.

In the Poetry Stage, a performing ensemble for which I auditioned and joined in the fall of upper year, I found the greatest learning experience of my time at Exeter. Under the direction of Exeter English teacher Dolores Kendrick, a published poet herself, our small cast of seven learned how to "perform" poems. For several years, Kendrick had made Poetry Stage an annual production. Once we understood Kendrick's instructions, we treated each poem as scripted dialogue and delivered each word with its own emphasis and expression. Her technique, which called for us to treat all poetry as though it had been written for the stage, gave me a new approach toward interpreting verse.

Through the second semester, our cast met weekly to prepare for our show in May. Apart from the method she directed us to employ, Kendrick educated us with the script she compiled for that season. Kendrick, then the only African American woman among Exeter's faculty, chose to focus on the poems of Gwendolyn Brooks, Lucille Clifton, and Ntozake Shange. In their writings, the three poets address disparate social issues pertaining to the African American community. Many of their poems, especially Brooks's, balance a tangible sense of hope on the edge of each stanza, a hope waiting either to be propped up or knocked down once and for all.

In a way very different from my other activities, Poetry Stage gave me the satisfaction of doing something I considered very important. The world will never hear enough of Brooks's message and the others', and at least I helped spotlight some of the works. Eventually Brooks came to visit campus, and we performed several of her poems for her. The whole cast panicked when we flubbed a few of the lines in a poem. We apologized immediately after the show, but Brooks laughed and said she had not noticed. She autographed our scripts for us, and I will always treasure mine.

As Ms. Kendrick compiled the program for our production that spring, she talked to us about dedicating our performance. We would dedicate it in part, she said, to a former castmate of ours who withdrew from Exeter. We missed our schoolmate and all agreed her name should appear on the program. What Kendrick said next, however, took me by surprise. She launched into a speech about how I had been a reliable hard worker and how she thought I deserved the rest of the dedication. Too startled to protest, I became misty-eyed and thanked Kendrick.

Roxane would later grill me when we discussed it: if I did not want to be set apart under such circumstances, why had I not protested? I told Roxane I had been awed by the good intentions before me; Kendrick had been so kind to me. Nonetheless, in her dedication and my acceptance, we had fallen into roles long cast for us. Thankfully, my health rarely set me apart from the rest of the performers at other times.

Of course, plenty else set me apart from the rest of the cast. As one of two Caucasians among a small cast of African Americans, I became hopelessly inept when we needed to interpret the works of the three poets. As we turned their poems into scenes, we needed to create atmospheres into which I did not easily fit. The cast eventually decided to give me a couple of what they called "jive lessons." They painstakingly taught me to walk with a rhythm that coincided with theirs, and then they taught me several expressions to use during our scenes. They made me yell "Yo!" and "Word!" until I no longer wondered what the syllables meant but rather said them with authority. Although after some rehearsals we still shook our heads and laughed at my poor showing, I did not stand out as much as before.

That spring, after one of our final rehearsals, Kendrick spoke to me alone.

"Isn't there a way for you to control that cough of yours? I didn't hear you cough once during *Godspell*." I promised I would do my best to achieve silence.

During our May performance I kept a large bottle of cough syrup backstage. I still coughed during performances, but not as often as I would have. During one show I grew so frustrated that I took cough medicine between every scene. A castmate remembered after a while that I had begun the show with a full bottle. Backstage he questioned me in a low voice.

"Haven't you been having an awful lot of that stuff, Terri?"

"Yeah, I guess so. Looks like about half the bottle, doesn't it?"

"How much are you supposed to have?"

I hunted for the dosage on the label and laughed when I found it. "Two teaspoons every six hours."

"Maybe you better not have any more."

"Maybe you're right."

The rest of the show went smoothly except for tell-tale coughing.

Afterward, as I walked the short path from the theater to the infirmary's back door, I began stumbling. Still alert, I puzzled over this sudden loss of control. I could not follow the path and found myself zig-zagging along. I glanced in all directions to make sure no one could see.

When I reached the infirmary, the head nurse marched up to me and started asking questions.

"Where have you been?"

"Onnnstage allll afffternooon."

She looked skeptical and gave me a stare. The administration regularly expelled students caught with alcohol.

I handed her my program.

"Loook, I'mmm fine. Jussst had a litttle tooo much cough syrrup, that'sss allll." She stared doubtfully until the infirmary elevator's door closed between us.

That afternoon Roxane found me lying flat on my bed, too dizzy to move. When I sat up for one of the treatment positions, I grabbed hold of the bed, afraid I would fall off it.

"I know you too well to think you're drunk," Roxane said. "But that's how you're acting."

"Allll we neeed is a deann," I giggled. "I could bee the firrst perrson bussted at the Acaademy for cough syrrup."

"That's right," Rox said. "You're too square to get yourself busted any other way."

We howled with laughter, attracting the head nurse. I let Roxane do the talking. I decided to use cough drops instead of syrup for the rest of the school year.

CHAPTER
❧ TWENTY-THREE

As the second semester progressed, I became increasingly preoccupied with my exile in the infirmary. For weeks Roxane, Sunny, and I tried to determine the channel through which I should seek help. We decided I would have the best chance of generating results if I presented my adviser and the deans with a concrete alternative to my living arrangement. The three of us formulated a plan: I would approach Andrew Hertig, head of the history department and one of my favorite teachers from my first fall at Exeter. I would ask him to help me move into the dormitory he supervised. Wheelwright Hall stood far enough away from the infirmary for me to be reasonably independent, yet close enough that I could assure faculty members I would be able to seek help if ever needed. I preferred Wheelwright because of its location and because I knew many of the girls who lived there. Nonetheless, my two cohorts and I listed the succession in which I would approach other dormitory heads until I received a positive response.

Roxane warned me to keep my hopes low. "He may be right," she said cautiously of my adviser. "Maybe none of these people will want to take you on."

Over and over, Rox and I practiced the conversations I would have with administrators; I defended my case while she raised all possible objections:

"Why can't you stay in the infirmary?"

"Because I'm isolated and unhappy and it's unhealthy for me to be there."

"What happens when you get sick?"

"You'll just have to trust me. I think I'm responsible enough to know when I need to seek medical help."

"What about Lamont? Isn't that where you lived before?"

Yes, it is, but the building is small enough that the noise of my cough will always be a problem there." I did not plan to tell of my adviser's opposition until I had found an ally.

When I felt confident with the rehearsed conversation, I walked over to Hertig's classroom one night early in spring. I had been told he would be working there, and I summoned the nerve to try my luck. When I reached his dark and empty classroom, I did not have the courage to try to find him elsewhere. I waited until several days later to return.

My anxiety stemmed from the important nature of my request and had nothing to do with Hertig. In fact, I considered him to be one of the kindliest and wisest teachers at Exeter and instinctively felt that if anyone at the school would help me, he would.

When finally I approached him in the classroom one night, I forgot all my drills with Roxane. I felt I had never asked about anything so critical. I would not spend another year in the infirmary, so my future at Exeter depended upon my gaining entry into a dorm. From all of our strategy meetings, I remembered only the need to convey a sense of urgency: the dean of students would be drawing up his housing plan for the next academic year and I needed to win my dorm slot in time. Also, I had to be sure my move did not amount to forgotten work on someone's desk; I would need time to find another school if necessary.

"Mr. Hertig? Hi. I was wondering if I could come in and talk to you."

Friendly, but unsmiling, perhaps because of my own solemn expression, he said, "Hello," and beckoned me to a chair at the end of the room's table.

I began, in a steady voice, to talk about the difficulties of life in the infirmary. I did not need to mention cystic fibrosis; Hertig had attended conferences during my first semester at Exeter during which Lamont advisers explained the illness to my teachers. He had been very understanding and even visited me at Children's on his way to Thanksgiving with relatives.

As I sat talking in his classroom, my frustration erupted. I cried and my voice soared a few octaves. I realized I had started rambling and repeating myself, but Hertig remained silent. I tried to force myself to think in concise unemotional terms and to make an effective argument, but with every word, I imagined myself losing ground. The tears stalled my thoughts.

A year and a half earlier, at the same table, Hertig and I had begun a tutoring session that ended as a conversation between friends. He had been told, as had all my teachers, the important details about my health. But he had never heard me talk about it until that long ago afternoon when I had explained the force that compelled me to attend Exeter. I had looked up to find tears in his eyes.

As I stated my case for housing, I calmly concluded my monologue. Had it been daylight, the infirmary would have loomed large out the window behind Hertig's chair. Hidden in the darkness, it stood as a monument only I could see to days and nights of quiet seclusion, to differences, to discrimination, and to a world I wanted to change.

When Hertig spoke, he raised the practical considerations that Roxane and I had anticipated. I relaxed slightly as we treaded familiar ground.

Would it be safe for me to leave the supervision of the infirmary behind?

What about the cough at night?

Had I tried to return to Lamont? Here I tried diplomatically to relate what my adviser told my father and me.

Did I have friends in Wheelwright? It seemed silly, but prepared for this, I mentioned about six names.

Did my adviser know? I told him I could not easily approach my adviser about the subject and begged Hertig to intervene. I avoided my adviser for the next few weeks.

The oxygen concentrator? Safe, safe, I promised.

He seemed tired at the end of the conversation. I knew our talk would be difficult for me but did not expect it to drain him as well. For this reason, Roxane and I speculated anxiously afterward: had he been unenthusiastic?

Hertig told me to pick up a dormitory change slip from the dean's office. I did so as soon as the forms became available and brought one to him to sign. Not until his pen hit the paper did I begin to feel hopeful. Then I looked at what he had written: "Andrew W. Hertig, if Terri can have room A."

Room A, tucked in a corner by itself on Wheelwright's first floor, would be perfect to contain the sound of my cough. Hertig had reservations about any room besides A, however.

Two problems existed with room A: first, it had been occupied for years by teaching fellows who, lacking their own apartments, had made do with the two-room suite and its kitchenette and bathroom; second, if the school turned the room over to students, they would want to make it a "double" because of its size.

When I went to see the dean of students about room A, I walked in as he ended a telephone conversation with our principal.

"That was Mr. Kurtz," he told me. "He says I need to find places for several more students."

I stood asking the dean to sacrifice a bedspace when somewhere between ten and twenty students had no quarters yet for fall.

The dean expressed a willingness to help but emphasized that he could make no promises. The school faced a routine space shortage due to higher matriculation than expected and the increasing size of the student body.

That same day at lunch, I found myself sitting across from Christopher Hertig, Mr. Hertig's son and a classmate with whom I had worked on the *Exonian*.

"Do you know that your dad gave me a conditional signature? I'm trying to move into Wheelwright, but unless the deans give up a bedspace and let me have room A, I may be out of luck."

"You're kidding. Well, you know, I'm going to be in France all next year. Heck you can have my bed!" It was not that simple, but we laughed.

I discussed my dilemma with a few other students and received a resounding measure of support. A lower I danced with said that if it came down to the bedspace, she would room with me in A. I considered my coughing and noisy oxygen concentrator reason enough to spare her if possible, but now I had an emergency plan. I reasoned that if we shared A, we could find a way to make the door and wall separating the two rooms of the suite into a sound barrier.

At last I had hope of a normal school year in the fall. Exeter began to hold out the same magic it had held for me when I arrived as a prep, except that this time I would find a social niche for myself. I began looking forward to the fall instead of dreading it.

At the paper, I gave Meg updates with each new development in my quest for housing. She, too, offered to room with me, but since she commuted already, the deans told her that she could not help the space shortage by sharing room A with me. As we waited for the dean's ruling on the situation, Meg and I began talking about the kind of tent we would buy to camp out in the quadrangle should we need to protest.

"A few nights with campfires and the deans would find a place for you," Meg promised. We even began recruiting other campers from the *Exonian* staff.

Eventually, the dean notified me that I had been placed, alone, in room A. The news spread that I would be moving to a dorm, and other students congratulated me for weeks after the decision. I spent more and more time with the girls I knew from Wheelwright. Sunny and Roxane expressed great relief that I would once again be with people my own age; both of them excitedly helped me make plans for fall.

"It's gonna be great," the two of them took turns saying. And I could not have agreed more.

CHAPTER
❖ TWENTY-FOUR

In the spring, when I first met my college placement adviser, he tried to sober me up about my options. The placement office had to work hard to discourage students from applying to Harvard, else the whole senior class may have applied each year. Since arriving as preps, we had been reminded over and over that small colleges offered more attention than large universities and that we should not limit our sights to the Ivy League. We came to regard seniors who avoided big name schools in their applications as strong in character and as champions of individuality.

Most students fell into three categories. First, each year found a large group of seniors intent on upholding family traditions to attend certain schools. These students had the confidence of knowing colleges would treat them as "legacies," but they also came under undue pressure. When rejected from such schools, they blamed only themselves for interrupting a family line. Second, most of us picked traditional competitive schools and applied to one or two Ivy League colleges. And third, many students each year would rebel against conservatism, and implicitly against Exeter, by rejecting the Ivy League and all its trappings. The year before I got to Exeter, a student council president chewed and apparently swallowed a Harvard application on the assembly stage to portray himself as a nonconformist. The incident lingered fresh in people's minds during my prep year; people still debated whether he had swallowed the application or spit it out after the assembly.

Exeter's college placement office had the difficult and unbecoming task of herding each senior class toward a formation that would provide the best statistics for the next year's catalogue. Many students believed decisions occurred in the placement office and had little to do with admissions offices, which would act on Exeter's recommendations. Some Exeter counselors, to be sure, advised students to pursue their own carefully researched goals. But because the Exeter student body competed with itself for admissions, and we knew many schools to have an "Exeter quota," other counselors could not help but be caught up in an odds game.

Into this fray I walked that spring, a very unusual Exeter student. I had not earned highest honors nor a varsity letter, and yet I wanted to apply early to the Harvard I had come to love during my many years at Children's. My counselor did not take this idea seriously and kept naming a school he said would be my perfect match. But I knew that school's main strengths to be drama and engineering, and I had just said I wanted to major in English and pursue writing. I could not get out of that first meeting without saying I would take his proposals very seriously. I did manage to make him explain why I should not apply early to Harvard, and I had to swallow his reply that I would not be a strong enough candidate for the early pool. He did not think I should apply to Harvard at all, but I knew the decision would be mine to make. Meg, meanwhile, got the clearance to apply early, and I told her to make a good showing for the rest of us regular decision folks.

In August my parents took me to visit six college campuses where I had scheduled interviews and tours. Harvard, however, had become my first choice soon after I began going to Children's.

Surrounded by medical students and interns in the hospital, I had found myself most impressed by the Harvard graduates I knew. Doctors-in-training would pull up chairs next to my bed and after our introductions, would rattle off their academic credentials at the first opportunity. Sometimes our talk turned to colleges, and I wondered then why anyone would ask an eleven-year-old about her long-term plans.

Eric Sorscher, a Harvard medical student I met during his year-long sabbatical to work on cystic fibrosis research, nurtured my interest in Harvard more than anyone else. After graduating from Yale, he came to Harvard for a medical degree, and two of his brothers attended Harvard as undergraduates. Eric, held in high regard by Shwachman, spoke openly with me about what he knew of the institution.

One brisk spring afternoon during my seventh-grade year, I had left the hospital for a few hours to let Eric guide Ted, Susan, my mother, and me around the Cambridge campus. I did not have to hide my wide-eyed awe from my friend because he knew how I felt. Onlookers smiled as our procession passed by: Eric led the way and carried a small Susan atop his shoulders, my mother and Ted walked in the middle, and I dragged behind looking every which way. Eric spent a long time pointing out landmarks to me and telling me stories he heard from his brothers. Eventually he would begin a career as a CF researcher at the University of Alabama. His encouragement and his confidence in me went a long way toward helping me find the courage to persist after my goals.

In stark contrast to the opposition I met when I looked at preparatory schools, a lack of protest characterized my discussions with friends and family as I began applying to colleges. Individuals who once insisted, "You'll never be able to manage so far from home," remained tactfully silent when I showed them college catalogues. Exeter worked well enough that I eliminated all objections to my attending a faraway college before they could be raised.

During my first college interview, at Swarthmore, I spoke about CF with none of the same apprehension I had felt at Hotchkiss. Even though upper year had been difficult, I ended it with more self-assurance than I had ever known. I no longer needed to hide my disorder or hide behind it. I would feel uncomfortable about CF and my cough often in the future, but I would never again be made to feel insecure. At Swarthmore, I mentioned my health at the beginning of our meeting instead of waiting until we both ran out of questions. I did not need to steady myself on the chair while I waited for the interviewer's response. If my directness received a negative reception, I would keep hunting for the college that would welcome me.

When Dad and I set out for the interviews, I knew none of the admissions officers could say anything to thwart my plans. To ensure that they all fully understood my problem, I presented them with the worst possible scenario: frequent leaves of absence for the hospital, my inability to take part in athletics or move easily around campus, and an awkward dormitory life because of the cough. It seemed unlikely any of the schools could claim to be unprepared for me because Exeter had already managed for two years, albeit awkwardly.

I left Swarthmore knowing that if I applied there, my health would not keep me out, something I never felt sure of during my prep school applications.

Although Harvard admissions officers routinely came to Exeter each winter to interview all applicants from the school in one round, I scheduled an interview at Harvard that summer. I needed to speak frankly with an admissions officer about my strengths and weaknesses, and determine whether Exeter's placement office had done well to discourage me. My father and I had reached Boston on our tour of colleges, and my mother drove to meet us before we visited Harvard. She left my grand-parents in charge of Ted, Susan, Elizabeth, and my new little brother, Timmy, who had been born in January. My family knew well the specters before me as we prepared to stop at Harvard: I had watched so many friends with CF lose all trace of their hopes and goals, and for them almost more than for me, I had to achieve a loosely defined measure of success. I had to get into Harvard not just because I wanted to be there but because my friends and I deserved better than the expectation—and all too often, the reality—that we would be full-time sick people by the time we left our teens.

I had no need to explain any of this to my parents, who quietly understood. They did their best to encourage me though they knew I would remain tense during this leg of our journey.

"You've come this far, and we're very proud of you," Mother said outside the admissions building. "Now go on in there and do your best and a little bit better."

When it came time to follow the director of admissions into her office, I found myself so nervous I could barely swallow. With her silence early in our interview, the director put me in the position of needing to ask more questions than she did in order to keep the conversation going. I asked her about the *Crimson*, the liberal-leaning daily paper published by Harvard undergraduates. She seemed not to like the paper much and said I should overlook it in favor of other campus publications if I came to Harvard. Ironically, I would later interview her regularly in my capacity as a *Crimson* reporter.

After circling the topics of campus life and medical services, we talked briefly about the school's approach to the chronically ill. The admissions director asked where else I planned to apply.

After I told her my list, which included Brown University, she startled me with her response.

"Oh, I think you would fit in much better at a place like Brown than at Harvard."

I did not mind her reference to Brown, which remained one of the schools I would have happily attended in place of Harvard; but I most definitely minded the implication that I would not fit in at Harvard. She specifically meant my health when she made this comment.

"Oh, really? How so?" I asked with the pleasant expression of a curious innocent and did not listen to her elaborate discussion of Brown's approach toward disabled students. To be sure I wanted to hear about this approach, but while on Brown's campus and not Harvard's. I tried to look fascinated while I struggled to understand the interviewer's mind-set. Although I reminded myself I might have been experiencing routine rejection, I got the distinct impression she did not want me to have anything to do with Harvard. I took as much comfort as I could in the fact that I still had test scores, recommendations, and the application ahead of me. I realized I would have to submit the best application possible to compensate for the negative tone of the interview.

Of the schools I applied to, Barnard and Brown each reported that they had one CF patient attending them. Later I would hear from the Children's grapevine that Harvard also had one CF patient among its undergraduate community, but my source swore me to secrecy. The young man with CF told no one about his health precisely because he wanted to do that thing the interviewer implied I could not do: he wanted to fit in.

CHAPTER ❦ TWENTY-FIVE

My senior year made amends for the two before it. I made
many friends in Wheelwright and finally had an adviser who
respected my judgment. I also found that students I knew from
classes or activities felt more comfortable stopping by my dorm
room than they had the infirmary; I had a steady flow of visitors.
The awkwardness created by my assembly address had begun to
dissipate, and although some students remembered my speech
all too well, I found others willing to let me make a fresh start.

Each time I returned to my new suite, I took comfort in the
freedom I had acquired. I would have been delighted with any
accommodation in a dorm but had been given a magnificent
suite to make my own. I covered the walls of the two rooms with
pictures of dancers and nature scenes; although many of the
prints had hung in the infirmary as well, they had seemed less
festive there. I had an armchair for studying, an extra bookshelf,
and expansive closet space to take the place of two tiny infirmary
lockers. I had an extra bed that I made into a couch. And as part
of what may have been the best student living arrangement on
campus, I had a kitchenette and bathroom to myself.

In addition to Meg, I found a close friend in Lane Wilder, the
daughter of one of Roxane's former schoolmates. I had been
hearing updates about Lane ever since she applied during my
first year; she came to Exeter as an upper. When we met, we

became fast friends, although we found it more convenient to spend time together as seniors. I grew to dearly love Lane, who completed a college application essay on historical turning points by writing about the breakup of the Beatles. We shared a similar sense of humor and spent long hours talking in the dining hall or in one of our rooms. Lane, a fledgling engineer, kept me sane through the required physics course we took together in the fall. In the spring I kept her from backing down when we both signed up for aerobics.

Despite my efforts, I made few friends of other seniors, perhaps because during our strained two years together, my classmates never had the chance to view me as one of them. Instead, I spent much of my time with lowers and uppers in Wheelwright, many of whom began the curious practice of coming to me for advice on academic and social matters. I told them my opinion when they sought it, but always laughingly reminded them my experience had not made me an authority on life at Exeter. I grew especially close to my nearest neighbor, Hertig's daughter Jenny. She and I often served as each other's sounding boards for her trials as a lower and mine as a senior.

I never again checked in early on a Saturday night but stayed out with Lane and others until the last possible minute. Our student center and our gym usually became social centers for the evening, and there we watched films or went to dances. Both Lane and Meg had more courage than I did when it came to pursuing recalcitrant members of the opposite sex; Meg had at least one short-term relationship during the year, and Lane had several. I felt pleased, however, that I had broken through my residual shyness at least enough to find dance partners or someone to talk to at parties.

When I rushed back to Wheelwright on Saturday nights, as Lane rushed to her own dorm, I found eleven o'clock check-in a comforting reminder that I lived among so many people who cared about each other. In Wheelwright, our three advisers made Saturday night check-in special. We lingered in one of the faculty apartments over ice cream or cookies and had the opportunity to visit with girls we had not seen in a while. Often I would continue a conversation with a dormmate well into Sunday morning. Then I would struggle to be ready for nine o'clock Mass and the Cotys, who continued to pick me up for church each Sunday.

Hertig made an excellent adviser and friend. During the week, he regularly held check-in in his study, and the room seemed always to be filled with girls seeking advice. Many times I went to him with imposing dilemmas, and he had only wise words to offer. Undoubtedly, I could not have passed physics or chemistry without his help. I gave my best to the year-long battle with the sciences but still needed a patient planner to help with course-passing strategy.

And when my college placement adviser sent me into a fit of depression in November, Hertig picked up the pieces. Based on a failing physics grade I would raise to C-range, the adviser said when I pressed him, "I'm not going to lie to you, Terri. I don't think you're going to get into college." To be told this at Exeter could make anyone miserable, although each year our competitive pool left several students with only rejections and in need of eleventh-hour help from the placement office. I cried for a few days, and although I continued with my applications, I began planning the year I would spend in Europe before reapplying to colleges. Hertig reminded me that the adviser had no crystal ball at his disposal and that I should focus almost exclusively on my physics grade.

My new adviser handled my health well from the start. At our first dormitory meeting of the year, I heard him say familiar-sounding words.

"For the benefit of new students, let me point out that Terri has an unusual living arrangement . . ."

A year earlier at a similar meeting my former adviser called me special. I had not spoken to Hertig about letting me keep a low profile in the dorm, so I forgave him for whatever he would say next and braced myself.

". . . she has a kitchen in her room and if you ever want to bake anything, she's the one to talk to." I waited, but he added nothing else. I felt an overwhelming relief and knew I had found a terrific ally.

Besides dorm life, I finally reached the point of being treated like anyone else in the classroom as well. My teachers made little mention of CF. Since I had no prolonged absences for hospitalization all year, I never had reason to discuss my health with them. I would only go to Children's during school breaks. I wanted nothing to set me apart from classmates.

I missed only four classes during the entire year, my best record since nursery school. This did not mean I always felt good enough to attend class; it meant that when I did not, I stayed away from the infirmary, where I could have gotten an excuse.

"Today's not looking too good," I would tell Roxane during chest percussion on particularly difficult mornings. "I think I'll head over to the infirmary." But we both knew I did not mean it and would not sacrifice any of my newly acquired independence. By the time my morning classes began, I would inevitably decide that sitting through a fifty-minute class would be preferable to making a trip to the medical building from which I had fought to be released. I made my one trip to the infirmary—the three other absences went unexcused—on a morning I knew I would not be able to control my cough.

"I can't stop coughing," I told a nurse. "Can you give me something to quiet me down?" She led me to the room by the second floor nurses' station with the blue walls and told me to sleep. I stayed there until the school doctor returned from a town pharmacy with some non-prescription cough drops. Roxane and I later decided the visit had been pointless.

Most days, however, I could control the cough with lozenges. Mr. Deardorff, my Russian teacher, and I often compared brands, and he frequently offered me some from the supply he kept for his ever-present respiratory ailments.

I returned to the infirmary two other times. The first time I had no choice but to respond to a summons from the head nurse: tucked into my post office box, the notice said I must go to the infirmary to schedule an appointment with the doctor there. And, of course, the notice said: "Failure to respond will result in an unexcused absence." We dreaded unexcused absences because accumulating more than three a semester incurred discipline.

The infirmary had a file on my case a few inches thick, and the staff knew that doctors at Children's followed my case. I could see no reason for my appointment with the infirmary's general practitioner except that the nurse had found one more means of control. I felt happier than ever that I had escaped to Wheelwright.

CHAPTER
❦ TWENTY-SIX

The night before winter break, Meg and I spent a remarkably incoherent but giddy night in my room. We stayed up all night tackling our respective problem sets, sorting out my college applications, and chattering away before we both left campus for the holidays.

Fittingly, we began the evening at the Wheelwright Christmas party, at which we remained until everyone else had left. My curfew of a year earlier lingered quite fresh in memory, and I felt pleased to stay as long as possible.

Hertig dressed as Santa for the party and gave out gag gifts selected by student proctors. When the distribution began and I saw the suitability of each gift—trashy novels for the girl seen hiding them under her pillow; a toy fire truck for the girl who set off the smoke alarm with her popcorn popper—I worried I might receive a bag of cough drops or some similar item. But Santa handed me a cake pan for my kitchen, and I relaxed.

After the party, Meg and I returned to my room to hit the books. I had physics homework to turn in the next morning, and Meg had chemistry. We had already loaded up on caffeine when Meg caught me dozing. She woke me up so we could go to the backup plan for when caffeine failed: we would exercise until we felt wide awake. We brought my tape deck into the Wheelwright common room, and from 1:15 until 2:30 A.M. we did aerobics to keep ourselves awake. A friend of ours from the *Exonian* joined us for a few minutes then gave in to fatigue.

Later while Meg struggled with her chemistry lab, concluding "hydrochloric acid is not good to drink," I sorted through dozens of college forms for the first time. I made multiple stacks of recommendation forms and envelopes and organized them to be delivered to teachers in a few hours. While I sorted, Meg generously offered to type the necessary envelopes.

Our conversation became less and less meaningful toward dawn. When I looked over the finished envelopes and found Meg's one mistake, the two of us laughed for several minutes with the low amusement threshold of the overtired. She had spelled the name of one of the schools incorrectly; when I discovered the error she ripped up the envelope and tossed it into the air like confetti, letting some of it land in my hair.

A few minutes before 5:30, we took part in a long-standing Exeter tradition: the early morning trip to Dunkin' Donuts after an all-nighter. Before we started the ten-minute walk, we stopped to see Dave Spraker, a friend of ours who lived in a dorm adjacent to Wheelwright. We entered Merrill Hall through a door that should have been locked and found a tired Dave awake and working in his first-floor room. From the doorway, although Meg defiantly crossed the threshold once to break the Exeter rule about visitations, we offered to bring Dave breakfast.

Meg and I trekked to the doughnut shop before the dawn's first light. Although we walked along a major road, we passed no more than two cars and had only the street lamps to help us negotiate our way through snow drifts. My boots kept my feet dry, while Meg's stylish suede shoes soon soaked through. The morning chill made both of us rush along.

Around a quarter to six, we found Dunkin' Donuts filled with our classmates. We did not stay long, however, and soon returned to campus with juice, muffins, and Dave's breakfast. This time we conceded to Meg's feet and painstakingly walked around all the snow instead of through it. To our great consternation, we found all the doors to Wheelwright locked and received no answer when we banged on the first-floor windows. Students did not have keys to the dorms, which remained locked between check-in and breakfast. We found the Merrill door strangely locked and thumped on the windows of the dorm's common room to no avail.

We found ourselves freezing, hungry, and stranded in the middle of the residential quadrangle. Roxane had a key to Wheelwright but would not arrive for forty-five minutes. The two of us spent an awfully long fifteen minutes keeping a close watch on the entries to five different dorms. We agreed to bolt for the first open door. To keep warm we did jumping jacks and marched around the quad.

When three of Dave's dormmates emerged into the dark morning, we ran to them screaming and waving our arms. If they had let the door shut behind them, we would still have been out of luck. They stared at us oddly as we darted past them into Merrill and started cheering.

Inside, we sat eating our cold muffins and talking to a sleeping Dave who had collapsed on a common room couch. He awoke mid-conversation and spent several seconds trying to become oriented.

"What are you two doing here?" he asked, not unreasonably.

"Eating breakfast. Have a doughnut."

Dave shook his head and wandered away to his room. Still munching, Meg and I greeted several residents of Merrill as they stepped periodically into their common room.

"Good morning!" we kept calling out cheerfully, smiling as their bleary eyes widened at the sight of us.

I did not see Roxane from the window until she had already turned the key and opened the door to Wheelwright. I entertained the silly fear that I would not be able to catch her before she received no answer at my door, left the building, and drove to work. I yelled to Meg that I had spotted her and sprinted out the door and across the quad in seconds. Rox did not believe at first that I managed to walk all the way to the doughnut shop so early in the morning, and Meg needed to verify my story.

Because of the all-night celebrating and packing across campus, few people stayed awake through our last Saturday morning classes before break. Meg and I counted ourselves among the many: she fell asleep in French and I fell asleep in physics. When my Russian class met to make Christmas cookies in Deardorff's kitchen, I ate Red Hots to keep myself awake.

When my parents arrived a few hours later to take me to Children's for a course of antibiotics, I had not even packed. I had little to say for myself, especially because in my state of exhaustion I could barely talk. Nonetheless, I felt happy. The sweetness of friendship made the morning a brilliant one. As we drove out of Exeter, the sun hit the snow, filling everywhere but the plowed roads with shiny white opals.

To Children's I brought a few wearable outfits, my typewriter, six college applications, and three weeks' worth of supplementary physics assignments, thoughtfully compiled by the teacher whose class left me baffled.

At the hospital I kept a radio and headsets tuned alternately to my favorite Boston stations and shut out the hospital environment as much as possible. As I tended to the applications, the deadlines loomed large because most items needed to be postmarked around the time I would be leaving Children's. I had never accomplished so much in a hospital before: I composed several essays and careful answers to all the questions and neatly typed each application.

For most of my stay, I had a two-bed room to myself. To get the work done, I limited my conversations with interns to ten words or less, asked no questions of anyone, and kept shutting my door every time someone opened it. I even made eating a secondary activity by keeping typewriter and notes atop my bedside table while I balanced food trays on my bed and ate quickly.

The crowded setting of a teaching hospital came in handy for the first time after I finished my essays: I found more proofreaders than I could have hoped to find elsewhere. I just handed the typewritten pages to anyone who walked into my room; since I had not communicated with anyone since my arrival, they all took an interest in this first insight into my personality.

My only harassment as I tried to work came from an unexpected source.

Each day, undaunted by closed door, clicking typewriter, my averted face, and the headphones I wore, two or three men in red suits would march into the room, wave and ho-ho-ho me to the point of exasperation, chat for a minute, and then leave—calling "Merrrrry Chrisssstmas!"—dragging out the words until they all sounded like sheep with colds. Under most other circumstances I would have been hospitable, but as I struggled to meet application deadlines, I felt I had more important things to think about than reindeer, toyshops, and sleighs. Still, I talked to them all and even managed a smile for the one who asked, "And what do you want for Christmas, sweetheart?"

"To get into college," I told him with the same wide-eyed expression he used when questioning me. "Got any connections, Santa?"

I told a nurse one day, "If I see one more Santa Claus this week, I'm going to belt him. Honest, I will." She laughed and excused herself to warn the elves.

Over the phone, Meg and I planned that she would visit and we would head downtown for a movie. Meg wondered if her mother should join us so we would have the adult presence required by the hospital for the outings of underage patients. Days before the outing, however, nurses told me I would be allowed to leave with Meg, even though neither of us had turned eighteen.

The morning of our trip, just minutes after Meg boarded her bus to Boston alone, a nurse entered my room wearing the determined expression of someone dedicated to enforcing hospital rules. "You won't be able to leave today with anyone under eighteen, okay Terri?" I managed half a nod in response before she left the room.

"I wish you'd called a little bit earlier," Mr. Riley said when I called their home. "Meg's mother could easily have taken the bus down."

My own nurse came in to offer an apologetic shrug. "There are only a few people on this floor who would stop you from leaving," she said. "We almost pulled it off, but one of them was standing at the nurses' station when someone asked when you were going." She leaned over my bedside table, frustrated. "There are so many more important things in this world to be worried about."

Scheming for a moment, she added, "Do you think she would notice if you just disappeared for a few hours? I could cover for you. If I were you, I'd just leave." She shrugged again, then hurried off to check on other patients.

I had to choose whether to break a hospital rule, spend the afternoon at Children's, or drag a hospital volunteer with us, if one could be found.

The doctor rotating on the pulmonary service stopped by my room during my deliberation. I told him my dilemma, not because I thought he could help but because I wanted to complain to someone.

"Is everything all right?" interns, and sometimes other doctors, will ask during rounds; "What can I do for you this morning?" Usually there is no appropriate answer; chances are you have not waited until rounds to sort out your problems. Often these questions would find me eating breakfast, brushing my teeth, or sorting out my wet hair after a shower. "I'm fine, thanks," I would mumble to the merry group that would expect an answer even if my mouth were full of toothpaste.

This time I had a problem to be solved, and the doctor reacted in an unexpectedly helpful way. He grabbed my bedside phone and called Dr. Richard Fox, who had been my doctor for a year and a half. As I listened with new hope, I heard him ask Fox to intervene for me. By the time Meg arrived, Fox had spoken to the nurses and taken full responsibility for my outing. Naturally, he would not be coming with us but signed the papers as though he were.

"Have a nice lunch with Uncle Rich," the rule-abiding nurse sulked as we left.

At a downtown movie theater near Boylston Street, we watched *Jewel of the Nile*, the sequel to *Romancing the Stone*, which had been a cult hit at Exeter. We became engrossed enough for me to forget about the hospital and for Meg to forget about the early decision letter from Harvard that she expected to receive that day.

After the film, Meg called her parents from a pay phone in the theater lobby to tell them she would be home later than expected.

The news came in a rush, and it was all I could do to interpret Meg's frantic hand signals and her end of the conversation: the letter had arrived, her parents had opened it, and Harvard had accepted her.

I had grown so close to Meg that I felt almost as though it had happened to me. It seemed so wonderful; one of us had our future, or the next four years of it, sorted out. We shared relief, expectation, and hopes that we would be there together. We began shrieking and jumping in a very unscholarly display. The clerk at the snack counter frowned at us as we skipped from the theater.

CHAPTER
❈ TWENTY-SEVEN

Back at Children's during spring break, I roomed with Antonella Leone, a pragmatic rebel of a CF patient and one of the strongest people I will ever know. She spoke several languages and acted as the only interpreter between her Italian-speaking family and her physicians. When diagnosed as a child, she wanted to protect her family from the truth: she told them she fought an asthma-like illness. An Italian-speaking doctor caused fireworks years later when he set the clan straight. Nellie had not been secretive out of deceit; she wanted to suffer alone. Although I do not approve of what she did, I know no one else who could have been strong enough to keep that secret.

For years Nellie and I had known of each other and shared mutual friends, but we first became acquainted when we roomed together that spring. The animated Antonella stood a little taller than my five feet three inches, with a stout but not heavy build, and left her wavy brown hair to fly about her brown eyes at will. She portrayed the perfect diplomat in most hospital matters but often exploded in private. Though we barely discussed it, she shared my discontent with a world in which her dishonesty about CF, with friends and with family, made things easier for her. There should have been no secrets to hide, no social expectations.

We clung with all our respective mights to the rituals of late adolescence; we embraced trends, laughed as often as possible. Much of the wardrobe I saw her wear for hospital leaves consisted of tight clothes with loud, stirring patterns. She had none of the same social inhibitions I continued to battle. She realized with detachment that boyfriends would take better to the concept of asthma than to CF. She had ground rules with her many suitors: none could visit her at Children's, but she would meet them elsewhere. They visited her often at her house and must have thought she had an uncommonly severe case of asthma.

Between us there instantly developed a foundation that made it as though we had known each other all our lives. We fought the same fight, had lived through the same battles, preserved the same cautious optimism. I could say anything to Nellie and know she would understand. And she felt the same. After so many years of shielding friends from my recurrent fears and sparing them complaints they would have found incomprehensible, candor came as a luxury for me.

Nellie and I first became friends when I transferred into her room from another floor during an episode of *Miami Vice*. We knew we would get along when both of us saved greetings and conversation for commercial breaks.

The next day we laid claim to the Division's portable tape deck. All too often in hospitals, people who share rooms can barely sustain a conversation, let alone agree on music. We would never have sought the tape deck if, for example, either of us had been rooming with a quiet patient in her thirties or a ten-year-old with vigilant parents. But we delightedly determined that we both wanted loud music to fill the room.

We rummaged through the tapes I brought for my cassette player and agreed on the Cars' *Greatest Hits*. In what must have been a sophisticated escapist exercise, we listened to that album for three days straight, from breakfast until we fell asleep. We managed to learn most of the words and kept shutting our door so we could sing with Ric Ocasek.

We started the volume at "two" for a few days and then worked up to four and five. Once, for half an hour, we let it stay at ten. Our door stayed shut, but through the windows we could see good-natured nurses and therapists dancing down the hall to our music. We planned the noise as a stunt that would last two or three minutes until someone important demanded silence, and we would comply. The lack of reaction startled us.

"This is a hospital, isn't it?"

"Yeah, I'm pretty sure it is."

"Okay. Just checking."

We settled on six as plenty daring, even with the door closed. Nellie took to dancing atop her bed and would attract a gallery of spectators.

"Please, get down," I would say slowly through a smile and clenched teeth when I became embarrassed by her antics. No doubt Nellie would have been even less restrained without my conservative influence.

The music kept us from thinking about other things.

As every new doctor affiliated with Harvard entered the room and shook my hand, I pictured an admissions officer in Cambridge frowning at my application.

Intravenous catheters, meanwhile, poked out of my veins almost daily, requiring that a new catheter be placed into another vein. My fragile veins made ever poorer targets. It became customary for me to spend several hours hunched over the table in the treatment room, begging the beginners not to touch me and the experts to keep trying.

"Please call someone from the [intensive care] unit," I would ask interns and senior residents who ventured to replace the catheter. The people who worked in the unit had much more experience in placing difficult IVs, and although I did not like to make myself into one more chore for those doing some of the hospital's most important work, I was always delighted when the catheter could be placed after only five or ten minutes in the treatment room.

Most interns and residents eagerly followed the chain of command, however, occasionally bringing military overtones to their refusal to call in an expert. They had a job to do, they would say. Often I grew tired of arguing and let a persistent resident dig two or three needles into my arms before he or she quit.

"I'm really sorry. I honestly thought I could get that one," he or she would inevitably say after an excruciating hour in the treatment room. I would pull my chair away from the examination table parked in the center of a room filled with medical supplies and leave in silence, too drained to speak. Sometimes I would be summoned to the treatment room three or four times in a day before someone successfully placed a new catheter.

Often during that admission, Nellie would be waiting near the treatment room when I emerged. She would quickly hustle me back to our room to play the Cars at top volume.

Needles and my college chances caused us none of the same anguish as did poor pulmonary tests. Nellie and I often found ourselves crying after we received lab results documenting the steady decline of our lung function. Nellie's numbers fell slightly lower than mine, which would not budge upward. The sickest patients learn not to ask for their numbers, but Nellie and I always looked for the recovery of lost ground or, at the very least, stability.

The numbers rarely pleased us, and we worked hard to keep ourselves in good cheer. A nurse entered our room one evening to find us both hurling boxes of hospital tissues at the closet door. We had found the most efficient way to throw a joint tantrum without breaking anything.

Yet our greatest pain that spring, the one loud music and tantrums could not remedy, came from another CF patient's conversations with Nellie. He told her that he thought he would die soon.

"What can I do?" she asked me, hoping I would somehow provide a practical approach to the situation.

I asked myself the same question until it echoed between us with never an answer; but rather than acknowledge helplessness, I made a suggestion.

"Talk him out of it."

"Yeah, I'm trying but he's pretty scared."

Each night Nellie cried herself to sleep as she despaired of helping her friend. I did not know him as well as she did and could think of no way to comfort her. But I felt her quiet sobs in the darkness as though they were mine. There seemed to be more pain on our tiny little ward than should have been able to fit there.

In one of the cruel ironies we all began to regard as typical, Nellie's friend belatedly decided he wanted a heart-lung transplant. The transplant, first performed in the mid-1980s, brings a new set of problems. Screening criteria, expenses, and the donor shortage remain prohibitive, and no one knows yet whether the heart-lung transplant will ever be a practical long-term solution to life-threatening respiratory problems. Nonetheless, the operation provides the only potential treatment we have for what doctors at meetings have chillingly labeled "end-stage" cystic fibrosis. We entered the 1990s with less than ten survivors of the operation in North America; at that time England had fared better, with about five times the number of survivors.

Every CF patient on Division 37 heard that one of the sickest among us wanted a transplant. We also heard that although surgeons deemed him too sick for the operation, hospital staff would do their best to make him believe otherwise through his last days.

We learned something else: Nellie's friend had a relative experienced in surgical matters. The relative instructed him to listen for the questions and phrases that would indicate how seriously he was being considered. Whatever Nellie's friend listened for in conversation with the surgeons, he did not hear it. The people acting as though he had been placed on a transplant waiting list failed in their ruse.

"He knows the truth and he's giving it up." We spoke of the matter in troubled whispers. Nellie's friend survived two more months.

Most nights Nellie and I walked downstairs to the snack bar in the hospital cafeteria. She would order french fries, and I would look for the most unusual flavor of yogurt. One evening she accompanied me grudgingly even though she did not want a snack. She did not prepare me for the way she would amuse herself.

We arrived about five minutes before the line opened and sat down with an off-duty cashier. The woman checked her watch and lit a cigarette.

"What about me?" Nellie asked. She laughed; the cashier laughed. "Aren't you going to offer me a smoke?"

"Nah. Are you kiddin'? I'm not supposed to be givin' out cigarettes to patients."

Nellie protested.

I laughed innocently at what I took to be Nellie's sarcasm. We all knew smoking to be the ultimate self-destructive act for a CF patient. We avoided secondary smoke as much as possible. Those who still chose to smoke did so with full knowledge that they contributed to their own worsening condition.

Nellie's performance stunned me.

She became a chatty diabetic in her twenties with a fictional name and fictional complaints. She said she liked to smoke every day but that the stupid hospital had taken away her cigarettes. She appealed to the cashier's sense of justice, saying: "I just don't think it's fair."

The cashier agreeably passed Nellie the lighter and a cigarette. After she heard me cough, the cashier turned to me.

"Now I know better than to give you a smoke. You're in for cystic fibrosis. I can tell." I nodded as the situation required but did not speak.

When I realized Nellie had every intention of smoking, I cleared my throat uneasily. I tried to catch her eye but failed. I did not want to interfere with her performance but definitely did not want her to light up.

Nellie handled the cigarette like a pack-a-day smoker. She did not cough once. She even kept some sort of conversation going, although I remained in shock and could not say much. When we left minutes later with my yogurt, the cashier remained fooled.

Outside the cafeteria, I whirled on her.

"Are you crazy? What was that all about back there?"

"I haven't had a smoke in years, not since my lungs started getting worse. I just wanted to see if I could still do it." I could not let her off so easily.

"I don't believe what I just saw. That's really going to push those pulmonary function tests right up there, you know? I mean, you're just going to have one happy group of doctors when they look at your lab results. Glad you guys all work as a team. . . ."

Nellie showed sound judgment at other times, however. When the pulmonary lab reported unusually high pulmonary function numbers for her, she remained skeptical while her doctors accepted the apparent improvement in her condition. Several figures in white came to stand at the foot of her bed and recommend that she be discharged.

"I want to go home. You know that." She repeated it often. "I just don't think I'm well enough yet." The chart holders would shrug and agree to let her make her own decision.

A week later the laboratory staff discovered their error and announced that Nellie's numbers had never improved. When the news came I went straight to the supply closet for tissue boxes. Between throws at our closet door, we listed all the doctors we knew, classifying them as bozos and non-bozos. Anyone who had been taken in by the faulty set of numbers fell into the former category, although we found it necessary to make a cool bozo category for those who seemed to mean well. We could name only one individual who had questioned the results. There were never enough non-bozos around when you needed them.

CHAPTER
❖ TWENTY-EIGHT

Winter at Exeter never seemed ready to end on March 21 but instead forced spring to wrestle with it. Each year as the seasons clashed, a new batch of seniors grew introspective and tense, awaiting word from colleges. Decision letters came at staggered intervals from the first early pools in December, but most of us waited for April.

After assemblies, when the student body made the great rush for the post office, it was understood throughout second semester that seniors should be allowed in first. Friends found each other with raised eyebrows, ready to offer congratulations or support. In one common scene, I saw a senior's dormmates gathered around him, chanting "Open it. Open it."

Early in winter, the dining hall filled with talk of colleges. Seniors asked each other about respectable safety schools or specifics about a particular place. Almost everyone had friends scattered throughout several colleges and had stories to tell about certain campuses. We knew how the two or three classes before us had fared with colleges and understood that we had subjected our fates to a quirky and unpredictable system.

By late winter many groups of seniors had put a moratorium on discussion of colleges. No longer did people want to consult each other or hear what others had to say. People stopped themselves as they began to relate a run-in with an admission office or a story about an interview. Seniors still thought very much about colleges, but only close friends continued to pursue the topic as the season approached.

In March and April few dared even mention college until the letters arrived. As seniors waited for news, the placement office began its meetings with the class of uppers.

During the long wait I prepared myself for the worst. After all, my placement adviser, an authority in his field, had told me he did not think I would get into college. I realized I made a strange profile among the Exeter pool and did not blame myself for the difficulty I expected to have. I had spent one semester as a prep, then, after my absence, had returned the next fall as an upper. Naturally I had received few of Exeter's hard-won As after joining a class with so much more experience than I had. Yet I maintained a respectable average and worked hard to contribute in the classroom and out of it. I knew colleges would have their own view of the situation. Although I felt frustrated by what looked to be impending rejection, I expected to reapply in a year if necessary.

Some of my anxiety lifted when two schools both let me know early that they had accepted me. Still, I nervously awaited decisions from the other four, especially Harvard. In my most optimistic moments, I imagined that in the fall I might be going to school with Meg, writing for the *Crimson*, and having Cambridge and my beloved Boston as backdrops to my education.

I rarely let myself hope, however. As the notification date for most schools neared, I forced myself to think of other things. For the week before the letters came, I spoke almost daily with my parents. Since I might have received four rejections, I prepared to fall back on my supportive family and my own self-esteem.

We expected the letters to be postmarked April 15 and take a few days to travel to Exeter. On Saturday, April 12, I woke up planning to spend a very relaxing weekend. After outings with friends and time away from campus, I would be better prepared to face the next week. As I left breakfast that morning, I caught up with a dormmate on her way to class. I convinced Tanya she had plenty of time to stop in with me at the post office. School notices, graded papers, and notes from other students all appeared in our mailboxes, and I expected to find one of these or a letter from home.

As Tanya and I walked the short way, our talk turned to the three staples of Exeter conversation: the weather, the workload, and our fatigue. I broke off in the middle of a sentence to fiddle with the combination lock to my mailbox and grope at a bulky white envelope.

When I had the envelope half out of my box, I saw the return address and froze. I stood still until Tanya approached. She and I had not spent much time discussing our hopes for college, but as she stood opposite me, taking an upside down look at the Harvard and Radcliffe shields in the envelope's corner, she knew how important the next few seconds would be.

"I can't open it, Tanya. I don't want to open it."

"Terri, you have to." She laughed but I could not.

She led me to the ledge table that lined one wall of the room, and I immediately ripped the envelope open with the savagery of an impatient toddler.

Rejection letters arrive in thin envelopes, as anyone can tell you after their first spring at Exeter. But I needed to see the decision in print. After hurriedly emptying the envelope onto the counter, I hunted for the official notice.

I read aloud the first words I saw and said them over and over in agony.

"We are very sorry . . ."

Tanya winced and I studied the black block letters typed onto the Harvard stationery, hoping they would reassemble themselves while I watched. I stared as hard as I could, but the message looked the same. When I gasped, I realized I had been holding my breath.

Another Wheelwright senior bounded up to us and picked up one of the pamphlets in the pile I had not touched since I let it fall from the envelope.

"Terri, look at this. It's for students," Jenny said. "You're not a student there unless you got in."

I stared at her until I comprehended, and then I made a high-pitched sound of glee. The two girls hugged me and about fifteen people passing through the room congratulated me.

When I summoned the courage, I looked again at the paragraph in front of me.

"WE ARE VERY SORRY THAT THE CERTIFICATE MENTIONED IN YOUR ADMISSIONS LETTER HAS BEEN DELAYED. IT WILL BE SENT TO YOU SHORTLY."

"They did that on purpose, scaring you like that," someone said.

I started back to Wheelwright but ran into another senior awaiting her Harvard letter. Lisa asked me to accompany her. She opened her similarly bulky envelope, and we made much more noise than I had the first time.

When I finally left the post office, I ran to the pay telephone in Wheelwright's basement. A busy signal kept me from talking to my mother, but I reached my dad in the emergency room. I screamed my news into the receiver.

"That's great. I'm glad to hear it," he said.

"That's it, Dad? You're not going to shriek or anything?"

"I'm standing in the middle of the emergency room right now," he said in his hospital voice, "so I can't start shrieking at the moment. I'll call Mom and tell her."

When Mother called she could not have been happier. She said she wanted to track down Eric Sorscher, whom we had not seen in years, to tell him.

Next I called Meg, who was spending the semester as a congressional intern. We would have so much to talk about when I saw her before our commencement and after, when we would spend a few weeks in Ireland with my parents. The two of us had both made it into Harvard and little else could have seemed so wonderful.

Teresa and Elizabeth

I had a busy day. With several other seniors I attended a rally against the Seabrook nuclear power plant, which had not provided a reasonable evacuation plan for the nearby Academy. Though we took the issue seriously, the day found most of us intoxicated with college news. Back on campus, I rushed to tend to my duties as assistant stage manager of the Dance Concert. After the show, the stage manager presented me with a congratulatory card signed by most of the company.

Then I went for ice cream with a dancer who had been accepted early to Harvard. We excitedly talked about what we wanted to do there and about what our first year might be like.

Hertig gave me a big hug at check-in that night. In my room I found a basket of goodies on my bed from the Rileys, Meg's family. In my absence, they had come by with champagne glasses and ginger ale.

I did not see Roxane until several days later when she returned from a trip to Las Vegas. When she entered the room, I smiled and nodded in response to the question that had been hovering before she left.

"Oh," she gasped, "this is wonderful!"

Overcast skies hung over commencement day at Exeter, so a crowd of five thousand converged in one of the school's gymnasiums. For the ceremony my class of 320 wore dress clothes sans gowns in keeping with tradition; we would earn our tassels in college. We carried balloons colored Exeter crimson, which out of deference to Harvard we always called maroon or dark red. A large delegation of my family and friends sat watching somewhere. Our student orchestra played loudly enough to jolt most of us into the reality of the moment.

For almost all of us, the ceremony brought relief. The great pressures placed upon us had subsided temporarily. Some might be unhappy with college decisions, but all of us could still revel in the day. A strange thing happened in the days leading to graduation: the cliques, the competition, the classism all seemed to vanish as seniors began realizing the bond created by attaining our common goal. I found myself talking to people I had never known well, and friends of mine reported the same. The new atmosphere of friendship went a long way toward helping me displace memories of infirmary exile. I hardly hold my classmates responsible for any of my isolation at Exeter; instead, I wish I had known them.

Ed, Teresa, and Pat at Exeter graduation

That day I carried with me my own vistas far from the pomp in the gym. I lingered at the river bank of my first fall at Exeter, where my hope nearly washed away with the rain. I feared then that my illness and trip to the hospital would convince everyone I could not endure an Exeter education. I knew I needed the Academy to prepare me for college and future independence. And I feared that by failing I would carve for myself a portrait of hopelessness. I could not imagine a future dictated by the limitations of chances lost.

In our principal's speech, he urged us to continue to be good people. I could not help but think of my hospital friends, most of whom would never finish high school, let alone contemplate college. Patients and staff from Division 37 had sent a huge box of long-stemmed flowers when news reached there that I had been accepted by Harvard.

A dean awarded a few dozen small scholarships, and despite my chemistry and physics grades, I won one whose criteria I never ascertained. We sang a song and hurried to the diplomas. Although awards identify the top five students in the graduating class, Exeter mercifully does not rank students.

When finally I clutched my envelope with the diploma and its dark red insignia, I felt an invigorating sense of accomplishment. Fleetingly, however, I felt something else that disturbed me. Later I would know the flickering cloud to be the dawning of a realization come too late.

For three years I had fought my battle and no one else's. I had made my way to graduation, but would others? I had been silent through my trials, seeking victory through diplomacy. As the first student with a serious chronic medical problem to attend the school, I had thought I would serve the cause just by being there. I had been content to be a token and gave no thought to institutional memory or long-term policy. The admissions office once told me they had never admitted anyone with a serious chronic illness before because no one had applied. I did not think to call on them to recruit qualified people who might otherwise believe such an education to be out of reach. As an upper I learned of a cystic fibrosis patient who wanted to attend Exeter after he heard about me. In his own deliberations, however, he decided no education could be worth entering what he regarded as such a hostile environment. I would have tried to change his mind if I could have tracked him down.

After graduation I felt most concerned that my year in the infirmary and my struggle to leave it behind might be forgotten. If ever another student with a chronic illness attended Exeter, and I hoped many would, he or she could easily be sent off to the infirmary as I had been. I wanted no one else to live that way.

Once during college I went to visit Roxane and stopped by the Academy to see Hertig. I wanted to walk through the infirmary to grasp at the harsh memory of a very important, if often forgettable, year of my life. A new infirmary staff filled the offices; the head nurse had left when a new doctor came to run the place. I went to climb the stairs, and the new doctor appeared.

"You can't go up there," she said. "You could catch something from one of our patients."

"Well, I lived up there for a year, and I just want to see it again really quickly."

"What are you talking about? No one ever lived up there."

She would not be convinced, so I shrugged and left. Then I remembered that according to the head nurse, I had not lived there or anywhere during upper year; I had been the infirmary's guest.

The next person who hopes to challenge the school's perception of the chronically ill will have to do it all alone. And with the same regret I felt when handed my diploma, I am sorry for it.

A few days after graduation, Meg, my parents, and I left for Ireland. We drove all over the small country—through Shannon and Cork and Dublin and Galway. We took time to talk to people and bag our lunches from country stores and walk until our feet were muddy. We visited Meg's relatives in Cork, and although we could not track down any of our own relatives, we knew that most of my family originally came from Ireland.

Something about our visit helped me to sort things out. Though an outsider, I felt more at peace in the country's rich green fields than I had in some time. I developed a fondness for the music of Christy Moore and Stockton's Wing, and I began reading more of the country's poets. In that my life is a search for answers, I found some there—one look at the seven-hundred-foot Cliffs of Moher, for example, leaves a person with the irrevocable sense that there is a beauty in the rugged and the barren and that there is a large scheme of nature into which we all somehow fall.

I spent the rest of my summer writing leisurely in my dad's office and then spending a month with Meg and her parents. Her father is such a gifted writer that every conversation with him was a learning experience; the several pots of coffee he prepared every day soon had me hooked on the stuff. Meg's mother helped me sort ideas; she had also been a writer and her suggestions were always insightful. We spent time sailing and sunning and lounging; we had our social escapades and our rides through the back roads of New Hampshire. Meg did her best to show me the basics of driving on the long driveway to her house, but I was too terrified then to do more than mechanically follow her directions. The month at Meg's house was a time during which I was overwhelmingly content.

So I was ready to smile my way through anything that would happen at Harvard. Good thing, too.

The first big scene came during an orientation week placement exam. A friend from Wheelwright lived near me in the Yard and introduced me to one of her roommates, Emily Mieras. Emily and I headed over to where all those in the first-year class would take the math placement test. I told Emily all about my cough, and she had been so understanding I felt braced for whatever dirty looks might come my way through tense test silence.

I sat in a nondescript auditorium, clutching my number two pencils, and the math problems made no sense to me. Emily sat nearby. I tried so hard not to cough that I was unable to concentrate. I coughed once, then again, again. The curiosity factor prevailed, and a few heads turned my way, but the noise did not stop; it was beyond my control. After a few minutes, it seemed as though everyone in the room had flashed a mean expression in my direction. The proctors huddled, and then one of them raced toward me.

We walked out of the room, through double doors, and stood talking in a stairwell. With as little ado as possible, we established that I would finish the test in an empty room.

Later in the test, the proctor brought me a note from the test's coordinator.

"Miss Mullen," incorrectly began the bureaucratic scrawl. Arrangements would be made, the note said, for me to take the remainder of my placement exams in private rooms. Good for Harvard. I sat hoping life would improve after the orientation business was over.

"You have as much of a right to be here as anyone else," my new friend Emily had said when I told her I worried what others might think of the cough. As I walked back to my room in Canaday Hall, I kept repeating her words to myself. It was an attitude I adopted right then and there, and it has since seen me through countless events that might otherwise have been traumatic.

CHAPTER
❧ TWENTY-NINE

The *Crimson*, Harvard's daily student newspaper, drew me into its environs within days of my arrival on campus. I dragged a newly made friend to the paper's headquarters at 14 Plympton Street in Cambridge. The building looked so large to me then with its many rooms: two business offices in its foyer; three editorial offices; the newsroom consisting of a few desks, a cluttered bulletin board, and a ledge table weighted down with books of all sorts; the glassed-in room filled with video display terminals; the photo lounge and two darkrooms; the enormous press; the basement rooms used for paste-up and production; and finally the "sanctum," a second-floor library with classic wooden floor, vinyl-covered armchairs and couches, overburdened book shelves, old-fashioned lamps, and the president's chair.

At first the juniors and seniors who barked at each other in their own strange language intimidated me, but I resolved to find a place for myself. The *Crimson* had one of its largest mastheads ever that year and a huge reportorial staff to match. The paper did a nearly thorough job of covering its many beats, which spanned Cambridge and Boston as well as our campus.

I joined the "comp," a two-month training program for new reporters. We wrote eight stories without bylines, then wrote ten more, including a longer feature, all while being carefully watched and tutored. Although the staff treated compers with

The Harvard Crimson

The Weather
Thanks for the All-night

XVI, No. 10   CAMBRIDGE, MASS., SATURDAY, FEBRUARY 13, 1987

some contempt—no one could remember our names, and everything we did carried the taint of having been done by a comper—I quickly became addicted to the place.

On my first assignment I wrote about how Robert Runcie, the Archbishop of Canterbury, visited campus while a small scandal about women in the church broiled at home. The conflict of interest that I had not fully understood at Exeter became quite clear to me then. I covered the event with someone who had met the archbishop, and because she liked him so much, she wanted to avoid any hint of controversy in the story. I learned my first lesson at Harvard when I recognized her bias as a hindrance to our work.

I worked hard on that story: when we needed to find articles in the *Times of London*, I chased around to a few different Harvard libraries, one of them quite far from the *Crimson*. Seeing that the issues we wanted had not yet reached the libraries, I hurried back to the paper. The editor authorized me to call the *Times* for help. Calling London made my first day at the paper a heady one.

I continued to work hard and did my best to fit in with everyone else in the newsroom. When asked about my cough, I attributed it to my allergies to Bogart, the beloved—if lazy—newsroom cat. Bogart, an overweight orange and white eavesdropper who slinked around the building seeking attention, did indeed make my eyes water. He created a handy excuse for my cough.

The *Crimson's* news day began at 2:00 P.M. We compers would arrive then, or a few minutes early to beat the rush, and check in

248

with the "day slotter," an editor who that day had charge of doling out stories to compers and keeping track of beat reporters. At 5:00 P.M. the day slotter ran a dummy meeting, at which the editors ordered the stories of the day, deciding where each article should appear in the paper.

The three-hour news day limited us but spawned ingenuity. Sometimes, we needed to reach people at other campuses for their reactions to the news we reported and for information about educational and institutional norms. As compers we soon learned which universities and institutions were located in earlier time zones, so that we could call after 5:00 P.M. if necessary. Often we called former Harvard faculty members who would be more candid with us than professors on our own campus.

Because of the time restraint, editors sometimes put together dummies that would be contingent on whether a reporter reached a crucial source at home that night. Harvard administrators and professors, if they had any desire to be cited regularly in the campus press, took calls from *Crimson* reporters at home. We rarely had enough time to reach all the necessary people before 5:00 P.M. We appreciated the faculty's cooperation and began all after-hours calls with the preface, "I'm very sorry to trouble you at home, but . . ."

After the dummy meeting, everyone wandered to dinner. Reporters faced a loose deadline that fell somewhere between 7:30 P.M. for compers and midnight for a star reporter compiling a big story. The stories went to our typesetter after being edited by a staff reporter and then an editor. Downstairs, Pat Sorrento, an outspoken *Crimson* employee who filled the building with his cigar smoke, pasted up the front page and arranged most inside copy. Pat occasionally showed his soft side to the many generations of *Crimson* editors who came to know him as they passed through the building, but everyone knew that a late paper guaranteed a grumpy Pat. To avoid his wrath and to get home before sunrise, editors rushed to assemble the feature, editorial, and sports pages.

When the editors finally "closed out" the paper, Pat and press operator Brian Byrne assisted the students who remained for press run. This group usually included an editor, an experienced staff writer, and a copy editor who was either a comper or someone newly elected to the ranks.

After all the preparations, Brian operated the press, usually sometime between 2:00 and 7:00 A.M. As the press filled the building with the sound of its churning, and as the freshly inked papers flicked out onto a conveyer belt to be grabbed by us and stacked, most of us felt awed by the process we had completed.

Legend held that there had once been regular "four-figure" close-outs, so called because they occurred before 1:00 A.M. The more time I spent at the paper, the more that seemed improbable. Putting the paper to bed early required the rare assembly of all the right conditions. When I became an executive editor my junior year, I struggled to urge writers to finish and editors to send copy to the typesetter. But we had no fixed deadline, and everyone knew it, so discipline never reigned. As long as we readied the bundles of papers by 6:00 or 7:00 A.M., the news stands and student deliverers picked up the papers without incident.

Junior year, I learned from a friend that our press operator's sister had died of cystic fibrosis at an early age. Brian did not mention his sister until I asked about her. She had been a patient of Shwachman's, and Brian and I shared a special bond after I knew. Everyone in the building had kept the well-known fact a secret from me because they did not want to upset me.

During that first fall, I kept my own secret. No one realized I had CF until I went to the hospital in December. Midway through my comp, I needed a course of IV antibiotics. I carefully kept this from everyone at the paper. I coordinated the IV antibiotics from my dorm room and arranged them so they would not interfere with the *Crimson's* news day. Even when my dorm supervisor insisted I stay briefly in the university infirmary with all my medicine, I went back and forth from the infirmary without telling anyone at the paper. I dressed in clothes that disguised the central venous line catheter taped in place where it entered my neck. Although I still had chest percussion each morning and evening, I asked the physical therapists who came to my room to come during dinner time. This way no one missed me at the paper.

When another comper caught a cold, the editors fussed over her and offered her extra time to complete her comp. I felt satisfied that I was not getting any special treatment. I had seen to it that my place there remained entirely independent of my health.

Teresa (left) with friends at Harvard

Even when I told some of the people there in December, the staff handled the news well and never made me feel self-conscious. Only once that year did anyone disappoint me. At a *Crimson* cookout in the spring, I stood talking to a group of seniors around the grill. A friend of mine became slightly distracted from his grill duty and suddenly had difficulty flipping the burgers in front of him.

"Tom's having trouble," a senior I did not know well said of my friend. He meant to make a joke of it. "He's got cystic fibrosis."

The group around the grill grew silent, and the senior did not seem to notice all the faces staring at him in shock.

"Uh, John?" someone said after a minute. "You know that Terri has cystic fibrosis, right?"

"Oh really?" said John. "What is cystic fibrosis?" He did not apologize.

"Well," I said with all the patience I could muster, "It's definitely not about coordination. When you think of cystic fibrosis, think of lungs. That's all that's wrong with us."

"But doesn't it impair your motor skills?" he asked. "You seem to be standing up okay."

"Yeah, I'm fine." I gave up and walked away.

The *Crimson* gave me an irreverent approach to academics at Harvard. For better or worse, student journalists who stayed writing and editing until 2:00 or 3:00 A.M. did not always wake up for morning classes. And although books pertaining to our coverage always lay strewn throughout the building, no one expected to accomplish any work for classes when we had a paper to publish.

Naturally everyone at the *Crimson* worked hard outside the building to maintain their academic obligations. Many left the paper and went home to study or read for several hours; most survived on little sleep. I balanced everything as best I could.

Spending time at the *Crimson* meant that I partially lost track of my classmates. Although I kept in close touch with Meg, I ate most meals with staff writers and other compers instead of joining the first-year class at the Harvard Union. I formed many lasting friendships with students in the classes ahead of me.

I rarely saw my roommate. Jeannette and I had our own bedrooms but shared a common room. She marveled at the hours I kept. I usually returned to our room around 1:00 A.M., exhausted but happy that one of my articles would be printed in the next day's paper. As soon as I awoke each morning, I grabbed the *Crimson* and read it from cover to cover. When I joined the staff, I began keeping even longer hours than during my comp, and as an editor my junior year, I spent an average of sixty hours a week in the building.

Steadfastly liberal in its editorial politics, the *Crimson* indelibly shaped my worldview. In its coverage the paper stayed ever mindful of the dearth of women and minority faculty throughout the university. For the first time I comprehended that I had a fight for equity on my hands, in much the same way that so many others did. I realized I could reject the passive role assigned to the chronically ill and had no need to submit to anyone as I had at Exeter. I had grown up feeling ashamed of my illness. At the *Crimson* I learned to trade shame for anger, and in anger I found strength.

One of my experiences as a comper gave me great occasion for introspection. Usually I got so caught up in a story that I did not think about much else. But one morning I attended a ten o'clock press conference for a staff writer who wanted to sleep late. Some professors at Harvard's Kennedy School of Government issued a report recommending a five-dollars-per-barrel tariff on

Teresa and friends enjoying a picnic in the dorm

oil imports into this country. I planned to listen to their remarks, read their report, then call experts who could critically evaluate their proposal.

I left my nine o'clock Russian class early and quickly made my way across campus. As I entered the main entrance of what undergraduates called the K-School, I fell in step with a friendly young reporter. As we ascended stairs, finding our way in spite of the building's complicated floor plan, we joked about how easy it would be to get lost there. We chatted about other things and finally stepped into the press-filled penthouse together, sharing an embarrassed smile over our lateness. One of the professors had already begun his remarks.

Concentrating, I fought to control my breathing. The brisk walk took my breath away, and I hoped anyone who noticed would simply think I rushed to the conference. My respirations would not slow down as quickly as someone with a healthy pair of lungs, and I did not want to call attention to myself.

While we had been stair-climbing, I briefly considered warning my new acquaintance about the cough. I thought the revelation might give me an ally in case I grew noisy in the conference. But I got much too caught up in the excitement of being a real reporter, talking to another real reporter, making my way to a real press conference.

Naturally, I brought a box of cough drops—one of twenty-seven boxes my uncle sent from England, where the lozenges seemed to be more powerful than those in the United States. It had not been easy to explain to Jeannette why the first care package either one of us received contained nothing but a few hundred cough drops. Now as I clutched one of those boxes in the conference room, I felt confident I could remain quiet.

No one would have paid much attention to me, the obvious amateur among the gathered journalists, if it had not been for the trouble I began having. I had no control over my cough and desperately tried to muffle the sound as it occurred with increasing frequency.

Then I began keeping track. The Associated Press reporter made the first eye contact, briefly staring me down with a "what-the-hell-are-you-doing-here?" look. That caused a chain reaction and within five minutes everyone in the room had glanced in my direction. I would have left, but I felt sure I could stop coughing and I had an assignment to cover. I grew increasingly self-conscious as more people took notice, and my face turned a dark scarlet. The channel 4 camera operator and his accompanying anchor looked prepared to interrupt the speakers to ask me to leave. I did not blame them for their hostility; I did not mean to interfere with their footage—although I could tell they already had enough sound bites to do without those drowned out by my cough. I kept mouthing the word "sorry" in response to the camera operator's nasty looks.

I could not go back to the paper without a story. At first my notes, taken in a personal shorthand I adopted at Exeter, stayed concise. But as the meeting progressed, I recorded everything in my notebook, even statistics I knew I would never use in my story, because I needed to think about something besides my cough and the angry looks. At the end of the presentation, I had gathered as much information as the *Crimson* would want from the speakers. I planned to drop off my Russian books in my room, then head to the paper to start calling economists who could assess the proposal.

Nonetheless, I lingered in the room for a moment. I felt as though I wanted to apologize to someone for coughing so much. There did not appear to be a single receptive face there, however, so I fled the room.

I tried to catch up to the reporter with whom I walked in, but his friendliness disappeared. He did not even look up as he passed me leaving the room, and although I was right behind him as we both left the building, he did not make the same attempts at conversation he had earlier. I wanted to speak to him, but like everyone else at the conference, he had assumed an unapproachable air as though I had wronged him.

When I reached the Square, I saw one of the women who had been in the room and I quickened pace, hoping to walk beside her and say a few words. I did not know what I would say, but I needed to hear a friendly voice. She did not see me, and I watched her rush down the steps to the subway (the "T").

On my way back to the dorm, I had to walk past Out-of-Town News, a well-stocked newsstand that usually boosted my spirits when I passed it. For the moment, however, it served mainly as a reminder that my bylines might always come harder to me than others. I had been traumatized in my attempt to fit in with my role models and then lost the chance to talk to someone about it. I might have gone straight to the *Crimson* or called there, but I had not yet told anyone I had CF.

Back in my room, I threw down my binder of Russian notes, watching loose papers fall in disarray, and sank to the floor without taking off my coat. Jeannette had gone to class. For a long time I cried and knew nothing but the wretched pain of exclusion.

Half an hour later, I took off my coat and called my mother. In a long-distance conversation that lasted more than an hour, I told her I thought it would be impossible for anyone with CF to be a reporter, or for that matter, a doctor, lawyer, or any professional whose job depended upon interacting with people.

"What am I doing here?" I posed the question to her after a long rambling speech about how I thought the quality of life for CF patients could never improve as long as those around us remained ignorant.

My mother did not interrupt but said all the right things to indicate she understood.

I went on to tell her it bothered me that the premedical students I met at Harvard had great ambitions as scientists but had no idea what kind of life I led. And I did not expect them to learn that in medical school.

Mother listened patiently as I screamed about the inefficient educational system, about how the priorities had shifted in medical training, and how the patient barely mattered anymore.

A few days before the press conference, a CF doctor, the same one who told Roxane I would not last long at Exeter, told me most of his patients who started at Harvard had dropped out of school. He told me it would be better for me to leave during my first year, to save my parents money and embarrassment. His attitude came as a stark change from the supportive one of Dr. Fox, who had left Children's for Minnesota. The new doctor asked how I could attend lectures if I coughed as much as I did during my appointment with him. I told him I just made noise and enemies, but he said that could not continue long.

In the same conversation, as he gave me a lift to campus, the doctor and I discussed the scheduled visit of journalist Nicholas Daniloff. Daniloff, who included Harvard on a speaking tour, had made headlines while held captive by the Soviet government in Moscow. The doctor told me I should not bother to study Russian; I would never be able to spend more than a month in the Soviet Union because of its sparse medical facilities. I had only been gushing about Daniloff, one of my heroes, and never said I wanted to live in the Soviet Union. The doctor made a brilliant clinician, but I will never understand why he discouraged me. I regarded his words as irresponsible. A patient with less experience might have been severely shaken.

When Jeannette finally made an entrance, I was crying into the phone and sounded hysterical. She looked frightened and shut the door to her room behind her.

In my agitated state I asked Mother if it would make any sense for me to leave Harvard and spend all my time educating people about CF. Who cared about a liberal arts degree when the world held us in such contempt?

Of course, I finally calmed down and found a better brand of cough drops. I had to learn and remember that I could never let myself be made to feel so insecure. After all, I had hardly disrupted the conference. Despite the other reporters and their varying expressions of resentment, I belonged finally, and I would not forget it.

CHAPTER ✸ THIRTY

The day should have been a milestone of my first year at Harvard. For weeks I looked forward to the gridiron confrontation between our football team and that of our New Haven neighbor. I reserved my ticket by deadline and made sure my crimson sweatshirt was fit to be worn. But I never made it to the Harvard-Yale game that year.

I awoke that Saturday to the same tap-tapping at my window I heard every morning: the physical therapists who came to do my chest percussion knew that my two alarm clocks could barely be heard over the hum of the oxygen concentrator with which I slept. The closed curtains in my room did little to filter out the late-morning sunshine, and I squinted as I stumbled through the common room to let in Kathleen, who came to pound my chest.

The chest percussion began much like so many other sessions. I moved into the different positions, tilted downward over a "slant board," and coughed groggily in response to Kathleen's spirited percussion. I did not fully awaken until I felt the unmistakable movement of liquid inside my chest; I startled Kathleen by alertly sitting up and cursing.

"'Scuse me," I mumbled, then spent several minutes coughing up blood. Without need to consult each other, we ended the percussion session. I sat down on my bed, and Kathleen swiftly folded the slant board and leaned it against a wall.

This small-scale medical crisis found me in a difficult situation. Around the time Fox left for Minnesota, the cystic fibrosis program at Children's had become considerably less dynamic than the one for which we had driven so many hours since 1980. The program reached a low point when Shwachman died that fall. With Fox gone, I looked to the CF program at Massachusetts General Hospital. Kathleen worked at Children's, however, and phoned the pulmonary physician on call there. She gave a brief explanation to the young doctor and then handed me the phone. I answered the woman's questions in monosyllables, then hung up the phone and yelled another obscenity.

"Well?" Kathleen said expectantly.

"She wants me to go to the ER," I said disgustedly, standing up and wincing at my disgruntled reflection in a full-length mirror.

Teresa, Elizabeth, and Susan in Harvard Square

"Come on, then," she said briskly as she rose from one of our floor cushions and put on her coat. I had hoped for a hot shower and time to make myself presentable but realized the haste with which Kathleen wanted me to act.

"Um," I droned. "It's not like this hasn't happened before, you know. I think it would make more sense for me to pick up some vitamin K and hang out in my room today. You know there's nothing they can do for me anyway."

In what is a fairly common occurrence for CF patients, one of the infections in my lungs had eroded through a bed of capillary vessels. A hospital could monitor the loss of blood or in severe cases, perform a bronchial artery embolization. The embolization, an operation I underwent twice during college, entails injecting pieces of synthetic foam into bronchial arteries, so that the foam blocks the blood supply to the capillaries. The morning's episode certainly did not warrant an embolization. I knew vitamin K, which causes blood to clot, to be the only possible treatment unless the bleeding grew worse.

Still, I did not have the self-possession so early in my day to argue with an anxious Kathleen. A few minutes later I crossed through the Yard with her, looking appropriately as though I had just rolled out of bed. On our way to the Square, we passed several groups of Yalies with blue hair, and I felt as though I had lived through this moment before. In the fall of 1983, when my low pulmonary numbers required me to leave Exeter that first time, my father and I left town just before the big game against Andover. We had passed hundreds of blue people then, too.

In the Square, Kathleen pushed me into a taxi and I realized I would lose most of the day.

I spent the next several hours at Children's waiting: for the ER paperwork when I arrived, for a nurse, for an intern, then for the pulmonary doctor on call. I made good progress on a medieval

romance assigned for a literature course; at least I had the presence of mind to grab a book about the famed lovers Tristan and
Isolde as I left my dorm room. I prided myself on being able to
concentrate despite all the commotion outside my little room. I
tried to limit conversation with ER staffers who kept peering in to
apologize for the wait and make sure my coughing had slowed
down, as I told them it had.

When the doctor finally arrived, I could think only of
Tristan and Isolde and the game; the bleeding had stopped
shortly after my arrival. When she suggested I be admitted right
then, I shook my head. I knew I had enough strength to wait
the few days until Thanksgiving, which would bring two days
of school break. When we finished our business, I headed
upstairs to see friends.

"You look like crap," said Derrick Bolling, a young member
of one of Boston's big political families, when I stepped into his
hospital room. We took such candor for granted between us. I
made a face at him but approached the bed and gave my skinny
friend a big hug.

Derrick and I had a friendship based on endurance. We had
lived through the unthinkable, including the death of Derrick's
adorable younger brother Bruce. We never talked about the hard
times, preferring to spend our energy to escape rather than reflect.
We did not think much about distributive genetics, either, but
Derrick and his brother were the only two African Americans with
CF I met at Children's.

The afternoon had dwindled away, and I had not eaten, so
Derrick let me have one of his stockpiled Twinkies and a grue-
some banana-flavored pastry item. I sat on his bed for a while,
then went downstairs to find a sandwich.

A few minutes later, while I munched, we discussed the
ingredients in the hospital chicken salad. Derrick cared

passionately about such things; after all, he had been the force behind a formal petition to Children's administrators calling for better scrutiny of the hospital's dietary system. Most patients had good-naturedly laughed at Derrick, to his face, for taking the issue so seriously. We had all benefitted, however, when the food on our meal trays arrived better prepared.

Now we talked seriously about our health: we both wanted a straight answer from the other about how we felt. Derrick told me, ambiguously, that he had been better but also worse. I told him I felt too well to be in a hospital. Little mattered more to me than keeping pace with my peers at Harvard, but I did not say that to Derrick.

Rolling his eyes, Derrick dismissed my claim and made emphatic use of an obscenity.

"Who do you think you're talking to here?" he said. "You need to be in this bed more than I do."

I reminded him I had transferred my care to Mass General. Genuinely concerned, he said that did not matter and I should start IV antibiotics as soon as possible. I nodded and changed the subject.

We talked about the outside world: family, school, and our short-term goals. I told Derrick most of my news except I did not want to depress him by recounting the awkward moments. I talked about some of my first *Crimson* assignments but said nothing of the the heartbreaking press conference earlier in the week. I told Derrick how thrilled I had been to interview the Archbishop of Canterbury and then Dudley Herschbach, a Harvard professor who won the Nobel Prize for chemistry. I did not tell Derrick that my coughing made both interviews difficult.

When I left Derrick's room, I made sure I was smiling.

Back in the Square, alumni wandered around waving their Crimson pennants. Harvard won the game, but I could not tell from any of the faces.

A mostly blue person whistled at me as I passed him in the Yard. When I looked at his face, he winked at me. I knew I still looked like I had just rolled out of bed. Yalies seemed an odd bunch to me.

The Monday after the Yale game, I spoke to my doctor at Mass General. He did not want to admit me, he said, because he already had too high a census, the number of patients staying in the hospital. But I pleaded my case; eventually we agreed I would be admitted on Wednesday afternoon to take full advantage of Thanksgiving and its two days of school holiday. The doctor told me that because I gave him such short notice, he would have to exaggerate the severity of my condition to find me a bed. I thought he should have been able to secure me a bed on the basis of my reduced pulmonary function alone, but all illnesses become relative. Since the lung infections remained a constant in my condition, they could rarely push my name to the top of a hospital admitting list. Even if I made arrangements weeks in advance, so they would coincide with vacations, I sometimes had to wait several days for a bed.

I convinced the reluctant doctor that he should let me leave the hospital on Sunday to continue administering IV antibiotics in my dorm. Few conservative doctors would have fully subscribed to this arrangement, and my doctor did not, but I persuaded him that I needed to attend classes when they resumed Monday.

My father, in a characteristic act of self-sacrifice, drove to town to help me settle into the hospital. While we waited in the admissions office, we caught up on two months of news. I babbled excitedly about the *Crimson*, and my father related the escapades of Elizabeth and Timmy, the two toddlers at home.

Finally we reached my nondescript quarters. From my window I had a view of other wings of the hospital. I did not even have a street or traffic light to entertain me. Little sun came through the window, so I needed the unpleasant fluorescent light above my bed.

I brought several weighty books with me from a core curriculum course called *Conceptions of Human Nature*. I had not been able to concentrate on the course since a day when I left the lecture early to attend an appointment with the new doctor. On that day, as I gathered my books together, wondering how crowded the T would be at lunchtime, the professor paraphrased the philosophy of Sir Francis Galton. In 1883 Galton invented the term eugenics for his scientific approach toward "bettering" the human race through selective breeding.

"Disease," I heard, "is Nature's way of improving the race."

The words wrenched me out of boredom. Until then I had found little to interest me in the course, which I took to fill a requirement. Eugenics angered me, and I hardly wanted its tenets revived in a classroom, even in the form of a history lesson.

So now, in the hospital bed, I found myself unable to care about what yesterday's Great Thinkers had thought. The books went back on my sea green, metal nightstand, and I read the day's *Boston Globe* until hospital business finally interrupted me.

An intern strode into my room and confidently crossed her legs as she sat in a chair by the end of my bed. A clipboard on her knee, she asked typical questions about medications and reason for admission. Then came the question that found me unprepared.

"And how long have you had cystic fibrosis?"

She measured out the syllables carefully, not wanting to mispronounce the name of the disorder.

A patient makes a choice when confronted with such ignorance. Some might have displayed the irritation I kept hidden.

Some might have enjoyed the situation: "Well it's been about a year now and it's just terrible; do you think I'll get over it soon?"

My response came instinctively. I would remain on the intern's good side if I acted as though she knew more than I did and as if I had not caught her mistake. For her benefit, I became a timid and wide-eyed patient who wanted to confirm my little knowledge with my intern, the expert.

"Well, 'course it's genetic and everything, and let's see, I guess I was diagnosed about the time I was four."

She seemed terrified I might realize she did not know which set of organs had been affected by CF. She asked very general questions and never made mention of my lungs.

I could see the relief emanating from her face when I staged a well-timed coughing fit.

"So, you've been having difficulty with your breathing?" she suddenly asked.

In this manner I continued to convey as much information as I could without embarrassing her.

A nurse quizzed me about my condition later, and in the course of our conversation, I learned why the intern had been so ill-informed. The nurse told me the hospital had only two other CF patients staying in it. She said I would be a learning experience for almost everyone with whom I came into contact. Indeed I had to teach my percussion routine to the therapists and had to spend all my laundry quarters on downstairs vending machines when I could not get enough food on the floor.

That night I closed my door, put on my sneakers and stereo headsets, and did my daily aerobics workout. Every night, besides a lot of stretching, I mainly jogged around in circles for half an hour. The hard floor made an excellent surface for my aerobics shoes.

Halfway through my routine, I spent a fun-filled five minutes explaining myself to a startled night nurse. The rest of his

Elizabeth visiting Teresa in the hospital

patients had retired for the night, and as he made rounds with his flashlight, he did not expect to find anyone awake, let alone doing aerobics.

"Well," I told him with grave face, "I think it's important for me to stay in shape while I'm here."

I had no more interruptions.

The next day I boycotted Thanksgiving. I did not feel depressed and knew I had plenty to be thankful for, but I had decided Thanksgiving as a holiday did not hold up well in the hospital. I had spent five or six of them in hospitals and considered myself an authority. An extra-long phone conversation with my family served as my only acknowledgement of the occasion.

Nurses kept asking if I wanted to watch the parades; I shrugged and told them no. The dietician tried hard to coax me into abandoning my protest so I would eat the same turkey dinner served to everyone else in the hospital. I told her I would have no part of the feast, but she ordered the meal for me anyway. Instead of touching the hospital tray, I made the clerk at the Pizza Pad down the street a very happy man. When I called to place my order, the phone rang for less than three seconds before someone grabbed the receiver. The man sounded deliriously happy to speak to me and kept me on the phone as long as he could. He would rush the pizza to the hospital lobby, he said, and he hoped I would feel better soon. I wondered whose idea it had been to keep a pizza restaurant open during Thanksgiving dinner.

More visitors than usual flitted through the hall, peering into every doorway as they tried to locate their hospitalized friends and relatives. The masses appeared taken aback by the sight of me with my pizza.

On Saturday my whole family came to town, bearing turkey sandwiches and the rest of Thanksgiving dinner proper on paper plates. While my parents and Ted and Susan sat talking to me, the little ones raced around the tiny room. They soon found it had little excitement to offer except for the television's remote control.

My family has missed Thanksgiving together so many times that we have our own historical theory: while some pilgrims went to shoot the turkey, the others must have stayed home and eaten pizza until everyone could be together.

Sunday we proceeded as planned, and I left the hospital. In my dorm room, we received a huge delivery of IV equipment. When Jeannette arrived, she found our common room converted into a tiny hospital ward. Gigantic boxes lined our walls, frozen bags of medication filled our freezer, and an IV pole adorned with bag and tubing loomed tall in the center of the room. Sitting on our floor cushions, a nurse and I spent the better part of an hour trying to put a catheter into one of my veins. We had to replace an IV that had not lasted the few hours since I left the hospital. An astonished Jeannette greeted my family, then quickly escaped into her bedroom.

Eventually the nurse left, my family left, and I sat all alone with the costly medical equipment. Though a common one for chronically ill patients, the arrangement would cost several thousand dollars. Our insurance would cover only 80 percent. At times, home IV care produced higher bills than hospital care because of all the equipment needed; on the other hand, the service eliminated the overhead cost of a day in the hospital. I saw much of my care in terms of the bills my family would incur. Although many of my Exeter and Harvard classmates spent lavish school breaks in Europe or tropical climates, I undoubtedly ran up a higher bill than they did each time I spent the same vacation period in a hospital.

With a port-a-cath or other implanted IV site or with a central venous line entering a major vein, I would have been given a pump. But because this IV sat nestled precariously in a small arm vein, the visiting nurses expected me to let the solution drip unaided from a bag into the tubing. Gravity administered the drugs very slowly. What could have taken little more than an hour took longer, and my 10:00 P.M. dose finished at 1:00 A.M. My parents and I should have insisted on having a pump to push the medication through during a programmed time period.

I did not hear my alarm, woke to the sound of one of my physical therapists knocking on my window, and ran my 6:00 A.M. IV dose an hour late. For a few days, I struggled to run IVs in my room. The chaos of that first cycle would continue as the three daily doses each took three hours from start to finish. In addition, one of the drugs had the side effect of keeping me continually tired. I missed most of my classes during that time. I felt determined to keep up with my work at the *Crimson*, however, and adjusted my schedule to fit the newsday.

Meanwhile, my fragile peripheral veins made the daily practice unbearably painful as the medicine somehow seeped outside a vein, causing redness and severe burning sensations. The visiting nurses reached their limit starting new IV lines, and I soon needed an anesthesiologist friend at Children's to place a central venous line in my neck.

My resident adviser or "proctor," third-year Harvard Medical student Maddie Wilson, eventually protested the IV arrangement; she wanted me to enter the university infirmary. The office of the dean of first-year students began pressuring me, at Maddie's insistence, to take my IV equipment to Stillman Infirmary. Exeter had humbled me more than I realized, and I did not feel bold enough to object.

One evening Maddie summoned a university security car, whose driver refused to help us lift my mammoth box of medical supplies into the car. Maddie and I stopped the first two strong-looking passersby outside our entryway and gained their assistance.

For about a week, I spent the bulk of my waking hours putting together stories for my *Crimson* comp and watching Stillman nurses as they set up my IVs.

I remained vigilant about the IV: I knew the dangers of having an IV line running from my jugular vein to my heart, and I would not take chances. The nurses treated me with great kindness but had no experience with central lines. We almost ran into trouble one morning when a nurse forgot to check the IV tubing for air before starting the medicine. At seven in the morning, I lay half asleep but groggily asked her to stop and clear the tubing, which was full of air, before connecting it to my line. She reluctantly did so. If that much air had been infused into my vein, my heart would have been thrown off balance.

Similar lapses occurred regularly, such as when nurses insisted I had received IV antibiotics during the night, when I could prove by counting the bags of my measured doses that I had not. The head of the infirmary came by my room each day to apologize for the latest improprieties.

In order to leave the infirmary, I enlisted the help of a doctor from Children's. He convinced the necessary officials it would be more efficient for me to run IVs from my room. I wanted very much to have a normal first year at Harvard, and I already had strong ties to Children's; these two factors made it seem easier to ask the Children's doctor to follow me than to return to the Mass General doctor who urged me to drop out of school. I explained to the Mass General doctor that I had a larger base of support at Children's than at Mass General. He agreed and actually seemed pleased.

I went to see the Children's doctor a few days before winter break, and we decided to end the course of IV antibiotics. The three weeks seemed pointless because my clinical status had remained the same. Although I began antibiotics because of my run-down state, I gained no improvement from the drugs. We removed my line, sutures, and all. I stared at the long catheter that had been lodged in my neck, and I hated it for ushering in antibiotics that had not worked.

Before I left, I took the opportunity to tell the Children's doctor about my approach to life with cystic fibrosis. I told him he was not allowed to give up on me, no matter what, and I looked forward to working with him.

The words that came back at me were chilling. With an untroubled calm he told me the disorder would run its course.

He drew some diagrams of respiratory airways to corroborate his point. He shrugged a few times and told me there was little he could do; my lungs had suffered irreversible damage. I had known this for years, of course, but he told me again anyway.

Had I not been medically educated enough to realize I was clinically stable and in no immediate peril, I would have despaired in the wake of his remarks. Instead, I had become so jaded that I looked for the political nuance that might be there. I had briefly left Children's for another hospital; I wondered whether I should consider this expression of apathy as my reprimand for shifting my loyalty.

I tried to give the conversation a positive direction. "Yes, but . . ." I interrupted him a few times with attempts at cautious optimism. Reality came crashing down around me when I was nine; I did not need for him to believe he was its first champion.

I could not rescue our discussion and left at my first opportunity. Our partnership remained intact, but I did not feel entirely happy with it.

Harry Shwachman had died earlier in the fall; multiple strokes forced him bit by bit out of the work he loved. Susan and I remained his patients for as long as he could treat us, and after that we regarded him for some time as an adviser. Near the end, his strokes made it difficult to communicate, but we would whenever possible.

When I made the break to Mass General, looking for a strong presence in a new doctor, I fell out of touch with my many friends at Children's. So I learned of his death some weeks afterward when a therapist mentioned it during chest percussion. The therapist brought in a photocopy of the obituary. I held the paper in my hand, stared at the gray likeness of a younger Harry with thick black glasses, and cried.

With Shwachman's passing we lost much more than an individual. Even in the midst of great in-house rivalry at Children's,

Shwachman saved his only real spite for cystic fibrosis. While others made some patients feel like statistics, or worse, pawns in a silly hospital showdown, Shwachman continued to be our soulmate. I believe he awoke in the morning feeling the same desperation, anger, and hatred toward the disorder that patients do; he made the struggle his own.

As I left Children's that afternoon, the chasm left by Shwachman's absence gaped wide. I wondered whether I could dare hope other clinicians would care as he did. How could any of us work successfully with a doctor who did only what was expected, performed only the stated requirements of the job, uttered the incredible postmortem oath "I did everything I could"? Such a person could achieve competence in many fields of medicine. But for the treatment of life-threatening illness, we had to ask more of a doctor.

Fair or not, we needed an individual who would never "recover" from losing that first patient, as we would never recover from losing our friends. We needed a doctor prepared to keep vigil for us. We had such standard symptoms and treatments we almost did not need doctors for their basic medical knowledge; many of us easily could have picked our own drugs and timed our own stays in the hospital. We deciphered medical abstracts and looked up medicines in the *Physician's Desk Reference* by ourselves. Instead, we needed weathered strategists to fight alongside us and feel our triumph or our loss. We could not tell young pulmonary fellows they had picked an easy field. They would learn soon enough, however, that what they lost in peace and comfort, they would gain back in a revitalized sense of wonder. A CF doctor had to have an unmitigated appreciation for life that equalled or exceeded that of all his or her peers.

During the T ride back to campus, I started to doubt my own instincts. I wondered if the doctor had been right to offer a negative prognosis. A few minutes later I decided against this after considering my current medical status and medical history. The fear he stirred in me had no foundation.

Still, I felt depressed. My favorite view in all Boston, as the train passed between Charles and Kendall stations, only heightened my anxiety. The Hancock and the Prudential buildings towered reliably behind the Charles River and the winter-smitten esplanade. Commuters paid no mind to the scene, but I found it spectacular as ever. That day I realized I would eventually have to leave Boston to find another Shwachman. I would find it difficult to part with his city, now my city, after college. When the time came, I could not look back; fortunately for the moment, however, I still had to get through the semester.

CHAPTER
⊞ THIRTY-ONE

The day after my visit with the new doctor, I awoke to find a strange rash covering my face. It remained there the next morning as well, but I felt more annoyed than alarmed. Then I described the rash to a friend over the telephone, and she diagnosed chicken pox.

Shwachman had kept me out of school for six weeks in the seventh grade during a chicken pox epidemic at St. Thomas. He knew the normally harmless childhood virus would threaten a CF patient's life; he said something at the time about the risk of developing internal pox on the lungs. Shwachman told us the risk increased as patients grew older, perhaps in part because the pain of pocks on the lungs interfered with clearing secretions.

Somehow I managed to avoid the virus, even when Ted and Susan caught it during the epidemic. Susan, fortunately, did not have any complications. In any case, Shwachman's warning to me had been so emphatic that I became truly fearful in my dorm that morning. On Division 39 I had watched chicken pox weaken a CF patient who died in short order.

Maddie, the proctor from upstairs, came with me to the Children's emergency room. There I sat wearing a surgical mask to keep from spreading chicken pox throughout the ward. The mask made it hard to breathe and made the forty-five-minute wait seem interminable. Maddie and I spent the time trading disjointed pieces of conversation about her favorite subject and my least, hospitals.

Finally I found myself talking to an intern whose byline later seemed to turn up all over the place as she wrote freelance articles about her experiences as a woman in medicine.

"Shwachman said I was in a lot of trouble if this ever happened," I told her. She did not seem to respond, so I began repeating myself and using my hands for emphasis.

We conferred in a tiny exam room near the ER desk. She stood while I sat, legs crossed, atop a table. I had sat on hundreds of similar tables and knew my position was intended to be passive; I was supposed to be listening to someone else's analysis of the situation. But I knew mine could not go unheard.

Somehow I had pictured that the intern would nod, having been taught about the danger of chicken pox in older CF patients. If not her, then someone upstairs surely would have a plan to fend off the dangers of which Shwachman had warned. It did not occur to me that I might be facing this peril without any fortification whatsoever; I believed too much in modern medicine to entertain the thought.

The intern amazed me with her reaction. She assured me I had nothing to fear from a simple childhood virus. Then she addressed my reference to Shwachman: "You and a lot of other patients just had a really big loss. You're going through a tough time, and I understand."

"You don't believe me."

"I believe you think he said something like that, and right now you want to hold onto that memory. That's only natural."

"Wait. Wait, I swear to you, this is not in my head." My hands flew out of control, and I spoke almost frantically. "He said it, he really said it, and there's gotta be someone around here who remembers."

But no one did. She admitted me to Division 37, and for the first few days, doctors patronized me, telling me I should not worry so much about chicken pox. I started to doubt my own memory until my mother assured me by phone that she too remembered. I felt eerily alone in the bustling hospital and old for my seventeen years. Even as I insisted to doctors and nurses that Shwachman had kept me out of school for so long for a reason, my word meant nothing.

I found the experience disillusioning for two reasons. First, I had taken great pains to be an educated patient and never made things up, so it surprised me my fears could be so easily dismissed. Second, I felt alarmed that no one involved in my care had ever treated a CF patient with chicken pox, and that as a teenager, I could have partial grasp of information unknown to anyone else in the hospital.

My complications happened more quickly than I expected, and fortunately my father soon arrived to help. Coughing hurt unbelievably, so I had difficulty clearing my airways. My appetite disappeared, and although I struggled to keep eating, I began losing what would amount to thirty pounds. My temperature hovered well above double digits Fahrenheit, and I began having alternate chills and heat spells. I started sleeping more than staying awake and, having quickly lost my aerobic fitness, found it difficult to get out of bed to walk to the sink or bathroom. In less than a week's time, I became completely dependent on other people.

"Believe me now?" I asked the doctors one morning when I had grown too sick to care much about their response. I found it difficult to talk because my respirations flew in and out so quickly; the three words required a focused effort from me.

"Yes, Terri, we believe you now," someone said.

When Christmas Eve suddenly dropped itself down into the march of unassuming hospital days, the doctors wanted to send me home for the holidays. Because I remained so sick, my family offered to celebrate Christmas in a Boston hotel room. I, too, thought it would be wise for me to remain in the hospital, perhaps taking a one-day leave for Christmas. The prospect of leaving medical help behind seemed foolhardy. With what strength I had, I diplomatically proposed to the doctors that I stay. They remained intent, however, on their efforts to clear the hospital for the holidays.

Dad drove me back to Allentown where my parents would administer my IV medications. In a haze, I sat still for the ride and then retired to my bedroom at home. During my years away, the room had stayed that of a small girl's, except for the Harvard poster hanging next to my desk.

On Christmas morning all the relatives, now used to unpredictability in their dealings with me, visited quietly downstairs while my mother tended to my many needs. She nonchalantly helped me sip drinks and stagger to the bathroom without ever acting as though the necessary vigil came as an inconvenience.

Naturally I stayed home from Christmas Mass; around midday our pastor brought me the Eucharist. He entered the room and said all the prayers for the sick I had heard so often. Then he uttered something that made me flash a look to my mother she understood well: it meant "get him out of here."

He said: "May Christ welcome you into His Heavenly Kingdom."

The priest meant perfectly well, but I did not have the energy to explain to him that I was working very hard to weather the crisis, to stay grounded in this world. I needed prayers for strength and recovery, but my appearance belied that.

My mother deftly steered the priest out of my room, then came back to sit with me. She knew without much talk between us that I needed her to help me fight my way through the crisis.

I sat up for Christmas dinner with my family but managed only a few mouthfuls while my relatives feasted. My mother's parents and two of her brothers and their families had all visited us, and various guests made attempts at conversation with me. I could not do much more than nod, shake my head, or utter a few syllables. I also found it hard to concentrate.

I slept through most of the week between Christmas and New Year's. It seemed as though every time I opened my eyes I would throw up and become so exhausted that I needed to lie back and sleep. For four days in a row, I coughed up and vomited frighteningly large quantities of blood, several ounces at a time.

During those four days, my mother placed several emergency telephone calls to Children's, but no one answered the pulmonary pages or returned her calls. My parents hurriedly consulted with doctors in Philadelphia, deciding I would head to the city for a transfusion if I lost much more blood.

There seemed to be little we could do other than pursue common sense measures: I kept drinking high-protein, high-calorie shakes; I took vitamin K tablets to slow the bleeding from tiny lung vessels; and I fought for mobility by moving around the house as much as possible. My parents continued to administer my IV medicines.

Beyond that, we rented the first *Rocky* movie, and I watched it three times on New Year's Eve. The film's portrayal of a fighter who proves almost everyone wrong in the course of overcoming unfavorable odds made it a favorite in our house. Ted and Susan and I missed the ball dropping in Times' Square because we sat watching Rocky train for his big boxing match.

I returned to Cambridge the day vacation ended in a state almost as pathetic as when I returned to Exeter my first spring there. I continued to run IVs in my dorm room. I did not recover fully for some months, but I decidedly had no time to be sick.

The call came late in the evening on the night before second semester classes began. It caught Jeannette and me scrambling around, straightening the room, and picking classes to attend during Harvard's two-week "shopping period."

I heard nothing in Meg's voice to warn me. She said her brief vacation between semesters had been fun, and she had gone skiing. Our conversation sounded like so many before it. While we filled twenty minutes with mindless gossip, I doodled in my course catalogue, made piles of old lecture notes, and balanced the phone on my shoulder as I rearranged my desktop.

Just when I thought the conversation would end soon, we came to the only part of it that remains clear in my memory. We would have to talk about the rooming thing, she said. Of course we would, I agreed. Meg and one of her roommates had asked me to live with them in the fall; we would be making the big move then to one of Harvard's twelve residential houses where undergraduates settle in after the first year.

The three of us had not yet picked a house and soon we would need to complete the paperwork registering our choice. I suggested that we should meet to sort things out over dinner and asked Meg when she thought we might be able to get together. I had my pen poised to jot down the time she would propose.

"That's not what I meant," she said, sounding nervous. She paused. "I didn't mean to do this over the phone."

Something definitely did not sound right. I did not know what had made her sound so serious, but I would help in any way I could.

I stopped moving around and doodling and devoted my full concentration to the conversation.

"Hmmm? What's up?"

"I really don't think we should room together next year."

In my response, I gave Meg the benefit of the doubt. I thought I understood her meaning and still had not become alarmed.

"Of course not; I thought we'd settled that. That's why you two will room together and I'll take a single somewhere. I'd never ask either of you to put up with the cough."

"That's not what I mean."

Meg began talking about how I had not been eating well or sleeping enough since I started spending so much time at the *Crimson*. She said that seeing me take poor care of myself made her worry; in the meantime, she said, her grades had suffered. She said her mother told her our friendship would hurt her stint in academia. And she said she agreed with her mother.

All of this found me quite unprepared. First of all, I had been trying hard to compensate for the grueling routine at the *Crimson*. I took frequent naps and kept a supply of protein—milk, tuna, and peanut butter—in my room. I could not remember Meg ever expressing such concern before. Her disclosure about her tumbling grades seemed peculiar enough by itself, if true, but I did not understand how, after all that time as friends, my health could deter Meg from living with me.

If it had not been her idea, I did not understand how it could come from her mother. I had come to know both her parents well the previous summer when I spent a month at their house. Both Rileys had sent me notes and postcards all through fall. I could not imagine Mrs. Riley blaming me for any drop in Meg's grades.

"Well," I said slowly, bewildered, "then I guess we'll just block together. Geez, Meg, why didn't you tell me there was all this other stuff going on? If you're worrying like that we should talk through it soon. It's not healthy, you know."

Meg began making excuses. She said we would not be able to find a place where I could live far enough away from everyone to keep from bothering people with my noisy cough and still live near my two blockmates.

I did not, I could not accept the dissolution of our friendship in this manner. I needed to know if she was being honest about her concerns or if she had used my health to camouflage something problematic about our friendship. If she had chosen the medical excuse for convenience, then we had little left; Meg knew how I resented being set apart. To cite cystic fibrosis in this situation would be mean-spirited.

Desperation made me believe we could still reach a compromise; I had an old friend on the phone, after all, and she herself had often teased me about being paranoid.

Of course we'd find a place, I said. We'd just tell the housing office what we wanted, and they would help us find a place.

"Look, Meg, we'll make it work."

"I don't think we should block together either."

She had made her meaning clear. I did not want to know why, I just wanted to get off the phone before I let Meg hear me crying. She started doing all of the talking, and I answered in monosyllables.

We'd still see lots of each other, Meg said, and this would be better for our friendship. She reassured herself more than me.

"Maybe we should talk about this some other time," I said, hoping to get off the phone. Meg missed my intent.

"Terri, I'm not going to change my mind about this."

Then she grew friendly again, practically nonchalant, trying to talk about nonsense. Hot tears burned into my face, but at least I knew Meg could not hear me crying. She said we would have to have a meal together during the week.

"Yeah. Give me a few days and I'll call you." I knew I would not.

With the conversation over, I sat sobbing in disbelief.

I knew that all across campus roommates and casual friends found themselves at odds over housing forms. Each year at Harvard, the housing system brought with it confusion and, for some, disenchantment. Floating, or entering the housing lottery alone, was an unfortunate fate that would most likely place you in the room of several unenthusiastic strangers. I would be one of the lucky few to become close friends with the women into whose room I unceremoniously floated my sophomore year.

These clashes over housing took place throughout Harvard Yard, where most first-year students reside. I knew people who, as juniors or seniors, still maintained grudges stemming from their own mistreatment prior to the housing lottery. If Meg had simply come up against legitimate obstacles to our rooming together, then I would have been foolish to react the way I did.

But there had been more in her words and her awkwardness than doubts about rooming with me. She seemed to be unsure of whether she still valued our friendship; she wanted to relegate me into her circle of acquaintances. Most alarming was the bigger picture: if part of my life troubled Meg, it was a part she had pretended to accept and a part I could not change. I began to worry that the world might be full of well-meaning Megs who would be unable to sustain friendships with people like me. One could fault them, but life without them would undoubtedly be lonelier.

Jeannette and I had been moving in different circles. Most nights she had gone upstairs to study with her boyfriend, while I stayed late at the *Crimson* or went to parties. On the night of the phone call, however, we began to grow close. Jeannette turned away from her work and listened to me babble endlessly about the void that had erupted into my life.

I told her I feared that I would always face difficulty in finding friends who would accept my medical problem. She said I did not need people like Meg anyway.

Then came the practical: I had done most of my socializing within the confines of the *Crimson* community and Meg's dorm. Jeannette stayed home many Friday and Saturday nights, but I had always been able to find something to do with Meg and her dormmates. In addition, I had begun to feel close to some of the people in her entry. I knew that night that I would not be able to face Meg anytime soon and that meant I would lose touch with that large group of people. Unfortunately, I would later learn that Meg told almost no one in the dorm what happened, and many of them thought I did not care to see the entire group anymore. By senior year, I retained only one friend from that group.

But I reasoned I had no way of explaining all this to these new friends, and Jeannette agreed.

The afternoon after the phone call I found a note and carnation propped against my door.

"It was the best thing, the best thing for me. That's Machiavellian, but I think it's a situation where I have to be selfish."

It was a silly thing to do, but I took the carnation into our room and stomped on it.

We talked, eventually, a few more times. Each time Meg seemed to think we were mending our friendship, and each time I grew incredulous at the things she said. My instinct about this being an irreparable problem proved truly accurate.

She said she did not find it hard to be friends with the woman who would have been our third roommate, but she found it hard to be my friend. She was sorry; that was just the way things were. It wasn't fair, she said. In our conversations after the call, she spoke of the true hardship of being my friend; I never realized it was such a sacrifice for her and was, in fact, appalled that I had been a catalyst for this strange brand of martyrdom.

Meg did say, when prodded repeatedly, that she thought our friendship had grown slightly stale. But then she said that we had never been friends really, just people who spent time together by default at Exeter. This from her made me cry in the middle of the huge dining hall for first-year students.

The more we talked, the more I felt something strange happening: I let Meg say what she wanted, but I sat there detached, no longer mourning our friendship. I wanted to know why this had happened to me and if it could happen to anyone else. Then I realized it probably happened all the time. Although Meg considered herself open-minded, she had just emerged from four years at our conservative alma mater, and she maintained a very like group of friends. She wanted comfort at Harvard, and she gathered people around her who could provide it. In her life-time she had been programmed to look for homogeneity in her circle of friends.

While she spoke I sat wondering if we would ever live in a world in which people would accept others with differences, manifest or not. Meg would drift from the topic at hand, begin discussing matters social, and I would think about tolerance and intolerance. I could not accept the new and diluted version of friendship she offered, but I also felt no anger toward her. She had been part of something bigger than she knew, and for decency's sake, our country would have to start raising children who loved each other unconditionally. The explanation did not take away the hurt.

Fortunately, my work at the *Crimson* gave me little time for reflection in the wake of Meg's decision. A group of about twenty-five of us passed our comp and joined the staff before winter break. Finishing the comp brought us a definite elevation in status. Although everyone called us "baby editors" for a time, other *Crimson* editors—staff reporters eligible to make the first edit of another student's story—began learning our names. In keeping with *Crimson* custom, we learned that as editors we had earned the right to use our initials; in memos and notes I became "TAM" instead of "Mullin."

Unfortunately, I had landed in the hospital during the time the incoming executive board assigned us beats, and my request for a beat had been inadvertently overlooked. But several sophomores suggested I ask to cover Harvard Business School (the B–School).

The advice turned out to be excellent because I entered the scene at a time when coverage of the school had been scarce for many years. As the sophomores told me, I could find my own footing rather than being confined to formulaic stories such as speeches. The Business School avoided publicity more than any other Harvard graduate school. While many of our other reporters had no choice but to cover certain press conferences and events, I could learn from creating my own timetable for stories and ferreting out news wherever it might be.

No one at the *Crimson* could tell me anything more about the Business School than the name of its dean, so converting the school into my beat presented an enticing challenge. I needed to do an enormous amount of legwork before I could write anything about the place. I spent hours just talking to people—B-School students, junior professors, and even the staffers at the public relations office. I learned that many important administrators and professors would invariably be in the middle of a "meeting" when the *Crimson* called, unless I convinced their secretaries it would be more prudent for them to come to the phone. I learned about alliances within a faculty and about planted stories designed to cast an institution in a favorable light.

I read the student paper, the weekly *Harbus*, and spoke often with its editors. I barraged the campus news office with background questions and gathered old press releases and interview transcripts to start my own files on the school. I spoke to so many

Teresa at Harvard Business School (1990)

professors that I eventually found the ones who would be sources of valuable information. At libraries I skimmed every business journal or magazine I could find, looking for references to Harvard.

Conversations with B-School students became the most helpful part of this acclimation process. They directed me to their professors, after having carefully explained the faculty members' politics. They wistfully told me their complaints about the school but apologetically explained they did not want to make a bad impression with prospective employers by speaking out about problems. I came across a few blatant sexists, such as the gentleman who paged through the *Sports Illustrated* swimsuit issue during an interview. Yet for the most part, I found a less conservative group than I expected. Although they usually did not want me to print their names, even in utterly innocuous stories, they made a candidly cynical bunch. In the era of insider trading scandals, most seemed to subscribe to the idea that the business world had begun to totter under the weight of all its moral dilemmas. They initiated me to the point where I knew investment banks and other institutions by their nicknames and could gauge the salary offers of recruiting season.

Not all of the stories I researched made their way into print. Some remained too comprehensive even for a sixty-inch feature story, some got stopped short by tight-mouthed sources, and some just got lost in the *Crimson* shuffle or my own academic damage control. But I never felt I had wasted my time. I had too much fun reporting and writing to seek a hefty byline count; nonetheless, I held my own with the aggressive reporters in my class.

I benefitted greatly from working with the juniors and sophomores who edited my stories and gave me guidance. Between deadlines, some of them became my close friends. We would slip out of the building for an hour and gossip over coffee in Harvard

Square, or we would round up a big group and tramp to dinner in a house dining hall. Almost always, we analyzed the day's news as reported by the *Boston Globe*, the *New York Times,* and the Associated Press. I would let older students make predictions about world events or criticize the reporting jobs of some articles while I listened.

Our small group of first-year students forged some strong friendships among ourselves as well. The sometimes exasperating comp experience bonded us together.

This group of first-year students, sophomores and juniors, and a few lingering seniors, helped me fill my time after Meg's change of heart. In the *Crimson* and out of it, I kept my mind off the loss. I had found, in my work at the paper, the situation that made me happiest.

CHAPTER
❧ THIRTY-TWO

Right before spring finals, my physical therapists told me Nellie had returned to Children's and they had never seen her in such poor spirits. I visited at my first opportunity.

When I reached her room, she seemed to be thwarting attacks from all directions. Everyone wanted Nellie to cheer up, but their aggressive efforts toward this end did not help.

"We need to talk about your anxiety management," said a figure approaching Nellie when I arrived. Clad in a lab coat, and holding a clipboard, the woman had tried to make a science of Nellie's state of mind.

"Thank you, but I'm dying, and I really don't think we have much to talk about," Nellie said without expression. Shock value, I decided. She could not believe these words and would do anything to get the lab coat out of the room.

Unnerved, lab coat left. The others hovering around Nellie's bed dispersed shortly.

I tried to get Nellie and her roommate, our old friend Suzy Ahlman, to talk about upbeat topics.

The press had been full of stories about the team of British researchers who thought they had isolated the cystic fibrosis gene. Actually, this first team apparently isolated the marker next to the gene; researchers in the United States and Canada isolated the gene itself two and a half years later, in the summer of 1989.

But for a short time, we thought the gene had been identified. Most patients with sense about them realized the discovery would not directly benefit any of us for quite some time. In fact, we underestimated the publicity blitz that later would shift all attention to the gene and away from the clinical research that might prolong lives.

In any case, the time had grown ripe for surface hope. I did not buy into it, but I needed to try to boost Nellie's spirits. So I began: "You know, they're saying it'll be five to ten years now till they find something to help us." A random number was this, getting tossed about irresponsibly in medical circles across the country.

Nellie tossed her head back and laughed. She waved her hand through the air, unimpressed, and repeated softly, "Five to ten years."

"Don't think about the ten, just think about the five," said Suzy, who planned to go home the next morning.

Before we said more, Nellie asked her nurse to be allowed down to the garden. She wanted me to wheel her and insisted to the nurse that I be the only one to accompany her. The nurse did not take well to such instruction; Nellie's condition remained fragile, and I hardly made the ideal attendant. Still, Nellie grew resolute about such things; she almost sounded like she meant to bark orders.

I knew a trip to the garden meant that Nellie wanted to tell me something she could not say on the floor. We made the short trip there in virtual silence.

As we stood parked in the garden, Nellie confirmed my worst expectations. She told me how frightened she had become. I had no power to help her. I could barely rouse her to daydream, let alone decide to fight.

I wanted to tell her what I really thought about that day. I felt angry that the apparent discovery of the gene had made the public consider patients to be in less danger. I felt angry that the breakthrough meant we might never get our overdue clinical answer. I felt angry that with so much money spent in the name of cystic fibrosis, so little went to concerns like finding the quickest way to save the Nellies of the world.

Had she been well, Nellie could have helped me sort out my thoughts on the matter. But I dared not even mention them just then. They remained specters in the garden as I looked to the buildings around us for solace.

After our conversation I could no longer fathom why I should return to Harvard to study for finals. I felt like the whole world should just stop its business long enough to solve the most basic of medical problems. Our slow-acting and predictable respiratory infection still flourished unchecked. But of course I went back and hit the books.

Nellie had said she admired Geraldine Ferraro. The former vice-presidential candidate had a daughter attending Harvard Business School, and I desperately tried to reach her. It seemed to be the only thing I could do, to try to arrange for Ferraro to contact Nellie, but I got no response.

I spoke to Nellie a few times on the phone in between finals. Then on the last Wednesday in May, my physical therapist told me during evening percussion that I should get myself over to Children's if I ever wanted to see Nellie again.

When I called the floor, the secretary fueled my fears. Antonella was asleep, he told me, but I should come visit if I possibly could. I said something about waiting until she was awake and taking visitors. "No," he said. "Come now." I had never visited a sleeping person before.

Flower shops close when the business day ends. I had never thought of that. When someone got sick, you sent them flowers. At Children's we received our flowers from the front desk at all hours, so I had the impression florists remained on call, awaiting catastrophe and your reaction to it. Although I had received hundreds of floral arrangements during all my times in the hospital, I had sent flowers only for birthdays or holidays, never to a sick person. I wanted a beautiful bouquet now, something that would send a nurse scurrying to find a vase to display them.

Then again, we might be past the time for flowers. Maybe a rose then, a single red rose. Or maybe white. But as I frantically scrambled past all the people in Harvard Square, I found every single plant shop closed. How could they be? A couple looked curiously at me when I burst into tears on reaching the dark door of the last store I knew.

I slowly walked back to the line of taxis on Massachusetts Avenue. As I rode to the hospital, I hoped the cab driver would say something. Anything. Maybe he would turn on the radio or check in with his dispatcher. But we rode in silence; I had only my destination to consider.

Children's had ceased to be "my" hospital. Shwachman's influence had vanished all too quickly, and I had learned that trust was for the helpless. Most of the staff I had met when I began going there had burned out and left. Children's made a cheerful working environment except for the way people kept dying.

Nellie had said she felt uneasy there. I wished I could change that. I wanted the best for all of us; I wanted so much to make everything different.

A nurse leaped out at me as I started down the hall to Nellie's room. She wanted to be sure it would be all right for me to enter the room and cleared it with someone. Such formality was a bad sign.

The hissing of the oxygen made the only sound as I walked into the unlit room. The door stayed open so the hall light could drift to the edge of Nellie's bed. She lay there alone, except for a nurse who lingered at her bedside and a brother I vaguely remembered meeting, who sat in a chair.

Nellie opened her eyes when the nurse told her in a low voice that I had entered the room. I needed to say something, I knew, but opened my mouth two or three times without managing words.

The nurse left us, promising Nellie she would be right back.

Unsure of my role here, I stood in the quiet room for about five minutes. Then Nellie spoke to me. Twice I could not hear her, and the third time I leaned close.

"Come back some other time, okay, Terri?" she whispered.

"Of course I will." I thought she wanted to make sure I would visit her again soon.

"Do you mind?" she asked, not impatiently, but sincerely. Then I realized she wanted me to leave.

"Of course not," I tried to say convincingly. I said good-bye and gave her a big hug. "I'll be back," I said finally, but I knew this was our farewell.

The nurse came back in time to hear the last three words and looked startled.

"You're leaving?"

"She asked me to." My voice squeaked, and I felt disgusted with myself. I understood that she did not want friends to see her like this, but leaving the room was one of the single most painful things I have ever had to do.

As soon as I spoke I had to turn away to hide the tears.

I staggered into the middle of the hall, just out of view of Nellie's brother, grabbed my sides, and sobbed as quietly as I could. I did not want anyone in the room behind me to hear. For several minutes the steaming hot tears came so fast I could not see anything, and when I started to move, I walked into a wall.

I leaned against the wall and kept crying. When I finally noticed my surroundings, I realized the hall was eerily quiet. There were no ringing phones, no pages over the loudspeaker, no interns scuffing around in their clogs. I could not hear any beeping machinery or patients talking in their rooms. It seemed as though Nellie's was the only occupied bed in the whole hospital.

Suddenly I made out someone in a bright color, red perhaps, approaching.

"She don't mean to upset you or anything," Nellie's brother said kindly. He wanted to say more, I thought, but the language barrier remained too great. I asked how he was holding up, but he did not understand and returned to his sister.

I turned and looked down the hall, then started toward the somber group of Italians sitting in the activity center.

"Antonella—you frienda?" asked a woman walking toward the room I had left.

"Uh-huh," I squeaked. I had never met this relative of Nellie's, except perhaps among a crowd of family members I had met when they descended for a visit with Nellie. But we shared a big, comforting hug.

Mrs. Leone, an older and sturdier version of her daughter, saw me coming and held out her arms as I walked toward her. We both started crying as we clasped each other.

Then about half a dozen relatives and I made small talk through the one daughter who could speak English. The delays while Antonella's older sister interpreted for us made the conversation seem more superficial than it already was. The family asked me about school, and how I liked it, and how I was feeling. I did not know how to say the things I really felt.

I waited and said those things to a nurse who drove me back to campus an hour later.

"It's too soon," I told him in the car.

Not that at eighteen she was too young, statistics would have contradicted me there; but that a week and a half was too short a time for Nellie's condition to worsen so dramatically. She had been scared but stable in the garden. Something else must have gone wrong.

"Well, her newest infection had baffled everyone," the nurse said. "No one could tell for certain what really happened," he added. I just kept arguing and shaking my head until he let me out in the Square.

Harvard seemed a strange place to me as I walked home through the Yard that night. Did I deserve to be there? And what about Nellie, what did she deserve? Why had such a brilliant mind lost the chance to pursue an education? Since 1938, when CF first got its name, we had been waiting for an answer.

"WHAT WILL IT TAKE?"

My bitter voice filled the deserted Yard. I floated down the path somehow, knowing nothing but hopelessness and the sympathetic stars. What would it take to make our lives into a genuine research priority?

I did not study for finals that night. Into the early morning hours I sat typing, drafting letters to science editors; I planned conversations with TV reporters who had contacted me about CF before.

In the morning I went into a public relations frenzy, trying to reach every news outlet I could and telling people the gene's discovery would change cystic fibrosis research forever. I said patients had developed a new perspective: We feared that genetic research would likely overshadow all efforts to find a clinical control for us. We did not want to be forgotten amid the trumpets.

I needed to do something and raising awareness seemed to be my only choice. I fancied I was somehow helping Nellie, or at least giving her something.

My efforts made no stir, and I understood. As a reporter I always avoided the "public relations" story, urged on the paper by someone who wanted to see their business or cause featured in print. Perhaps we were not news, after all.

The call came at 10:05 the next Saturday. I had been sitting on our floor, wading madly through a semester's Russian notes.

I had called the hospital several times since Wednesday evening. Even when they started giving Nellie morphine, another very bad sign, the nurses had told me not to give up hope. But I felt so frustrated that I would have hung up the telephone on the next person to say "You never know."

Then one time they offered no more hope.

"I have some bad news," a nurse said.

"When?"

"Oh, about twenty minutes ago. She died in her sleep. I'm sorry to have to tell you this over the phone. You were on the list of people to call."

I remained in shock for the rest of finals and received some pretty terrible grades for my distraction. At least the work of helping to assemble the *Crimson's* commencement issue would soon make me feel productive and useful again.

For Nellie, I could do only one more thing. I had to tell the world about her, about us, and by default about me. Where my attempts to write about my experiences had faltered before, I now saw the urgency of it all. Until that spring, time in the hospital had numbed me to tragedy. It had all seemed inevitable; now I saw it as unjust. Somehow Nellie's vitality and the loss of it made me realize the horror of the state of affairs we in the hospital took for granted.

Through the way she lived, Nellie taught me to fight for the acceptance that had evaded me all my life. She showed me I must never be passive again. I think of her often, and believe I know what she would want me to say.

We will not live in a civilized society until we tend to the disenfranchised among us. In this time when women, people of color, the gay and lesbian community, and the disabled all continue to struggle for basic civil rights, there is another, uncounted minority. The chronically ill, especially those of us with life-threatening illnesses, have spent too many years on the fringes of American society. No matter how content we have been in our own lives, almost all of us in this country have grown up shunned and discouraged. The enlightened among us have learned to hate the word "concern" as a euphemism for discrimination.

Our ranks have little in common save illness. We may never bond together because all of us need to fight our own battles and few wish to identify with the ranks of the chronically ill.

We do not yet care about equal representation on college faculties and within law firms; we are still fighting for the right, the opportunity, to attend school. We contend with a stereotype every waking moment of our days, yet none of us can charge bias because we have not been recognized as deserving of the same treatment accorded our peers.

As a group, we are defenseless right now. We need healthy people everywhere to consider our dilemma and to help us. If, for a short while, we could give the same attention to medical research we have given to matters of defense, space exploration, or any of our new technologies, we could create a much more civil world.

We would reward the world that saved us with several hundred thousand lives geared toward making a contribution. We already give as much as we can, but we need more help.

Good-bye, Antonella. You've taught me well.

EPILOGUE

When our daughter Teresa was still very young, she won a trophy for collecting the most money for a Cystic Fibrosis Foundation Bike-A-Thon in Allentown. She did this by knocking on hundreds of doors and by being supported by wonderful family members and friends. She was so very proud of her trophy. It was a symbol to her that she was a champion. She could go on to accomplish anything. From that day on, nothing ever stopped her from reaching for the stars.

When we think of Teresa, the thought that always surfaces is her drive, determination, and courage. She had the conviction that she would fight this disease with everything in her—and that maybe things just might work out. In many ways, she was a pretty intense person. Only toward the end of her

Teresa sailing on Chesapeake Bay, summer 1990

life, after repeated hospitalizations and bouts of illness, did she voice the thought that perhaps the disease might win, when she simply said, "Please don't forget me."

For a parent, forgetting a child is not possible. Even after time, memories of our daughters are as vivid as if they had been here last week. There will always be an emptiness in our hearts as long as we breathe, and there is still intense pain when we look at pictures of them, so full of life and hope.

Our family went on a religious pilgrimage in 1983 to Lourdes, France, where our children bathed in the miraculous healing waters. Before we left Lourdes, both of our girls told us that it was no longer necessary to pray for a miracle for them; they both felt so intensely grounded in the belief that God would give them the strength that they needed for whatever the future might hold for them.

Teresa had an unwavering focus on her health. She frequently referred to herself in military terms—like a soldier battling an

A favorite photo of Teresa and Ted

The Boston Globe

BUSINESS

Frank, at Harvard, cites losses for li

By Teresa Mullin
Special to the Globe

Rep. Barney Frank told 100 supporters at the Harvard-Radcliffe Hillel yesterday that liberalism has lost ground despite many popular issues.

"If you go issue by issue, liberalism is popular," said Frank, the Democratic congressman from Newton who has come under f after acknowledging that he employed a male prostitute.

In a speech focusing on J voting patterns, Frank said the eralism "in general has ma give a poor impression of

"There are people who

that Jewish-Americans should be deterred from making the choices that made."

that although he are "begin- conser-

have one character They are men."

Frank also to prayer.

"I have not f Orthodox Jews w prayer in the sc mple reason," xpect scho Hebr

B-Schooler Talks; Scandal Revealed

By TERESA A. MULLIN

Charges this week that two major investm firms took part in illegal insider tradin testimony of an anonymous source 1971 Business School graduate.
Federal prosecutors are h testimony of "CS-1," to the case suspec Inc. official M
Siegel depa

banking on the k is a the

A striker waves a flag while listening to Jesse Jack

Medical issues touch

By Teresa Mullin
Contributing Reporter

The telephone workers who rallied in such huge numbers in Boston yesterday said their strike has attracted such impassioned support because the issues on the table, including medical benefits, represent a battle being waged now in workplaces across the country.

Members of dozens of local and regional unions, many of them from out of state, joined the ranks of the Nynex Corp. strikers at the rally. Workers said they have come together behind the issue of

medical coverage – part of w Nynex has proposed emplo pay for – because it is a perce workplace issue.

"We've had enough," sa Adele Stacy, business agent fo the clerical force of the Local 222 of the International Brotherhood of Electrical Workers. The issue of medical benefits "hits every employee. The fact is that unions are realizing we have to all be together because what hits one will hit the next," Stacy said.

"They're taking something away now that we've fought for for the last 20 years," said Timo

Harvard Business School graduates cheer – and the man in the foreground waves a dollar bill – after graduation yeste

Harvard MBAs urged to serve public, not s

By Teresa Mullin
Contributing Reporter

Harvard Business School Dean John H. McArthur yesterday urged the school's 765 graduating MBAs to find ways to serve the public, and told them, "Don't go through life focused only on No. 1. "I hope you will keep in front of you a sense of responsibility . . . It

is really not enough for the fortunate few that we represent to simply go through life making money. McArthur told the MBAs and eight doctoral recipients. In addition to mere professional accomplishments, people such as you and I . . . must also seek out ways to become involved" in public service.

The dean said it is important for the MBAs to "recognize that things will not get better for the world's oppressed "multitude without the private sector getting involved.

In perhaps the only event this year not carefully orchestrated by a school administration that runs itself according to a corporate line

chart, rain fo indoors. Abou Bright Hockey not been so vard's hockey

The schoo for the down chairs, simila ments and p HARVARD, Pa

Some of Teresa's Boston Globe *and* Harvard Crimson *articles*

enemy. She really did not like to cut corners with her treatments, be it clapping (chest percussion) or IV antibiotics. Even when we were exhausted after a trip, she would admonish us if we tried to abbreviate her chest percussion therapy sessions. Better than most, she knew the stakes.

As for the title of her book, Teresa made reference to a book of poems about Northern Ireland. A particular poem refers to a promontory of Ireland jutting out into the North Atlantic, trying to withstand the waves. It's a lonely struggle and only "the stones applaud" because there is no one else present to witness the battle—and all know that ultimately the waves will win. But the land fights on nonetheless, because that is the nature of things.

Teresa pleasantly dealt with the physical struggles of packing and unpacking during her trips to college. She always tried to minimize her differences from any other students, despite her constant cough. She worked for the student newspaper, the *Harvard Crimson*, and during her summer breaks, the *Boston Globe*. She had a number of articles published in the local section, and also a handful on the front page of the *Globe*. Heavy stuff for a freshman reporter. She was so proud of her reporting and, if the truth be told, she was good at it. She got the story in a first paragraph

Home for Christmas, 1990

that grabbed the reader, and her writing had just the right quotes. She seemed to have the knack for reporting.

Despite intermittent hospitalizations, home IVs, and the constant cough, Teresa made it through Harvard. Like any student, she was excited by the academic status of the visiting professors and faculty. Following each new semester meeting with faculty advisors and resident house masters, she found genuine support at her dormitories, especially at Quincy House. She was very proud of her work with the *Crimson* and the status of senior reporter. We shared that pride.

Teresa was turned down for consideration of a lung transplant at Johns Hopkins on the basis that she was not sick enough at that stage of her disease to justify the risk of the surgery. Undeterred, she decided that her best shot at a transplant was in the UK. They had the best survival statistics and experience with lung transplants at that time. She did the analysis and made the bold decision alone.

After graduating from Harvard in 1990, Teresa traveled to England and Scotland, hoping to find a job as a reporter—a daunting challenge when such jobs were usually reserved for citizens of the United Kingdom. Ultimately, after networking with fellow reporters and offering to do any menial newspaper task, she did find a job in London, but her health was failing. We have often thought that we never would have had that drive and courage at her age. She was a strong and determined person—not easily discouraged. We were sometimes in awe of her courage, but tried to continue in our difficult role as the supporting parents.

Before she left for England in the fall of 1990, Teresa made a point of watching the fireworks on the Fourth of July in Washington, D.C., saying that it would be the last time she would see them—a reference to the fact that the UK did not celebrate our Independence Day. She was right about not seeing the fireworks again, but for another reason.

Teresa had been through so many hospitalizations that we had lost count. We had already seen her rally so many times from what appeared to be serious bouts of respiratory illness that we could not come to believe that she might not rally yet again. Even as she struggled with respiratory fatigue and her lungs were failing her, we did not really grasp what was happening until the moment it occurred.

Teresa died in the Royal Brompton Hospital in London, on the morning of May 9, 1991. She was twenty-two years old. Coincidentally, that also happened to be the feast day (in the Catholic Church) of the Ascension.

Ted went on to graduate from the United States Naval Academy and serve in the military, including two tours of Iraq. He recently married.

Susan attended Bryn Mawr College, traveled extensively, and was happily married to Sean Patrick Boyle until she died of cystic fibrosis at the age of twenty-three.

Elizabeth graduated from Mount Holyoke College and was married in 2006.

Tim is a student at Muhlenberg College in Pennsylvania.

Ed is a urologic surgeon in private practice, and Pat remains at home with her mother, Mary Terese Dugan, who celebrated her ninety-third birthday in September 2006.

All of our children served as an inspiration for the creation of Camelot House—a daytime gathering place in Allentown, Pennsylvania, for seriously, chronically, and terminally ill children and their families. The parent organization of Camelot, Dream Come True (founded by Kostas Kalogeropoulos), presented Teresa with the computer on which she wrote this book.

Our last family portrait, October 1990. Front (left to right): Elizabeth and Tim. Center: Ed, Pat, and grandmother Mary Terese Dugan. Standing: Susan, Ted, and Teresa.

Speaking for our entire family—parents, brothers Ted and Tim, and sister Elizabeth—we can tell you that Teresa's and Susan's lives were a precious gift to all of us. We do not recall Teresa or Susan ever complaining about having a fatal illness. They would tell people they were "living with CF, not dying from it." And we all believed a cure would come in time to save them both.

As parents, we feel strongly that we were blessed with the five most precious children on earth. They have all traveled along a sometimes very bumpy road; but their courage and faith have carried them through each day. They were always, *always* there for each other—cheering each other on. We mourn the loss of our daughters, Teresa and Susan, but we thank God for the gift of their lives. And we pray they will live on in the hearts of all who knew them. We congratulate our surviving children, Ted, Elizabeth, and Tim, on a job well done. They have always been compassionate and loving, and we wish them continued strength, courage, good health, and happiness in all the days ahead.

It is our wish that our children never be forgotten, so we established the Teresa Mullin Memorial Fund and the Susan Mullin Boyle Memorial Fund. We have been able to help support the Cystic Fibrosis Foundation—hoping to find a cure for this horrific disease. We have sponsored bricks, chairs, a bike-a-thon, and hundreds of Camelot for Children camp trophies—where the goal is not winning but in being there for each other. Monsignor John P. Murphy, our pastor at St. Thomas More, presents a special journalism award in memory of Teresa to a member of the graduating class of the parish grammar school each June, and an award has also been established at the Harvard *Crimson*. We have sponsored a concert and Allentown's 2000 St. Patrick's Day Parade, and we have planted trees and donated books, artwork, hand bells (to the Moravian Academy bell choir), and defibrillators to our church and school.

We have also funded a thirty-minute video by Scott Stoneback of The Media People, entitled *Teresa Mullin, A Profile in Courage* and have set up a Web site at teresamullin.org. Many other memorial donations have been given to church, school, hospital, and community organizations. And now, we have published Teresa's book, *The Stones Applaud.*

Our family plans to continue to honor the memory of Teresa and Susan by helping other people as we think they would have wanted us to. Our children will live on in the hearts and minds of their family and friends—and now yours, too. Although we would like to recognize in writing everyone who helped Teresa in so very many ways—you know who you are—we are reluctant to list people and risk leaving someone out. Thank you for being there for Teresa and also for allowing us to share her story.

To those of you who continue in the battle with cystic fibrosis, know that you will be in our thoughts and prayers. There

The Stones Applaud served as the basis for an award-winning documentary, *Teresa Anne Mullin—A Profile in Courage*, by The Media People. Produced by Scott Stoneback, the 2004 documentary features interviews with the Mullin family, fellow students, family friends, former teachers, medical professionals, and journalists with whom Teresa worked. It also includes a special appearance by actress Susan Lucci of *All My Children*.

Narrated by Teresa's brother Ted and filmed on location at Phillips Exeter Academy, Harvard University, Children's Hospital of Boston, the *Boston Globe*, and in Allentown, Pennsylvania, the thirty-minute film also showcases Teresa herself in home movies, videos, and an insightful interview taped while she was writing *The Stones Applaud*.

Poignant without being maudlin, *Teresa Anne Mullin—A Profile in Courage* reveals the impact cystic fibrosis had on one family and how two sisters, Teresa and Susan, lived lives of courage, determination, and hope.

Teresa Anne Mullin—A Profile in Courage is available on DVD from:

Teresa Anne Mullin Memorial Fund
Susan Patricia Mullin Boyle Memorial Fund
P.O. Box 40
Center Valley, PA 18034
www.teresamullin.org

have been many helpful advances in cystic fibrosis research in recent years. Know that our family remains committed to helping find a cure for this devastating disease. We look forward to the day when we can finally—and so very happily—march in a victory parade with you. Know that we care.

Patricia and Edward Mullin

The Mullin family may be contacted at
P. O. Box 40
Center Valley, PA 18034